A MYSTIC ON
THE PRUSSIAN THRONE

FREDERICK-WILLIAM II

BY

GILBERT STANHOPE

AUTHOR OF "WHEN LOVE KNOCKS"

WITH TWELVE ILLUSTRATIONS

MILLS & BOON, LIMITED
49 RUPERT STREET
LONDON, W.

CONTENTS

LIST OF ILLUSTRATIONS

A MYSTIC

ON THE PRUSSIAN THRONE

INTRODUCTION

A PERIOD of modern German history that is very little known to the ordinary English reader is that of the brief reign—eleven years in all—of Frederick-William II of Prussia.

The reasons for this are obvious. It fills an intermediate space between the careers of two men of vivid and remarkable personality who, each in his turn, filled the centre of the stage of European history and concentrated upon himself the interest of civilised nations—two men, moreover, who were the greatest military geniuses of modern times.

Lying thus, a point of shadow between two brilliant lights, this period has not unnaturally been frequently overlooked. The eighteenth century belongs to Frederick the Great, the soldier of unconquerable spirit who held half Europe at bay; the philosopher-king who loved to gather choice spirits around him, and found leisure for literary correspondence and composition in the midst of war's turmoils; the recluse of Sans Souci, about whose eccentric ways and doings such innumerable stories were told.

B

A MYSTIC ON THE PRUSSIAN THRONE

And he had not been long in his grave before there began to appear above the horizon a star of still greater magnitude; before wondering Europe saw a Corsican lieutenant carve out an empire for himself with the sword, hand over kingdoms to his relations and followers, and parcel out the old Germanic Empire after his will.

Frederick-William's reign lasted only eleven years, and for much of that time the eyes of a fascinated and horrified world were drawn to the terrible drama being played out in France, where amid the flames of the Revolution the old *régime* was destroyed, and men were anxiously looking to see what would arise out of its ashes. We find authors who start out to write the history of Frederick-William drawn on to describing details of the Reign of Terror; it seems impossible to look away from that awful spectacle.

Neither have German historians been tempted to linger over a period, during which there set in that decline of Prussia's power and influence, which became so painfully manifest during the Napoleonic domination. It is pleasanter to hurry over the interval between the time when the Prussian army, under a leader who demanded miracles from his men—and got them—and that other time when Germany began to arise as if regenerated by her cruel disasters; when the painful story of her humiliation under the feet of an insolent victor is lightened by the heroic efforts of her patriotic sons.

And the personality of Frederick-William II is not one that could arouse even a biographer to actual

INTRODUCTION

enthusiasm.[1] We have neither the spectacle of a "good man struggling with adversity," nor the study (to many people even more interesting) of a picturesque villain. His virtues were of the every-day order and his failings were inglorious. And he died before the catastrophe for which his slack tension of the reins of government had helped to prepare the way.

There is a seemingly ineradicable tendency on the part of a biographer to glorify his hero or whitewash his villain, not wholly due to the desire to justify one's choice of the subject of a book. A better reason for it may be found in the fact that the close study of any man's whole life, an intimate knowledge of his surroundings and of the forces that affect the moulding of his character inevitably tend to make one realise what odds our poor imperfect human nature has to struggle against, and therefore to take no harsh view of his shortcomings.

And Frederick-William, if not very remarkable as a man, was certainly placed in a very remarkable position. To be the follower of Frederick the Great upon the throne of Prussia was a task that might well have staggered the boldest. It is proverbially difficult to be the successor of a great man, and of all rulers Frederick must have been about the most difficult to succeed. For his had been a one-man government, a system that was foredoomed to failure unless he could ensure that his successors

---

[1] It has, however, done so in the case of Herr Paulig, whose *Life of Frederick-William II* was published in 1881.

should have his own aims, his own ruthless determination, his own clearness of insight and untiring industry, together with that appreciation of the new spirit ushering in the new times, in which Frederick himself was wholly lacking.

It is true that he had some few upright and able men among his ministers, but they were merely well-trained officials accustomed to carry out his will. They had not been allowed any independence of judgment; to think for themselves was a crime. They did not work together; there was no council of State. Frederick himself was the brains of each department. The government of his day was like a necklace of beads of which the king was the connecting link; at his removal they fell apart.

Such a system could only succeed under the keen eye that let nothing pass, the ceaseless activity that found no detail too slight, the inexorable severity of a Frederick. The best qualities of Frederick-William—his sense of justice to individuals, his easy benevolence, his desire to see those about him happy—were just those for which the Frederician system had no use. And his worst qualities were just those that stood out in sharpest contrast to the merits of his predecessor.

At the beginning of his reign Prussia's position and *prestige* were truly remarkable considering its size and population. Its neighbour, Poland, that for want of unity and settled government was going to pieces, was actually much larger and had double its population. Prussia's infinitely more important position was due to two strong men, Frederick-

INTRODUCTION

William I and Frederick II. It was a triumph of the power of personality.

Frederick-William I, a simple, narrow-minded, God-fearing, autocratic ruler, had left behind him a well-drilled State, maintained in almost the same state of discipline as the admirable army he had trained but never used.

Frederick the Great, though more tolerant and large-minded, was not less of an autocrat in spite of his intellectual dallyings with the new ideas of liberty and the rights of man. He considered that he knew what was good for his people better than they did themselves, and he insisted on their having it.

He left behind him a country whose every resource had been strained to the uttermost to bring about great effects with inadequate means, and an outworn system of government that needed reconstruction, but was so artificially adjusted that to remove one of the pillars supporting the structure was to throw the whole into confusion.

And he left it at a time when, though there was actually a lull in the strife of nations, the spirit of unrest was abroad and active, and unsuspected forces were at work beneath the surface that were soon to break out in violent upheavals.

"Never," wrote the French ambassador Ségur in 1808, looking back upon this time, "never was so stormy an epoch preceded by a calm so universal. And the most far-seeing politician could scarcely at that time discern the feeble sparks that were soon to burst out in so terrible a conflagration."

A MYSTIC ON THE PRUSSIAN THRONE

Frederick-William's own country was far less
disturbed than any other by the revolutionary
movement; and a clever, ambitious and unscrupulous Prussian sovereign might have taken great
advantage of the internal dissensions of his
neighbours.

But Frederick-William, in spite of his moral
weaknesses, had much that was fine and chivalrous
in his nature. The interference in Holland, undertaken on his sister's account, was not pursued
aggressively. In the French campaign his most
ardent desire was to save Louis XVI and Marie
Antoinette from the hands of the mob and to uphold
the cause of monarchy.

German historians lament to this day that he
threw away the excellent cards he had in his hand,
for there was a time when Prussia held the balance
among European Powers, and an astute ruler might
have utilised the moment to advantage. There was
another time when Prussia might conceivably have
diverted the Empire from the Habsburg house, and
by crippling its Austrian rival have gained the first
rank among the Germanic nations.

But the firm, continuous and unswerving policy
that might have achieved such things was lacking.
At one time Hertzberg, at others Lucchesini,
Bischoffswerder and Haugwitz were his advisers in
foreign politics, and there was no continuity in his
policy.

He left behind him a country much increased in
size by the two further partitions of Poland, as well
as the natural accretion of the Ansbach and Bay-

reuth Margravate; but the new eastern territory, acquired but not assimilated, was only a source of weakness, and proved a drain instead of an assistance to the exhausted treasury.

Increased in size was the country when he left it, but very much fallen in public esteem. The army had lost its *prestige* for invincibility. The popularity among his own people that he had so earnestly desired was swamped by the hatred felt for the favourites who held sway over him. And his matrimonial aberrations lowered the character of the Hohenzollern dynasty, that had in the last two reigns been so conspicuous for decency and purity in an age that had seen a Louis XV, a Peter, a Catherine and an Augustus III of Saxony.

Beginning his reign with the sincere desire to please all, he ended it by disappointing everybody.

His earlier measures for the relief of taxation, especially the abolishment of the hated " Régie," were greeted with delight, but the taxes introduced later on to replenish the exhausted treasury were found equally burdensome.

The Court and the nobility generally were particularly exasperated that low-born outsiders, who did not belong to their charmed circle, should stand so high in his favour.

The learned classes, philosophers, journalists and writers, mostly held rationalistic views, and the ill-judged attempts of Wöllner and Hermes to drive them by rigour into the orthodox fold were bitterly resented. And as these were the classes whose voices were loudest and reached furthest, it is not surprising that the succeeding generation should have had an exaggerated idea of the King's failings.

And the changes of foreign policy in his reign, though not inexplicable when the situations are studied, exasperated both friends and foes. In the disputes with England as to the carrying out of the treaty of 1794, his standpoint, as explained by Professor Seeley in his *Life of Stein*, is comprehensible enough to us now, though it seemed to Lord Malmesbury, the English ambassador at the time, utterly indefensible.

His sympathy with the earlier struggles for liberty in France and the Austrian dependencies was followed later on by a decided reactionary tendency, but that is scarcely remarkable. Even without the influence of Bischoffswerder, to whom it was usually attributed, it is easily conceivable that the excesses of the Revolution and the fear of its spreading might tend to drive an absolute ruler to more repressive measures.

The continuity of his policy was greatly affected by his own readiness to grant what was asked of him. Those who saw him personally usually expected to get more from him than they afterwards obtained, when ministers and councillors had the handling of the matter and pointed out difficulties and objections.

Financially his reign was disastrous, for he began it with a sum that has been variously estimated as sixty-six or seventy-two million thalers in the treasury, and he finished it with a debt of twenty-two millions.

INTRODUCTION

Yet Treitschke deliberately declares that "the pleasure-loving Court was far from extravagant." It must be remembered that Frederick in his last years had doled out money very sparingly—when he did not absolutely refuse it—even for useful and necessary projects. He was deaf in that ear, he was wont to say when it was a question of a grant. Therefore a greater outlay had become necessary; money was needed on all sides; science, the fine arts, education, military and benevolent institutions, all demanded a loosening of the purse-strings. The Holland campaign, tho mobilisation on the frontier in 1790, and then the repeated French campaigns drained the treasury.

The finances on his accession were in confusion. Frederick, with all his other talents, was no financier, and it was impossible at first to find out how matters really stood in his exchequer, for he had allowed no one an insight into the whole. Each minister knew only what passed through his own department, and Frederick kept his own counsel about the rest. His personal expenses (except in the matter of snuff-boxes) had been reduced to an extraordinarily low level; and his privy purse (when used at all) was used for purposes of State.

The income of the State was smaller during Frederick-William's reign, due partly to bad harvests, that of 1794 being the worst on record, and partly to well-meant but not wisely carried out fiscal reforms. The new domains were not exploited for the benefit of the treasury. Hardenberg's policy in administrating the affairs of Ansbach

9

and Bayreuth for the ultimate good of the country rather than for increase of revenue had Frederick-William's approval. And in the sparing of forests a wise discretion was shown.

Where he did display a foolish liberality was in the giving away of crown lands, especially after the partition of Poland. The one really satisfactory work that Wöllner accomplished was the introduction of better order into the financial arrangements.

The reforms Frederick-William intended to bring in were mostly strangled in their birth by the manipulations of those to whom their carrying out was entrusted, or they fell through from the opposition against them in the country. The same weakness of moral fibre that left him at the mercy of his strong passions, surrendered him, when indulgence was followed by remorse, into the hands of those whom he looked upon as his spiritual leaders, some of whom had no scruples in playing upon his credulity and superstition. His reign is an object-lesson in the futility of good intentions, unless accompanied by sufficient resolution to carry them out in the face of opposition.

Frederick-William's piety was sincere, and not the hypocrisy it was labelled by some who saw it divorced from morality, and though its naïve display very possibly encouraged hypocrisy in others.

It is a matter for regret that no better word than "mystic" has been found to designate the various men of very different stamp, alike only in that they professed an interest in "the things of the spirit," who gathered about the Prussian Court.

INTRODUCTION

The word "mystic" has been used as a label for
some of the very finest characters the world has ever
known.   If by mystic we mean the man who
believes himself to be in direct spiritual communion
with a higher unseen power, then under the head
of mystics come most of the personalities whose
moral force—apart from their actions—has left a
deep impress upon the minds of all succeeding
generations.

But the same word has also to do duty both for
men, like Frederick-William, whose keen desire for
some definite and tangible assurance of the things
unseen made them uncritical as to the means
employed, and for the unscrupulous agents who
imposed upon their craving for the marvellous.

Rationalism and materialism had had their sway
during the middle of the eighteenth century, and
men's minds were in revolt against the dry, rigid
utilitarianism into which the movement known as
the "Aufklärung" had degenerated.   And now the
swing of the pendulum carried it too far in the
opposite direction.   A period of credulity followed
the period of scepticism.   The Secret Orders made
a strong appeal to those who felt the higher part of
their natures unsatisfied; and the ranks of the
Rosicrucians, Illuminati and the rest were swelled
by many earnest seekers after truth, as well as by
the herd of those who gape after every novelty.
And in an age when dupes are ready at hand there
is never any lack of fraudulent impostors.

The dupe and the impostor are ever with us, but
what is often only a fashionable craze became little

short of a national calamity when a sovereign, on whose authority no constitutional limits were yet set, chose his advisers among the members of these Secret Orders, and Prussia's destinies really lay in the power of a handful of men, some of whom were doubtless sincere and only self-deceived, while others made unscrupulous use of the influence they had over him.

It is one of the ironies of history that Frederick-William II should have been credited with a pusillanimous foreign policy. His personal bravery was never for a moment thrown into doubt. He had a longing for military glory, and saw himself mentally (and was pictured by his flatterers) as a sort of champion of Christendom, taking up arms for the established order against the forces of destruction, unaware that these were but clearing the way for a new era. A leader of a lost cause, he was an aristocrat in his mental outlook, and belonged to the times that were fast slipping away. He did not understand the drift of the currents that surrounded him. He still believed in the shadowy thing that had once been the German Empire. His Treaty of Basle has been blamed as a craven abandonment of German interests, but recent historians have shown how strongly he had at heart the cause for which he took up arms against France, how long he resisted the pressure put upon him from every side, and how he believed himself to be still acting as champion of the smaller states when the consent to negotiate was at length dragged out of him.

INTRODUCTION

Frederick-William II has been unfortunate in his chroniclers. The most widely-read descriptions of his Court and reign were those in which he was most libelled and traduced. Mirabeau's *Secret History of the Prussian Court* had an immense circulation, and though recognised afterwards as a spiteful caricature, had doubtless a great influence on the estimation in which Frederick-William was popularly held.

The amount of reliance to be placed upon Mirabeau's statements may be judged from a few instances : he counts the Duke Karl August of Saxe-Weimar, that most manly and high-minded of princes, among the servile throng who flattered the King for their own ends. He accuses Frederick-William of avarice as well as of extravagance. He declares that "no power on earth would compel him to read forty lines in succession," while it is well known that even in the pleasure-loving days before his accession Frederick-William was conferring both with Hertzberg and Wöllner over the policy of the future, and the notes and marginal remarks to hundreds of documents in the Prussian archives as well as his correspondence bear abundant witness to the contrary. Even Philippson, who is a bitter critic of his reactionary religious policy, and ruthlessly exposes his weakness and Wöllner's perfidy, incidentally disproves this theory.

Mirabeau himself gives us the source from which he obtained his information, from which we can judge of its value. "I know all," he says, "that can be learned from subaltern spies, from valets, courtiers, secretaries and the intemperate tongue of Prince Henry."[1]

In the beginning of his stay in Berlin when he still had hopes of gaining an influence over Frederick-William, his judgment was not so severe as it became when he found his hopes disappointed and wrote: "Every foreigner of merit is kept at a distance." While the latter part was written he was begging and praying to be sent elsewhere. "The man is judged," he wrote; "his creatures are judged; the system is judged." He was conscious that his mission had utterly failed.

Two other works in their time did their share towards stamping on the popular mind the opinion of Frederick-William II that long held sway. *Vertraute Briefe über die inneren Verhältnisse am preussischen Hofe seit dem Tode Friedrichs II* ("Confidential Letters on the inside Life of the Prussian Court since the death of Frederick II"), by Freiherr von Cölln, is a book of slight merit, little regarded by competent historians.

The *Life of Frederick-William II*, by the Comte de Ségur, is really more a history of the revolutionary upheaval in Europe, and written very obviously from the standpoint of the French republican. He was the ambassador who was sent to detach Frederick-William from the Austrian alliance and bring about a *rapprochement* with France, in which mission he failed signally.

And in Lord Malmesbury's Diary and Letters, the picture he incidentally gives of Frederick-

[1] Mirabeau, Eng. trans., I, 118. (1789.)

INTRODUCTION

William is not a flattering one, though he is perhaps less severe on him than on Frederick the Great, with whom he had so long fought a political duel. The Treaty of Basle so thwarted the plans of the English Government that it seemed to Malmesbury an infamy of the deepest dye.

Nor was Frederick-William fortunate in his apologists. Mirabeau's book called forth two answers, one from the historian Posselt, the other from the notorious Baron Trenck, who tried to show by this means his gratitude for the kindness shown to him. But abuse of an author is no contradiction of his statements, and may only avail to make him more widely read; moreover, neither of these writers had the biting wit that made Mirabeau's caricature so telling.

A highly eulogistic biography of him was written in 1811 by Dampmartin, who had been tutor to his children by the Countess Lichtenau.

Philippson's *Geschichte des preussischen Staatswesens vom Tode Friedrichs des Grossen bis zu den Freiheitskriegen* gives a full description of the development of the State during this period, which he describes as a peculiarly interesting one, since in it we see the commencement of those strivings for the restriction of absolutism which found their final issue in constitutional government; but Philippson only dwells on the character of the ruler in so far as it affected the course of affairs.

Within the last thirty years several writers have taken up the cudgels in defence of Frederick-William II. Paul Cassel published in 1886 a vindication of the Religious Edict, the principal cause of his later unpopularity, and declares that it needed more moral courage to start this reform than to fight a campaign. In F. R. Paulig's life of this King, published in 1909, the author's theological bias is plainly evident. For Frederick, the freethinker, he seems to have a feeling of personal hatred, while the piety of Frederick-William has his unstinted praise. His digression from his subject to prophecies regarding the millennium detract from the merit of his book as a history.

Historians like Treitschke and Heigel take a more fair-minded and impartial view of Frederick-William II, and while not glozing over his faults, do not lay on his shoulders and those of his advisers the blame for the errors of a whole generation.

Heigel especially does much to counteract the former harsher view. The complicated character of Frederick-William, he says, is not one to be dismissed with a phrase. "Of superficial education and disinclined to earnest studies, Frederick-William had not" (Heigel writes) "the knowledge that lightens the labours of a statesman, but he possessed the sound, manly understanding which enabled him to grasp the right even in difficult complications; in spite of being usually indolent, he was a sharp observer; he was long in weighing matters, and hesitating and careful in coming to a decision, but in that as to which he had once satisfied himself, he was quite firm and obstinate."[1]

Stein, Prussia's regenerator in later days, who

[1] Heigel, p. 161.

writes of this period of its decay as "that unhappy time that we lived through, that consumed our best years," yet describes the king in whose reign the decadence started with discriminating generosity. He was fond of drawing characters, says his biographer, Professor Seeley, but is unusually unsparingly severe. This is what he writes of Frederick-William : "He combined a lively feeling of his dignity with a strong memory enriched by the study of history, a just understanding and a noble, benevolent character; but these good qualities were clouded by sensuality, which gave his mistresses ascendancy over him; by a love of the marvellous and of spiritualism, which caused commonplace, designing men to gain influence over his mind; and by want of perseverance. Yet a great part of the errors of his reign ought to be ascribed to the nation, which cringed at once, without reserve or decency, before his favourites, Bischoffswerder and Wöllner, and before his mistresses, who in the sequel frustrated his better political designs and abused his generosity in a dishonourable manner in the matter of the granting away of the Polish lands."[1]

The kindest—and quite possibly the truest—descriptions of his character are given by two of his contemporaries, who as far as personal considerations are concerned had no cause to regard him favourably. H. von Boyen, a soldier of the Frederician school, who obtained very slow promotion during Frederick-William's reign, thus writes of

[1] Seeley's *Life of Stein*, p. 193.

him : He was "royally equipped by Nature, physic-
ally and mentally; there are rarely kings who
know so skilfully how to unite royal dignity with
amiability in conduct; except for too great stoutness
he was at his accession one of the finest men in the
country. To a clear understanding and great goodness of heart he united a very lively striving to
distinguish himself through kingly deeds and to
make his people really happy. Only these excellent qualities were frustrated by others, which
brought it about that affairs fell into the hands of
unworthy favourites. The immorality and extravagance which prevailed in the circle round him, was
unfortunately not without influence on the nation,
and this must be looked on as the turning-point in
which the last remains of the serious and thrifty
habits founded by Frederick-William I's severity
were quite overpowered by frivolous ones." [1]

And Kant, who had been practically silenced for
a time by Wöllner's persecuting zeal, who had
received on his publication of *Religion within the
Limits of Pure Reason* a royal rescript threatening
him with "our highest displeasure" if he repeated
the offence, was not embittered by the treatment
meted out to him, but with the discrimination of an
unprejudiced thinker describes Frederick-William
as "a brave, honest, humane and—putting aside
certain peculiarities of temperament—a thoroughly
excellent Prince." [2]

[1] H. von Boyen, p. 106.　　[2] Seeley's *Life of Stein*, p. 194.

CHAPTER I

On the 16th of August, in the year 1786, a lonely old man of seventy-four was fighting out his last weary fight with the one unconquerable foe, upheld by the same stern courage and grim, stoical endurance with which he had faced throughout a long life a host of implacable enemies and a series of almost impossible tasks.

There was no man of his generation whose personality had made so vivid an impression upon men's minds. Not only Prussia, but all Europe was on the alert to catch any rumour that came from that secluded spot, for it was known that the end could not be far off; but though his strength had been failing ever since his review of the army in Silesia the preceding summer, the strong hand of Frederick II was still all-potent in the guidance of his country's affairs and in the councils of Europe, and increasing weakness had never been allowed to interfere with his untiring attention to the duties of his position.

His end has been so often and fully described that we can easily see in imagination the little bent figure sitting forward in the chair he had scarcely been able to leave for weeks, partly supported now by the arms of the old hussar attendant. An old red velvet dressing-gown had taken the place of the familiar blue uniform with red facings and the snuff-bestrewed yellow waistcoat, but the big three-cornered hat, crushed into softness, still shaded the furrowed face with its protruding nose and jaw, close lips and keen eyes; and though one swollen and shapeless leg had to be wrapped in linen, on the other he still wore the high military boot.

Up to the day before he had with undiminished mental activity, though ever increasing bodily weakness, carried out the business of the State, dictated complicated diplomatic correspondence and planned military manœuvres that showed no lack of his usual skill and keenness. But that morning, when his ministers came at the usual hour to receive his directions, he had been half unconscious and they had been told to wait. Later on he had for the first time found himself unable to give the order of the day to General Rohdich, the commandant of the garrison, and had desisted with a sigh from the fruitless effort; the old General turning away with a tear in his eye as he realised that "alter Fritz" would give him the word of command no more.

The little shivering Italian greyhounds, the favourite companions of his later years, were by his side; the last sentence he spoke was on missing one of them at midnight, when he directed that the dog should be put back on its chair and covered with a quilt. They say his eyes had not even then lost all of their old fire.

It was at two o'clock on the morning of the 17th

of August that the last spark went out of that life that had meant so much for his country.

In Spartan self-denial Frederick had lived, writes Philippson, and in Spartan self-denial he died.

The furniture of the room—it was in his favourite dwelling of Sans Souci—was in keeping with the shabby, well-worn garments of the old King. When urged to have mended or renewed the velvet and fringes that had been torn by his greyhounds, he had argued that it would be useless, they would only tear the new stuff likewise. "After all," he once observed, "they cost me much less to keep than a Madame de Pompadour, and are much more faithful and devoted!"

His one great extravagance was snuff. He imported some special mixture from Spain, and always carried on his person at least two handsome snuff-boxes set with jewels, while others stood about on tables handy; he liked to change them continually, giving all a turn. It is characteristic that though it was with difficulty that a whole shirt could be found with which to cover his body, and though the wardrobe he left behind was valued at 400 thalers only, there were no less than a hundred and thirty snuff-boxes found in his possession, ranging in value from 2,000 to 10,000 thalers (about £300 to £1,500)!

For years past the world, even the Berlin world, had seen very little of Frederick. More than ever he hated and avoided in these last years all ceremonies. The untiring brain was as active as ever at seventy-four, and was still capable of carrying on, practically, the whole government of the country;

though now everything else save the power of work seemed to have fallen from him.

Music had been a passion with him; it is said that some of his best schemes and inspirations came to him while he was stepping about the room improvising on the flute in the hours he devoted to that practice; but with the loss of some of his teeth flute-playing had become impossible to him. His old teacher and concert-director, Quantz, had died some nine years before.

All his old friends were either dead or estranged, and of late years he had not been able to gather about him the witty society in which he delighted. Even those companions whom he tolerated mostly because they served as butts for his sometimes cruel shafts of humour and satire had more peaceful hours latterly; time had blunted the weapons he was wont to use against them; the old jokes were worn out.

Though he lived on to be seventy-four, he was already a prematurely aged man when he returned from the last campaign of the Seven Years' War twenty years earlier. The long fight against tremendous odds had not failed to tell upon him; the black moments of despair when any man but Frederick would have given up the fight, but which were for him the occasions for displaying his amazing rapidity of decision and resource, had left their mark.

And there were no "piping times of peace" for Frederick. Nicolai, who wrote the *Anekdoten von Friedrich II* in 1788, speaks feelingly from recollection of the terrible first seven years after the

FREDERICK THE GREAT.

war, when the industries of the country were almost at a standstill, when many of the clearest-sighted patriots thought the country's wounds were past healing, and Frederick was almost the only one who never lost courage. The work of restoring the impoverished country, which had been drained of its manhood and ruined by the presence of contending armies, as well as of colonising and settling the new provinces, was such as to demand the same great qualities, the same untiring zeal and devotion as had been needed for the formation and maintenance of that army which had brought Prussia into the forefront of European politics.

When, in the reign of Louis XIV, Prussia (or, more properly, Brandenburg) under its great Elector declared war against France, the monarch was scarcely aware that one more had been added to the number of his foes, so insignificant was the place that Prussia then held among the European states. The French still loved to speak of Frederick as the " Marquis de Brandenbourg "; it was long before they could learn to look upon this little state so recently erected into a kingdom as anything like a serious rival to their ancient monarchy.

But the Prussia that Frederick left behind him loomed very large in the eyes of the world. With a population less than a fourth of that of the United Kingdom at the time, it had an army more than four times as great. It is true that his father, Frederick-William I, was the one who first realised the fact that for a small and poor country, as Prussia then was, consisting of detached provinces scattered

among rival states and with no natural barrier to
protect it from more powerful neighbours, the one
way of safety lay in possessing an army that should
command the respect of friend and foe alike. He
had started the work, and his rigid parsimony had
left his son a well-filled war-chest. Two strong
men, ruling in succession, had wrought this change.

The reputation of the Prussian army with Frederick in command was now such that bold indeed
was the nation that would venture to attack him
single-handed; while his shrewd brain and keen
insight made it difficult for any one to outwit him in
the subtler arts of diplomacy and statecraft.

Up to the last day of his life he held the reins
of government in his own hands. Every department
of the State had his personal attention. He spared
himself no more than he had spared others.

Now the reins had at last to drop from the nerve-
less fingers. The world was anxious to know what
manner of man it was to whom it had fallen to take
up the task left behind him by Frederick the Great.

Meanwhile the royal family in Berlin were
awaiting, like the rest of the world, the issue of the
last fight of the tough old veteran whom death alone
could subdue.

Characteristically he had contested every inch of
ground and endeavoured to avoid any confession of
increasing illness. Except when obliged to use a
state carriage for some ceremonial, he still preferred
to be seen on horseback; it was within a few weeks
of his death that he took his last ride on Condé,

the English horse that was his favourite. When bad health sometimes compelled him to make the journey between Berlin and Potsdam in a closed carriage, he preferred to travel at night or in the small hours of the morning, so that the manner of his transit was not observed. Some say he even used rouge on his cheeks, to hide the alteration that increasing illness made in his appearance.

The Comte de Ségur, who saw him some eighteen months before his death, said that the fire of his glance showed no signs of age. Though evidently infirm in health, he looked as if he could still fight like a young soldier, and in spite of garments as old and worn as the man beneath them, his appearance was imposing.

On that same night—the night of August 16th to 17th—in Schönhausen, her summer residence near Berlin, Frederick's wife, Elizabeth Christine, was holding her usual court and supper-party. On her, since soon after the beginning of his reign, had devolved the carrying out of all the punctilious ceremonial of Prussian Court etiquette. That was the part allotted to her. She had no share in his life, in his labours or sorrows or joys.

It was many years now since Frederick had exchanged a word with her. The fiftieth anniversary of their wedding had passed unnoticed a few years before. It was twenty years since he had for the last time paid her even the annual visit of ceremony on her birthday, which had once been a custom with him if he happened to be anywhere near Berlin at the time.

A MYSTIC ON THE PRUSSIAN THRONE

On these occasions, and on these occasions only, it was remarked that he used to discard the high boots up to the knee, which formed part of his habitual attire, for low shoes and black silk stockings—evidently an effort to show her outward respect. Moreover, he always severely reproved those who permitted themselves to treat her with any lack of the deference due to her position as Queen.

Schönhausen, the summer residence he had given her soon after his accession, was rarely, if ever, visited by him; if he joined the supper-party at the Berlin Palace, it was his habit to turn and bow to her before sitting down, and again on rising to depart, but never to exchange with her a single word.

It caused an extraordinary excitement and a vast amount of comment in Berlin when once, in the early 'seventies, on hearing that she was suffering from a severe attack of gout, he showed some concern and made polite inquiries after her health.

Yet there was apparently never any quarrel between them. When he first saw, in the days of his youth, the bride his father had selected for him, he appears to have been agreeably surprised. In a letter to his sister he confessed to being rather pleased with her delicate features and complexion of lilies and roses, though he thought her style of dress and manner left something to be desired, but he adds that he kept this approval of his a secret from his despotic father, in order to enhance the merit of his obedience to his will! [1]

[1] Hahnke: *Elizabeth Cristine*, p. 14.

FREDERICK THE GREAT

The daughter of Duke Ferdinand of Brunswick-Bevern, Elizabeth Christine appears to have been rather a colourless person, and to have had very little influence upon those about her. A biography of her, written by Friedrich von Hahnke in 1848, is of necessity almost restricted to descriptions of the court functions in which she took part, and to the births, deaths and marriages in her family circle.

For the first ten years of their married life they had lived sometimes together, but soon after Frederick's accession he presented her with the Schönhausen residence she had once admired; and for the rest of her life, except when the appearance of the enemy in Berlin on several occasions drove the royal family into temporary exile, she never left the vicinity of the capital.

Husband and wife corresponded politely for many years, with inquiries after each other's health and occasional interchanges of good wishes upon anniversaries; but she was never allowed to go to Sans Souci; and the new buildings in Potsdam, which must have been constantly mentioned and admired in her presence, she had never been permitted to see.

Yet when Frederick, having no heirs of his own, insisted on his next brother, Augustus William, getting married, it was Louisa Amelia, the sister of his own Queen, whom he chose for that brother's bride. He had at least found his wife gentle and complaisant, anxious in all things to please him, and without any craving to meddle in affairs of State;

and he probably thought that just such another wife would be most suitable for his brother.

That Elizabeth Christine's feelings were deeply wounded by the way in which she was left out when all the other members of the royal family were gathered together, may be seen from her letters to her favourite brother Ferdinand; that it finally embittered and soured her we may infer from the allusions to her trying temper in her old age, which the discreet Countess von Voss occasionally permits herself in the diary of her life at the Court of three Prussian monarchs.

Neither his wife nor any other member of his family was permitted to come and bid farewell to the dying King. His nephew, the Prince of Prussia, as the heir to the throne was then called, had come to a neighbouring palace so as to be at hand if summoned; but no summons came. Frederick had long before this given up the hope that his successor would ever become a man of his own stamp and follow in his footsteps; and disappointment had led to actual dislike.

His younger nephew, Henry, had been Frederick's favourite. Of him he wrote that "he was endowed with every quality that one could wish a young man to possess." He had kept him a great deal under his own eye and advanced him in military service, building much upon his early promise. But in 1767 the young man, only twenty years of age, had, while bringing his cuirassiers from the garrison in Kyritz to Potsdam for a review, fallen victim to an attack of small-pox and died after a brief illness.

28

FREDERICK THE GREAT

His death had been the greatest sorrow of Frederick's later life, and from that time he seems to have cared less and less to see any of his family.

Of Frederick's own generation two brothers and a sister were still living in or near the capital.

His favourite sister, Wilhelmina, had died in 1758. She was the Margravine of Bayreuth, the writer of those graphic reminiscences of the early life of Frederick and herself, which Carlyle quotes so often, but also often shows to be far from accurate. The two had been close friends in youth, drawn together by the suffering they had both endured at the hands of their stern father, who seems to have kept all his severity for the two eldest of his large family.

The brother next in age to himself, Augustus William, the father of that successor of Frederick's with whom we shall be mostly concerned, had died during the Seven Years' War; and the manner of his death had been the cause of unending bitterness between Frederick and the rest of his family. For it was his unmeasured severity after Augustus William's disastrous retreat from Bohemia that so dispirited that gifted and very popular young Prince that he retired from the army a despairing, broken man, and succumbed in the following year to an illness he had no heart to resist.

Another sister, Ulrica, wife of the King of Sweden, had died in 1782. Charlotte, who had married the Duke of Brunswick, was still alive at his death, and was the recipient of the last letter of a domestic character that he wrote.

A MYSTIC ON THE PRUSSIAN THRONE

Henry, the eldest surviving brother, was a man who has been variously described by his contemporaries. Mirabeau's slighting epithet: "Small in person and small in mind," was possibly dictated by a personal grudge [1]; the Prince was at any rate large-minded enough to be only amused at the unflattering portrait of himself the Frenchman had given in his *Histoire sécrète de la cour de Prusse*. He even bought sixteen copies of the book, which he distributed among his friends, asking if the picture resembled him. Thiébault, a French professor at the Academy sometimes employed by Frederick, has much to say in Henry's favour. The Countess von Voss owns to disliking him as sincerely as she worshipped his wife.

He was undoubtedly keen and clever; as a general he distinguished himself by the remarkable celerity of some of his marches, and won from Frederick the praise of being the only one among them all who never made a mistake. But he had not Frederick's broader grasp of mind, nor his insight into the real position of affairs as regarded Prussia and its relation to the Empire and the other Continental Powers; like the rest of the family, he was never in sympathy with Frederick's bold and far-reaching schemes, and they formed an opposition party of whose discontent the King must always have been conscious. The brothers all put their opinions on one side and fought in his wars for the sake of the family honour and the safety of the country, but it was often with heavy hearts and

[1] Thiébault, II, 70.

an utter disbelief in the wisdom and justice of his cause.

Henry lived at Rheinsberg, the place where Frederick had spent the happiest years of his life before he came to the throne. The brothers corresponded occasionally and sometimes met, but quarrels were frequent between them, and Henry did not conceal from his friends, or even from strangers, his bitterness against the King.

The youngest brother, Ferdinand, had never been strong, and he played no important part in the history of the time. Though never actually wounded, the Seven Years' War had left him weakened and ruined in health. He had asked to be allowed to see Frederick a few weeks before his death, hearing that the end was near, but his wish was not granted.

The one unmarried sister, Amelia, Abbess of the Protestant foundation of Quedlinberg, was also living in Berlin. Once the beauty of the Court and the heroine of a romantic love-story, she was now prematurely aged and disfigured by illness, and possessed of a temper that made her the dread of all who came about her. She and her brother Henry were on particularly bad terms; he usually spoke of her as the "wicked fairy" (*la fée malfaisante*); and her caprices and outbursts of temper made her as much disliked in her old age as she had been in her youth admired for her beauty and wit.

Carlyle has expressed his utter disbelief in the romantic story of her attachment to Baron Trenck,

but contemporary writers speak of the affair as of
a thing perfectly well known and undisputed.
There is a story of a piece of gold fringe sur-
reptitiously abstracted from the handsome guards-
man's sash when he was on duty at the Palace, of
a whispered hint where the missing article might
be found, of stolen interviews and of how the rash
lover was finally arrested on a different charge and
suffered long imprisonment.

But all this was forty years ago, and Princess
Amelia, at the time of Frederick's death, was
terribly afflicted and infirm, with distorted limbs, a
head she could scarcely lift, and a hoarse, strangled
voice. She had something of her brother's sarcastic
humour, and was never happy in company unless
she had a victim on whom to vent her spleen.

Frederick was too clear-sighted not to be well
aware that after a reign of forty-six years a large
section of the public was ready to welcome a change.
He wrote to Voltaire: "There are many who are
inclined to think that I have lived too long," and
he knew that the eyes of the ambitious were turning
from the setting to the rising sun.

He had known the height of fame and the depths
of detraction and abuse. There had been no man
more admired in his generation, and probably no
man more cordially hated and dreaded. There
were times when all northern Europe had looked
on him as the great Protestant hero and champion.
The fame of his prowess in arms brought adven-
turous spirits from all nations to Prussia asking

32

leave to fight under his banner. His reputation for wit and learning attracted men of intellect to his Court.

On the other hand, he was dreaded and hated by those who had known the secrecy with which he prepared his plans and the swiftness and suddenness of his attacks. The orthodox religious were deeply shocked by his scepticism.

And his well-meant but despotic measures for the advancement of his country were by no means always such as were approved of by the people for whom he toiled. They might be proud of their sovereign as the hero of a hundred fights, who was looked on as one of the wonders of the age; but in spite of a winning charm that he could exercise at will, there was much in Frederick that made for unpopularity — his openly expressed scorn of humanity; his capricious harshness towards many men who deserved better treatment at his hands; his contempt for German society, the German language, learning and literature, and his preference for all things French.

He never learned to write his native language correctly; having conceived a prejudice against it in his youth from the heavy and involved style of the books from which his instruction was received, he never realised that it was already being shaped into a powerful instrument by the hands of such master-craftsmen as Lessing, Goethe and Schiller.

Of his chosen associates and correspondents two were of British nationality, Keith and Mitchell; several of Italian, as Algarotti, Bastiani and

Lucchesini, and the great majority French—
d'Argens, Voltaire, Valori, d'Alembert. Of Germans he had only about him a few old generals
and those ministers who took their instructions
constantly from him, as Hertzberg and Görtz.

Moreover Frederick, though theoretically interested in the new ideas of liberty that were now
fermenting in men's minds and were soon to break
out into upheavals of the old order, was very far
from permitting in the government of his own
country any innovations that tended to greater
liberty. On the contrary, he destroyed the last
vestige of self-government that the civic magis-
trature had enjoyed. Though he upheld and carried
out into practice the theory that the ruler is but the
chief servant of the State, yet a more despotic
government than his would be difficult to find. All
was done *for* the people, but nothing *through* the
people. He knew no ruth, no mercy where he considered the welfare of the State to be concerned.
The individual was nothing; the State was all.

It was small wonder that many hoped for a
gentler sway, for a successor who should be more
human, have more consideration for the happiness
of those around him, even if he lacked the sterner
virtues in which his predecessor excelled.

34

CHAPTER II

FREDERICK-WILLIAM was already forty-two years old when he was called upon to fill the place left vacant by Frederick the Great.

It was known that for many years past he had not been on good terms with his uncle, who, disappointed in his nephew, now ignored him as much as possible, neither consulting nor even informing him of what was being done in foreign or home affairs. By Frederick's enemies this was attributed to jealousy, but it was much more probably his usual impatience of incapacity. Not that the Prince was without intelligence and a certain amount of sound judgment when he exercised it uninfluenced; but he lacked clearness of insight and above all strength of will.

Now indecision was, in Frederick's eyes, of all things most lamentable. In a letter to his brother Henry he once wrote: "Adopt a resolution, what resolution you like, but stand by it and execute it with your whole strength. I conjure you, take a fixed resolution; better a bad, than none at all."

The Prince's extravagance, too, was abominable in the eyes of the old King, who knew the poverty of the country and its needs, whose habits of parsimony grew on him with advancing years till at last he could hardly bear to pay out money even for the good of that country whose welfare was his one thought.

It was known, too, that the Prince was fond of pleasure and a slave to his own passions. Frederick himself was no great stickler for morality, and he might have forgiven the frequent *amours* but for the fact that his nephew allowed himself to be influenced by his favourites, a fact that was fatal to such firm consistency of policy as was necessary if Prussia was to remain at the height she had attained.

The Prince was popular in Berlin. He was easier of access than his uncle, less capricious in temper, though also, like most of his family, given to sudden outbursts of rage. It was particularly noticed that he spoke to his associates with the polite " Sie," instead of always using the " Er " that marked their inferiority to himself, as Frederick did; and trifles like that make a great impression in a society so ceremonious as the Prussian.

He was known to be just, humane, with a strong sense of gratitude to all who had befriended him, and lavishly generous—a fault that goes a long way to make up for other deficiencies in a venal society.

And Berlin was—if we are to believe the description given by James Harris (afterwards first Earl of Malmesbury) when he was accredited there in 1773 —a city where morality was at a discount. He found neither honesty among men nor virtue among women. "The men," he wrote, "were entirely military, uninformed on every other subject. . . .

FREDERICK-WILLIAM'S BIRTH

A total corruption of morals reigns throughout both sexes in every class of life."[1]

And if Malmesbury's views were a little coloured by his anti-Prussian bias—not unnatural considering that his diplomatic career was one long effort to uphold English as against Prussian interests—we have Frederick's own admission of the deterioration of manners that had set in, which German writers also deplore and ascribe to the influence of France and the spread of scepticism.

The Prince had already been married a second time, having divorced his first wife, but had not yet entered into the curiously complicated matrimonial arrangements which were soon to follow.

In person Frederick-William was tall and broad, over six feet in height and already inclining to that corpulence which afterwards so troubled him and gained him the name of " der Dicke " (the Stout).

Malmesbury described him as having "more the air of a stout foot-soldier than a great prince." But other writers speak much more favourably of his personal appearance. Joseph II of Austria called him the "handsomest man that could be seen "; and Prince Albert of Teschen wrote of him: "The Crown Prince displays with the strength and size of a giant a readiness for the greatest exertions. He has an open, majestic type of face, and is full of courage and spirit."[2]

---

[1] Malmesbury : *Letters*, p. 255 ; *Diary* I, p. 97.
[2] "Der schönste Mann den man nur sehen könne" " Der Kronprinz zeigt in einem starken und riesenmässigen Körper eine Seele für die grössten Strapazen. Er hat eine offene, majestätische Gesichtsbildung und ist voller Heldenmut und Geist." Philippson, 33.

A MYSTIC ON THE PRUSSIAN THRONE

His portraits show a broad, high forehead and large, intellectual-looking eyes; but they are the eyes of a dreamer, not a man of action, having nothing of the keenness or the fire of Frederick's glance; and the lower part of the face is heavy and sensual.

Such was the man who had to step into Frederick's shoes. Let us go back two-and-forty years to the time of his birth, and see what parentage and what surroundings have combined to make him the manner of man he was.

Frederick-William's father was of a very different stamp from his famous brother, having many of the graces that Frederick lacked, but wanting in his sterner qualities. He had not, like Frederick, been trained and hardened to endurance by harsh treatment meted out to him in his youth; and while in outward appearance more bountifully favoured by nature, he was without Frederick's dauntless energy and resolution. Indeed, Frederick seems to have absorbed to his own share all the determination that should have fitted out the Hohenzollerns of his own and the two succeeding generations.

A fine, handsome man of great intelligence and most winning manners, Augustus William was a favourite with all; and his misfortunes and early death aroused the deepest sympathy of the whole nation. Even the stern old father, who had shown such merciless severity to Frederick in his youth, seems to have found a softer place in his heart for his younger children, and more especially for Augustus William, who was the acknowledged favourite.

FREDERICK-WILLIAM'S BIRTH

Thiébault says of him that his wit and talents and his irresistible kindliness were enhanced by a modesty that almost verged on timidity.

He was ten years younger than Frederick and only eighteen at the time of the latter's accession to the throne. He had, of course, received a military training, and in that army which Frederick and his predecessor wrought into such a wonderful machine for the raising of Prussia in the rank of the nations the duties of an officer were not to be taken lightly. Drill was strict, and leave very difficult to obtain; the young Princes at Potsdam had to slip out in disguise when they wanted to visit the capital.

The dowager Queen Sophia Dorothea had her residence in Monbijou, which was the great meeting-place for the members of her family. This was a small château in Berlin, but on the farther side of the Spree, with a small garden round it, and facing a willow-shaded road and a meadow that in winter was often completely submerged.

Sophia Dorothea was, it will be remembered, the daughter of our George I and that unhappy Queen Sophia Dorothea who was immured for thirty-two years in the castle of Ahlen in Hanover on suspicion of an intrigue with Count Königsmark.

Her love of the arts, of luxury and pleasure had been sternly restricted throughout her married life by her rough, frugal-minded husband, who hated all finery and display. Now she was able to wear her jewels without having to conceal them hurriedly

39

on notice of his approach. She had grown in later life so enormously stout that special arm-chairs had to be constructed for her.

She seems to have retained to the end the love of all her children. With Frederick's wife, too— that Elizabeth Christine whose entry into the family had at first been most unwelcome to her, for she had set her heart upon an English alliance for him—she became completely reconciled, and in her correspondence with her brother Ferdinand the younger Queen speaks most gratefully of her mother-in-law's kindness.

Here at Monbijou she held her little court, always visited by Frederick when he came to Berlin. The handsome and charming Augustus William, we learn, wrought terrible havoc upon the hearts of her ladies-in-waiting. To one of them—of whom we shall hear later in connection with this same Prince —we are indebted for the following description of the widowed Queen—

"I was seven years at the court of Queen Sophie Dorothea, and was devoted to her with the greatest veneration. She had never been beautiful, but she was stately and distinguished, and she retained all her dignity in her old age. Possibly she had more *esprit acquit* than *esprit inné*, but she was very well educated and well-bred, could converse with every one, and intercourse with her was delightful. She was uncommonly fond of splendour and of society; she liked to have company every afternoon and evening, and to sit a long time at meals, which was sometimes wearisome to us, her ladies-in-waiting.

FREDERICK-WILLIAM'S BIRTH

It was beautiful to see what great and respectful tenderness the King had for her." [1]

The Countess von Voss, from whose autobiographical notes the above lines are translated, was closely connected with the Prussian court for no less than sixty-nine years, and her diary and notes will often be drawn from in the following pages. She was a lively, vivacious lady of unimpeachable morals, and must have been possessed of uncommon qualities, for she won the respect and even affection of three men of such totally different type as the three successive occupants of the Prussian throne. In her childhood she knew the Court of Frederick-William I, and sixty years later she held in her arms the infant who was one day to be acclaimed at Versailles as William I, German Emperor.

Her father was General Pannewitz and her mother a favourite lady-in-waiting to Queen Sophia Dorothea. As she would not always be parted from her little daughter, the child was admitted to the palace. There is a story told of her, as a bright, pretty child of eleven, that she met the old King one day on the winding staircase that led to the Queen's apartments, and that he, never given to gallantry as a rule, tried to snatch a kiss from the little elf, but she defended herself by giving such a resounding box on the royal ears that it was heard by those below! The old King only laughed good-humouredly at his repulse.

She describes him as looking kingly in spite of his small stature, and as not being really of a bad

[1] Voss: *Neun und sechzig Jahre am Preussischen Hofe*, p. 10.

41

disposition, though he had violent outbreaks of temper, when his wife and children suffered hard treatment at his hands.

General Pannewitz was called to serve in the first Silesian war, and the family left Berlin; but at fourteen Fräulein Pannewitz was appointed lady-in-waiting to the Dowager Queen, and soon took up her residence entirely at Court, following the royal lady also in her annual summer visit to her second son at Oranienberg, where we shall hear of her later.

Frederick, being childless, was beginning to feel anxious to see the succession assured, and though Augustus William was not yet twenty years of age, he desired him to marry. From the same ducal house that had furnished him with his own wife he selected another sister, Louisa Amelia, to be his brother's bride. From Hanover had come suggestions for an English alliance for the Prince, but both Frederick and his wife were very anxious for this Brunswick marriage, which accordingly took place on the 6th of January, 1742.

Frederick had now been two years on the throne. The first Silesian war, entered upon against the protests of ministers and generals and under the disapproval of the public, was against all expectations turning out successfully. His hands were full at this time with diplomatic intrigues and secret treaties; he was proving his skill at playing off one nation against another, holding fast to his own unswerving aims all the time.

It is not intended here to deal with Frederick's

campaigns or his foreign politics, which have received exhaustive treatment at the hands of historians and writers on military matters. But it is important to note that Augustus William and his younger brothers were from the beginning and all throughout agreed in condemnation of Frederick's ambitious plans, being under the impression, from his father's treatment of him, that he had wild, reckless tendencies likely to be dangerous to the country.

With Silesia completely overrun by his troops and with his mind occupied with the ever-shifting political combinations of the time, Frederick was yet able to spend a few months of this winter in Berlin, and to be present at his brother's wedding.

It was celebrated with great magnificence, and the winter in the capital was a gay one; the members of the house of Brunswick, now to be yet more closely united with the Prussian royal family, were entertained there with a succession of balls, masquerades and assemblies.

Twelve days after the marriage Frederick rejoined his army for the short but glorious campaign that terminated in the Peace of Breslau in May 1742, when Maria Theresa was compelled to yield that province of Silesia which was to cost him years of struggle against overwhelming foes before he could rest unquestionably secure in its possession.

Frederick had presented his brother with the country seat of Oranienberg, lying to the north of Berlin, and here the newly married pair spent a couple of peaceful years. The mansion had stood

43

empty during the preceding reign; the large gardens, laid out originally after a plan of the famous Le Nôtre, had been left to themselves for many years, and the once carefully shorn beech hedges had now grown up into high walls of verdure, with over-arching roofs that shaded even in hottest summer days the cool green paths beneath. These smooth spaces and broad alleys, either with the arrows of sunlight piercing through the foliage, or illuminated with lamps at night, made a charming background for the fanciful dances that we read of in Countess von Voss's pages: the sarabands, rigodons, "passe-pieds" and "aimable vainqueurs," for the concerts, ballets and comedies, in all of which Augustus William's wit and inventive talent found abundant play.

But the scene was soon to change from the gay but innocent amusements of Oranienberg to the stern realities of war.

Austria, under its high-spirited young Duchess, was not likely to submit tamely to the loss of a province like Silesia. The Prussian nation had for-given Frederick for the boldness of his undertaking when they found how his success had increased the *prestige* of Prussian arms in the eyes of Europe; but his French and Bavarian allies had been dis-gusted at his making a separate treaty, which left them to uphold the claims of Charles VII against Austria without his aid.

Frederick had meanwhile been unceasing in his efforts for the increase and improvement of his army, and had kept a close watch on the issues of the campaign, seeing with some apprehension how favourably it was turning out for Austria. He foresaw now that she would probably turn her weapons against him. His great rule was never to wait to be attacked, but to take the initiative and startle his opponent by a bold move before the measures planned against him were complete.

His brothers, little as they were in sympathy with Frederick's policy, were, of course, as Princes of the House of Hohenzollern, officers in the Prussian army and men of undoubted personal bravery, ready to follow the call to arms; and in August 1744 Augustus William and Henry joined Frederick's army of 80,000 men in their march into Bohemia.

This was only two months before the birth of Augustus William's son, the future Frederick-William II.

The Princess of Prussia, as well as her sister, Frederick's Queen, had manifold causes of anxiety at this time. Not only their husbands and their husbands' brothers, but also three out of their own eight soldier brothers, were fighting in this campaign —Ferdinand, who was to attain such celebrity later, and Albert, who as a youthful volunteer was learning his profession in the Prussian army; while an elder brother, Ludwig, was in the Austrian service.

The brothers were much attached to one another, and on one occasion the chances of war unexpectedly permitted a brief meeting. The opposing forces were at no great distance from one another, and a Prussian officer who had ventured past the enemies' outposts had been shot. Ferdinand sent under a flag of truce a request for permission to take back the body for burial, which he received with the further news that his brother Ludwig was waiting at the outpost in the hopes of a meeting. Ferdinand and Albert hurried to the spot, and the three brothers welcomed with delight the brief glimpse of one another that was all the exigencies of the time permitted.

There was also at this time a good deal of uncertainty as to the safety of Berlin and the neighbourhood, which could not hope to offer much resistance if exposed to an attack. Writing to her brother in the following year, the Queen mentioned that there was only one regiment in the garrison, and that not of seasoned troops, but of peasants who had been pressed into the service, and who looked queer enough mounting guard without uniforms, some in their shirts. The plate in the palace, she continued, was guarded by one man! [1]

On September 19th there reached Berlin the good news of the capture of Prague after a six days' siege, which caused great rejoicing, though this initial success turned out to be but the beginning of Frederick's difficulties in Bohemia.

Six days later, on the 25th of September, Frederick-William was born.

The King and his brother were in the camp at Tabor when the news reached them. Prince Ferdinand wrote to his sister: "The master's joy and content are written on his face, and every one displays the liveliest delight and satisfaction." He

[1] Hahnke, p. 99.

46

was an enthusiastic admirer of his brother-in-law, and in his letters to his sister frequently speaks of him as " the master."

On October 11th the Queen wrote to her brother : " The King seems delighted at the birth of his nephew. He has written my sister a most kind and charming letter. She and her dear boy are, thank God! very well. To-morrow the child is to be baptised. The Queen-mother will hold him at the font. I shall also be godmother, and the other sponsors are the three Duchesses (of Brunswick), the mother, the grandmother and the reigning Duchess, the Duke, the Empress of Russia, the King of France and the Prince of Sweden." [1]

Not till two months later was Augustus William able to see his child. On the 14th of December the King re-entered Berlin, and with his two brothers went at once to see the happy mother. Frederick took his nephew in his arms and kissed him; and two days later he again appeared at his brother's palace, and hung round the infant's neck the Prussian Order of the Black Eagle.

Four days afterwards the royal brothers rejoined the army, where things had been going very badly for Prussia ever since those first captures of fortresses.

Early in the next year the death of Charles VII, the unlucky Bavarian Prince whose election as Emperor had brought him nothing but disaster, made Frederick's position yet more difficult. He had no longer the pretext of fighting in the imperial

[1] Hahnke, p. 96.

47

cause. The successor to the Bavarian Electorate made peace with Austria, leaving the troops in that country free to attack Frederick, who was maintaining himself with difficulty in a hostile district. He would gladly now have made peace with Austria, but that country, having made a quadruple alliance with England, Holland and Saxony in January 1795, was in a position to win back all she had lost in former campaigns. The Czarina Elizabeth of Russia had turned against Frederick, and Louis XV paid no attention to his requests for assistance. The intervention of Saxony added greatly to his difficulties, since it lay between his capital and Bohemia.

It was always when Frederick was hemmed in with numerous foes and thrown inexorably on his own resources that he rose to his highest flights of daring and won his greatest successes, or, according to the opposition party, that his good luck helped him out of the difficulties into which his rashness had led him.

But though Frederick well knew in what a precarious position he stood, and that, before the brilliant victory of Hohenfriedberg put a different complexion upon affairs, it had been a question less of the loss of Silesia than of the very existence of Prussia itself, at the Court of Berlin there had been very little realisation of the danger or doubt of the ultimate result.

The Queen-mother made a pleasure-journey to Oranienberg and thence to Rheinberg, accompanied by nearly the whole of the Court, the reigning Queen being as usual the one left out. Relays of three hundred horses were requisitioned for the conveyance of the party. It was one of the great hardships endured by the agricultural population of those days that they had not only to provide horses for military purposes, but also for the travels of the Sovereign and Court. One of the good measures to be placed to the credit of Frederick-William II was the forbidding of such misuse of this custom as sometimes occurred, when courtiers and others took advantage of it for their own private purposes. There were occasions later on when the land was so reduced that the royal party could not all travel together because of the difficulty of finding sufficient horses for their transport.

Part of this summer was spent by the royal sisters at Schönhausen, where the Queen gave a festival in honour of the Hohenfriedberg victory; they were back in Berlin in August, where the news of further glory gained at Sohr reached them in the next month, saddened for them by the tidings of the death of their young brother Albert.

The King's first account of the battle made no mention of the loss, a fact on which Elizabeth Christine commented very bitterly in a letter to her brother Ferdinand.

"Has the master," she wrote, "been touched at all by the death of the dear lost one? He has been cruel enough not to write a word either to my sister or myself. I am accustomed to his ways, but I cannot help feeling it, especially on such an occasion when one of my brothers has lost his life in his service; it is too cruel to behave in this way." Later on in the same letter she added: "I have just received a letter from the King, in which he writes to me as follows: 'You will have heard what happened the day before yesterday. I am sorry for those who lost their lives and regret them; my brother's and Prince Ferdinand are very well; Prince Louis is said to be wounded.' I beg you to let me know if it is dangerous. It seems as if this battle were destined to throw all our family into grief, and that each one of our brothers must have his part!" [1]

That the Princess of Prussia shared her grief and indignation may safely be conjectured, for the sisters were closely united. To her later on Frederick wrote, possibly in reply to some remonstrance: "I have grieved for the loss of your brother, Prince Albert, but he died the death of a brave man, though it came about needlessly through his own light-hearted carelessness ('*quoiqu'il se soit fait tuer de gaieté de cœur et sans nécessité*'). I am sorry for the grief it is only natural you should feel at the death of your relatives, but these are events for which there is no remedy." [2]

The end of this year (1745) brought the wished-for peace, Frederick retaining Silesia and guaranteed in its possession, but agreeing, in his capacity as Elector of Brandenburg, to the election of Maria Theresa's husband, Francis of Lorraine, Grand-

[1] Hahnke, p. 413.   [2] *Ibid.*, p. 103.

ELIZABETH CHRISTINE, WIFE OF FREDERICK THE GREAT.

Duke of Tuscany, to the imperial crown. Frederick's ministers were astounded at his moderation after such victories, but Frederick was cured of his youthful hunger after fame and military glory, and saw that nothing was to be gained by Prussia carrying on the conflict.

Though it ended in a virtual triumph of Austrian policy, yet the moral effect of the Prussian victories was immense. Prussia was no longer one of the insignificant states of that Empire, which under its successive Habsburg rulers had sunk so low. It ranked now as an independent country. It marked a further step in the disintegration of that curious and effete anomaly, the Holy Roman Empire, which had to be broken up before a real union of the German states could come into being. The Prussian army had established its reputation as the first in the world, and Frederick's subjects were fired with such an enthusiasm for him as had never before been displayed for a Brandenburg Prince.

The city of Berlin prepared a triumphant reception for him on his return there on December 28th. The laurel-bedecked carriage containing the King and his two brothers could scarcely make its way through the welcoming throng.

Augustus William was now promoted to the rank of general, and he divided his time between his country-house of Oranienberg and Berlin, where his military duties now lay. His wife spent much of her time in Schönhausen with her sister, who found in her society and doubtless in the childish prattle of the young Prince some consolation for the neglect with which she was treated.

An annual break in their retirement came with the review of troops at Tempelhof, which took place always in May. The sisters drove each in an open carriage drawn by eight horses, preceded by field-marshals, and with the Princess of Prussia was the young Prince. After the review the troops were always paraded past the royal carriages.

Of Frederick-William's mother we find very little notice in the chronicles of the day. Thiébault describes her as "gentle and good, averse from all scheming and intrigue," "of uniform and quiet conduct," and says that she never ventured out of the circle of her daily occupations.[1] At her death in 1780 Lord Malmesbury wrote of her : "Everybody is agreed in giving her the very high though simple panegyric that she had made many persons happy, and never given pain to a living soul."[2]

In the eyes of Augustus William, however, she does not appear to have been a desirable wife. She is said to have treated him with coldness, and to have withdrawn from him as much as possible. He was still only twenty-three when he fell a victim to that passion for Sophie von Pannewitz which so greatly embittered his life.

The Prince was a great deal in Monbijou with his mother, who was devoted to him, and here he was necessarily thrown into the society of this youthful lady-in-waiting, then only seventeen.

[1] Thiébault : *Mes Souvenirs*, I, 301, 311. [2] *Letters*, p. 448.

FREDERICK-WILLIAM'S BIRTH

"Before I even knew that he noticed me," writes the Countess, "he had conceived a passion that was a great misfortune both for his whole life and mine."[1]

She did her utmost, she asserts, to combat this feeling on his part, but it only grew in intensity. Her own heart was traitor to her; she might treat him with outward coldness, but she acknowledges in her simple, natural words that she could not do otherwise than return an affection that showed itself in such delicate and tender attentions.

She went with the old Queen to Oranienberg and Rheinsberg—to her last days the Countess retained tender recollections of the beech glades of the former—but wherever they went the Prince followed them, and every morning brought her a letter from him. Young as she was and deeply as she loved the handsome and winning Prince, whose passion was enduring as well as ardent, she remained true to her principles. She was willing to have married a Count Neipperg who courted her to escape from the painful situation, but the Prince managed to prevent the necessary royal consent to the wedding.

Five years passed in this struggle between her feelings and her sense of duty. The Prince was willing to divorce his wife and marry her; he begged her not to leave the Court. The King himself became uneasy at his brother's absorption in this unhappy affection; and the young girl at last

[1] Voss, p. 17.

summoned sufficient resolution to marry her cousin, Count von Voss, who had been an envoy at Dresden, and was now in high favour with the King.

The marriage festivities were, she writes, of the usual kind : crowds of guests, and much noise and gaiety that left her no time for thought. The Prince was in despair; he insisted on being present at the ceremony, but during its progress he fell unconscious to the ground, and had to be carried away. The guests all accompanied the bride in a festal procession to the bridegroom's house, which they all again visited the next morning to wish them good luck. There followed a dinner at the house of the bride's mother, and the next day the married couple turned their backs upon Berlin.

Thiébault describes the Countess as tall and slender, with the figure of a Diana and the fairness of a Venus, as charming, innocent and amiable as she was beautiful—a worthy subject for such devotion; and he admires the strength of character and resolution she showed all the more for his knowledge of the warmth of her heart and the depth of her feelings.

During the next two years she sometimes visited Berlin with her husband, but lived as much retired as possible, and the Prince apparently made no effort to seek her out. In 1753 her husband was appointed President of the Ministry of Justice at Magdeburg, and she left with the deepest regret the place where she had known such happy and yet such troubled times.

FREDERICK-WILLIAM'S BIRTH

She never saw the Prince again. But she kept always the tenderest recollection of the man who had so deeply loved her; his son and grandson found in her a faithful friend, and both showed that they knew how to value her services.

CHAPTER III

RECOGNISED from his birth as the future ruler of Prussia, the young Prince Frederick-William was scarcely three years old when petticoat government was pronounced to be no longer suitable for him; he was removed from the care of his female relatives, and a talented young Swiss professor, Nicholas Beguelin, was appointed his tutor.

French was the language then in general use at Court. It was in French that he was taught, and, like his uncle, he never became so thoroughly master of his native language as to write it with grammatical correctness.

He had by now a younger brother, for in 1747 a second son had been born to Augustus William—that Henry whose death just on reaching manhood was such a blow to Frederick's hopes.

It is most probable that the two young Princes —Frederick-William then a boy of six—saw something of that famous Carrousel which the King gave in August 1750, in honour of his favourite sister the Margravine of Ansbach.

There were four jousting parties, each consisting of about sixty cavaliers dressed as Romans, Carthaginians, Greeks and Persians, the first headed by Prince Augustus William, the rest by other Princes of the Blood. The Princess Amelia, then in her youthful bloom, gave away the prizes. There was tilting at the ring and at the Turk's head, as well as other mediæval sports such as must have delighted the heart of a boy.

Voltaire was there; it was the time when Frederick had at last induced him to take up his residence at Sans Souci; a step they both soon had cause to regret. Sir Jonas Hanway wrote home a description of it. Barberina, the dancer who had aroused so much enthusiasm in Berlin some years before, was again seen there on this occasion.

Hers is so curious a story that we are tempted to insert it here. Frederick, whose ceaseless activity left no department untouched, was particularly interested in the success of the new opera-house he had built. No detail was too small for his notice, and he even wrote anonymous dramatic criticisms in the Berlin newspapers, of which there already existed two.

Of actors and musicians he had plenty, but the ballet was not well represented; and hearing of an Italian dancer whose beauty and grace had made her the rage in London a short time before, he set his envoys in different foreign countries to work to find out whither the beautiful Barberina had gone. Count Gaetani, his representative at Venice, discovered her there, and induced her to sign an agreement to come to Berlin.

Time passed, however, and there were no signs

of her appearance. Gaetani went to her again, and found that having aroused an ardent love in the heart of a young Scotchman who was anxious to marry her, she had no intention of carrying out her contract, but was on the point of leaving Italy to accompany him to his northern home. German writers speak of this gentleman as " Lord Stuart Mackenzie "; he was in reality the grandson of the famous advocate, Sir James Mackenzie, and younger brother of the Mackenzie who afterwards became Earl of Bute.

It was difficult to persuade the lovers that Frederick of Prussia was not a man to be trifled with. He was determined to have his dancer. The Venetian republic turned at first a deaf ear to his request for intervention in such a trivial matter, but Frederick had his own methods for exacting compliance with his will.

A Venetian ambassador happened to be passing through Berlin. The King gave orders that his luggage was to be seized and held to ransom till the republic had found means to enforce the carrying out of the Barberina's contract !

Great, of course, was the outcry at this high-handed proceeding, but Frederick cared not one whit. It had the desired effect. The Venetian Government seized the person of the fair dancer, and she was sent in a post-chaise under armed escort to Vienna and thence to Berlin.

Her lover followed her all the way as closely as he was allowed, offered large sums of money to be permitted an interview with her, and applied to

Frederick himself to have her set free, but in vain. There are still three yellow faded letters in the Berlin archives, wherein the hapless lover poured out his heart in assurances of undying affection, which never reached the hands for which they were intended; and a letter to Frederick entreating that she might be restored to him bears the marginal note in his handwriting: " Reponatur." [1]   The King soon found means to bring about Mackenzie's return home.

The dancer's success in Berlin was great.   This was in 1744.   The Queen wrote of her to her brother Ferdinand—

" The Barberina danced on Wednesday and was much admired. . . . She is really beautiful, the K. was a little touched by her. She is an amiable creature; one cannot help liking her when one sees her." [2]

One wonders if the Barberina ever in her heart forgave Frederick for his summary frustration of her intended marriage with the gallant Scotchman. Outwardly she had to submit, and evidently did so with a good grace, winning golden opinions from Court and public. Frederick appears to have taken pleasure in her society; we read of his drinking tea with her.   But after four years she left Berlin against his will, giving up the salary, really magnificent for the period, which he gave her; and later, in spite of his strong disapproval of such a *mésalliance*, she married the son of the Chancellor Cocceji.

[1] Paulig, p. 18.   [2] Hahnke, p. 145.

A MYSTIC ON THE PRUSSIAN THRONE

The German theatre was never patronised by Frederick, and his wife, probably in deference to his opinion, did not visit it either. The Princess of Prussia, however, and the other ladies of the royal family gave it the encouragement of their presence soon after its opening, and at a performance given by children in May 1754 both the young princes were present.

Frederick-William was then ten years old. Three years previously the King had given him a military tutor in Major Count von Borcke, a nobleman who had had a scientific as well as a military training, and distinguished himself at the battle of Kesselsdorf. Frederick himself worked out a plan of instruction for him, carrying on a long and detailed correspondence with his brother on the subject. The end aimed at was to be the development of character and judgment rather than the acquirement of a mass of learning.

The Court preacher Sack was his teacher in religious matters; and Frederick specially recommended that, in view of his having to rule over so many Catholic subjects, he should be brought up to take tolerant views. Intercourse with men as well as with boys of his own age was considered advisable for him, and officers—often French prisoners of war—were invited to share his meals.

Major von Kleist, the soldier-poet, was one of those invited to his table in 1756, and he found that the twelve-year-old Prince had received a comprehensive course of training, and was sufficiently advanced in Latin to understand something of Virgil.

The boy showed great attachment to his teachers, and in after life he always bore them in grateful recollection.

Like most of his family he had great talent for music. The gamba was his first instrument; afterwards he learned to play the violoncello and attained great proficiency. For the greater part of his life music occupied a portion of his time every day.

Riding and military exercises formed part of his training at the earliest possible moment. The following anecdote shows how anxious Frederick was that he should possess a truly martial spirit.

Rumours had reached the Prussian King of a hope expressed by the young Archduke of Austria, afterwards Joseph II, that when a peace-loving prince, such as Frederick-William was reported to be, came to the throne, it might be possible for Austria to win back the province Frederick had wrested from her.

Frederick arranged that some one should repeat this speech before the young prince when drinking coffee with him by special invitation, and set himself to watch how he took the intelligence.

When the boy jumped up so hastily as to throw down his coffee-cup and declared angrily that it was not true, that the inheritance of his fathers should never be lessened through him, the uncle was so delighted that he rewarded him with rich presents before letting him go.[1]

[1] Kosmann: *Leben und Thaten Friedrich-Wilhelms II*, 7.

A MYSTIC ON THE PRUSSIAN THRONE

In 1751 Frederick-William's only sister was born, Wilhelmina, who afterwards married the Prince of Orange and Nassau. It was in her defence that he undertook that campaign in Holland, which was the first and the only successful one of his military expeditions.

The next glimpse we have of the young prince is that of a twelve-year-old boy, up at five o'clock on an August morning in the year 1756, watching the regiments of the Potsdam garrison as they parade before the keen eyes of the soldier-King.

But this was no ordinary muster, for, the inspection over, the word to march was given, and the boy saw the gleaming columns file off into the dim unknown, to wage such warfare as falls to the lot of few, and to leave—the great majority of them—their bones on the battlefields of the Seven Years' War.

To a boy of that age such events usually offer a pleasurable excitement, and even when a father and four uncles are among those taking part in the chances of war, sanguine youth is not wont to picture possible disasters.

But, young as the prince was, he can hardly have failed to be aware that the King was blamed by all his family for rushing, as they thought, precipitately into an unjust and unnecessary war.

Since the close of the last campaign Frederick had been looked upon by Austria, Russia and Saxony as a dangerous neighbour of predatory instincts, on whose movements a careful watch must be kept. He knew that Russia and Austria had entered into an alliance that was directed against him; that the Elector of Saxony was ready to join them at once on the breaking out of hostilities; that Austria was even entering into friendly relations with her old enemy France.

For years past he had been on the alert, noting every *rapprochement* of foreign Courts, every unusual movement of troops. He was not anxious for war; the old thirst for glory had died out in his youth, and he knew it would be a life and death struggle; but he was determined that Prussia should give a good account of herself if war were indeed inevitable.

In Russia he had a bitterer enemy than he knew; to the Czarina Elizabeth's ears had reached some of Frederick's sarcastic and contemptuous references to her and her Chancellor Bestusheff. Indeed Frederick's quick and lively temperament (in spite of the wonderful powers of persuasion testified to alike by friend and foe) made him ill adapted for diplomatic intercourse with foreign statesmen or ambassadors. He was carried away by his brilliant conversational powers to say more than he intended or than was wise. Later on he recognised this, and avoided personal intercourse with foreign envoys. Even in writing, his literary gifts sometimes swamped his better judgment.

In France there was a party for him, but the Pompadour—one of the three women with whom, as Frederick remarked, he was destined to be always in conflict—fostered the Austrian influence, which finally prevailed, and a defensive alliance between Louis XV and Maria-Theresa was formed in May 1756.

There seems no doubt of the fact that a strong coalition had been formed against Prussia, though whether there would have been no attack if Frederick had not taken the first step, or whether at the first favourable opportunity they would have broken out upon him, is a question which has been disputed from that time to this.

At any rate Frederick took the latter view, and knowing that the Austrians were, as usual, behind-hand with their preparations and would not be ready for another year, he resolved in the fearful odds against him to have at least the advantage of the first move.

To the English Ambassador—it was probably Sir Andrew Mitchell, with whom he was closely be-friended, who accompanied him through much of this war—he said: "Does my nose look like one that was made to be tweaked? By God! I will not have it. Maria-Theresa wants war, and she shall have it at once. I cannot prevent it; all I can do is to forestall my enemies." [1]

It was in August 1756 that he crossed over the Saxon frontier, and there began that long and arduous struggle, too famous to need recapitulation here.

The young prince must have known his father's

[1] Philippson, " Friedrich der Grosse " in *Der Neue Plutarch*, 143. " Sieht meine Nase danach aus, als wäre sie gemacht, Nasen-stüber in Empfang zu nehmen? " etc.

views and heard something of the protests that all three of Frederick's younger brothers made against his design. Frederick at last said in his annoyance to Prince Henry that if he were afraid, he had better remain at home, to which the latter replied that they would all know how to subordinate their opinions to their sense of duty. So the four brothers each took their share in the campaign.

Frederick-William grew up in the firm belief that his uncle's action at this time was an uncalled-for aggression, an opinion that he seems to have clung to throughout his life, and that undoubtedly influenced his later policy.

Saxony was in no position to withstand Frederick and his army of 70,000 men. Its vain and spendthrift ruler, Augustus III, had been entirely under the domination of his minister Brühl, whose extravagance was even greater than that of his master. To a man who prided himself on wearing a new suit every day and kept twelve tailors constantly at work for him, had been entrusted the finances of the country; and Brühl had dipped his hand into the national treasury to pay for his own and his master's whims and follies.

The army had been reduced from 60,000 to 20,000 men, and on the advance of Frederick both King and minister fled to Warsaw. Still the Saxon army resisted bravely, till Frederick's defeat of the rescuing Austrians at Lobositz compelled it to surrender, when many of the soldiers were incorporated in the Prussian army.

The King had ordered that this victory should

be celebrated in Berlin, and the Queen and Queen-mother gave festivities at which they received the congratulations of the nobility and foreigners of distinction. Elizabeth-Christine has been blamed for heartlessness in that there were gaieties at Court while her husband and brothers were risking their lives, and often when the fortune of war was going against them; but it was not infrequently at Frederick's wish, and in order to throw dust in the eyes of the foreign ambassadors.

The next year brought dark days indeed to Prussia. In January Frederick paid a short visit to Berlin, hurrying over from his winter quarters at Dresden, accompanied by Prince Henry, but not by Augustus William. He saw his mother then for the last time, for she died in June of this same year, and it was six long years before the King set foot in his capital again.

One blow after another fell upon him. His attack upon Saxony put him wrong in the eyes of the other members of the German Empire, of which he, as Elector of Brandenburg, still formed a part; and at the Diet held at Regensburg in January he was put under the ban of the empire, and war against him was resolved upon.

Russia promised eighty thousand troops to Austria as well as the help of her fleet. France also formally decided in Austria's favour, and engaged to send a hundred thousand men as well as subsidies. Sweden, against the wishes of its sovereign, whose wife was Frederick's sister, joined the coalition. English help was all he had to rely upon,

66

but on neither side was the treaty of January 1757 carried out in a manner satisfactory to the other party.

June of this year was one of the blackest months in Frederick's annals, when after the dearly bought victory of Prague and the siege of that city, he suffered a grievous defeat at the hands of Marshal Daun at Kolin. At the same time the Russians were gaining ground in East Prussia, the Swedes in Pomerania; and the English and Hanoverian army was giving way under the French attack.

It was ten days after the Kolin disaster that the royal family suffered a great loss in the death of the Queen-mother, whom happily the news of that misfortune never reached.

But yet another disaster was to come that more directly affected the young prince. After Kolin Frederick gave to his brother, in the place of Maurice of Dessau, the command of the army, now 30,000 strong, that was to retire towards the Lausitz, securing the strong places along their route, above all Zittau, where was their magazine as well as their provisions.

Seventy thousand Austrians under Charles of Lorraine and Daun had crossed the Elbe, and Augustus William retired before them. Frederick seems not to have believed that the main Austrian attack was directed against this army, and in one of his letters remarked that if they went on retreating, they would come bang upon Berlin at last!

The Prince's was undoubtedly a difficult position, and he had not Frederick's readiness of decision.

F 2 67

He called a council of war, at which he and his generals (with the exception of Winterfeld, who was absent) ended by choosing the worst of the three possible courses open to them, the circuitous route over the mountains towards Zittau, which after a seven days' march of extraordinary hardships, constantly attacked by flying bodies of Pandours, without food, shelter, and sometimes even without water, they reached in miserable condition, only to find the Austrians there before them, on a hill that commanded the city.

They were in no condition to attack the Austrians. A futile effort was made to get bread from the doomed city which, unfortified as it was, suffered bombardment with red-hot cannon-balls from Charles of Lorraine, and was burned to the ground.

Augustus William marched with the remnant of his army to Bautzen, where the King met him. That memorable meeting became tragic from its consequences. Frederick was never ready to forgive failure, and in this instance the disastrous retreat had left the gates of Silesia and Saxony open before the Austrian army. Winterfeld and Goltz had already joined the King, bringing him their story of the unfortunate march.

As the two brothers approached one another, the King drew bridle at some distance and dismounted. Augustus William and his generals did the same and saluted. But no answering salutation came from Frederick. He sat down on the ground as if awaiting further detachments.

Presently Goltz came over bearing a message,

which he delivered to the Prince and his generals in the even, expressionless tones of an official communication, to the effect that his Majesty had cause to be greatly displeased with them, that trial by court-martial was what they deserved, which would mean a death-sentence for them all, but that the King would not carry the matter so far, being unable to forget that in the general he had also a brother.

One must be a Prussian officer of that period, when a military career was the only one open to a man of rank, when prowess in arms was the chief glory of the nation; one must belong to a family like the Hohenzollerns, who had risen by virtue of their fighting qualities to a commanding position in Europe, to whom the glory of their name was dearer than life itself, before one can realise what this open humiliation meant to Augustus William.

It is said that he and his generals stood stiffly as they heard the message. Probably not one of them but would have received an Austrian bullet in his heart rather than have listened to those scathing words.

The Prince seems never really to have rallied from the blow. Letters passed between the two brothers that only widened the estrangement. The Prince begged for a court-martial, which he believed would have justified him. Frederick's ink, as Mitchell expressed it, was turned into gall.

The Prince then asked for leave to retire, his health having suffered from the hardships of the campaign. This was granted, and he was never recalled to take part in the war.

Meanwhile the safety of the capital had been suddenly threatened by the appearance before it of Haddick, a Croatian general, with a small force. The royal family under the escort of the garrison was hastily removed to the fortress of Spandau, and the enemy entered the city. But hearing that Maurice of Dessau was coming to the rescue, they judged it too precarious to remain, and left it next day, demanding a ransom of £27,000 and two dozen pairs of gloves for Maria-Theresa. Frederick was probably not annoyed to learn that when the latter part of the booty reached the Empress, it was discovered that all the gloves were for the left hand!

It was not considered advisable for the royal party to remain in a capital so incapable of a serious defence, and at the King's command the whole Court, with the royal children, the treasury and the ministry of foreign affairs, removed to Magdeburg. They had not been there a month before the tension of anxiety was relieved by the news of the great Prussian victory of Rossbach.

Frederick had written to his friend d'Argens: "To save the country I will attempt and risk impossible things." And indeed his achievements at this time were little short of miraculous; the boldness with which he flung his small force upon the French and imperial armies and beat them at Rossbach, and then, hurrying back into Silesia, which the Austrians had already begun to look upon as a reconquered country, won the astounding victory of Leuthen over a foe of three times his strength.

The good news was celebrated in Magdeburg by

a service in the cathedral, and at the singing of the *Te Deum* the bells were rung, three shots boomed out from the big cannon and a triple *feu-de-joie* was fired by the garrison.

Christmas brought the further good tidings of the recapture of Breslau, and early in the following year the Queen and Court returned to Berlin, Prince Frederick-William and his younger brother following with their tutor in February.

It was in this summer, twelve months after his disastrous retreat, that Augustus William died, succumbing to an illness that might not have been fatal if a keen desire to live had seconded the efforts of the physician. But hard fortune both in love and war had robbed him of all desire for life. He was tenderly nursed and deeply regretted by his family. In October his widow gave birth to another son, who, however, only lived a few months.

Though Frederick had written of him to his sister Wilhelmina that "he sulked and must be left to his caprices," his death seems to have reawakened all the old affection. Those around him say that his grief was inconsolable. To his reader, de Catt, he wrote—

" I cannot get the loss of this brother out of my mind; in spite of all my efforts to busy myself with other matters, his image is ever before my mind to torture me."[1]

Prince Henry never forgave the King for his harsh treatment of this brother, but always looked on him as answerable for his death. He rendered

[1] Philippson, p. 252.

him, of course, military obedience, and though occasional quarrels took place there was no open rupture between them. But his hatred of Frederick was well known to his own circle and no secret to foreigners who visited the Court.

One way in which he displayed it was only calculated to make himself ridiculous. He erected an obelisk in the grounds of his Rheinsberg residence to the memory of the heroes of the Seven Years' War, on which appeared the names of all those who had distinguished themselves—except Frederick and his favourite general, Winterfeld!

CHAPTER IV

YOUTH AND FIRST MARRIAGE

AFTER the death of Augustus William, Frederick entrusted to the guardianship of Marshal von Kalckstein the three children he had left. In December the young Prince was given the title of Prince of Prussia. Military training was now more than ever to take the first place in his round of duties. He had to be present daily at the regimental drill.

At fifteen the Prince must have been old enough to share in the wild excitement in Berlin when the disastrous news of Kunersdorf reached that capital (Aug. 13, 1759). The five couriers whom Frederick dispatched, telling first of victory and then of blackest disaster, did not arrive in the order in which they were sent off, so that the greatest confusion prevailed, and while some were rejoicing in wild enthusiasm over a great victory, others were in despair at a terrible loss, and no one knew what to believe. But it soon became too evident that Frederick had sustained a crushing defeat at the hands of the combined Austrian and Russian troops.

More alarming still was the news that Frederick himself had for a time given way to despair. Surrounded on all sides by enemies, having exhausted all means of help, he saw nothing before him but

73

the destruction of his country, which he was resolved not to outlive. It was known that he carried poison about with him, and when there came the news that he had shut himself up in the Reitweiner Schloss for two days, seeing no one and issuing no orders, that despair and confusion reigned in his camp, the worst was feared.

Couriers passed constantly between Berlin and Reitwein, great was the tension of suspense, and when at last they brought the news that the King had again picked up the reins he had momentarily let drop, had taken again upon his shoulders the burden of affairs, immense relief was felt all round, and probably by no one more than the young Prince, who would have found himself suddenly called to the throne at such a crisis as this.

One of the precautionary measures that Frederick ordered was the removal of the court to Magdeburg; they returned in November, but the following year they had again to take flight; and this time the Russians and Austrians actually occupied the city, where much depredation was done by the latter.

Prince Frederick-William and his brother had been continuing their education in Magdeburg, and in 1760 they were allowed to visit the King in his winter quarters at Leipzig. A more hopeful atmosphere prevailed there now. After the remarkable march into Silesia, which Carlyle has so graphically described, and the victory of Torgau, Frederick was able to relax a little from the strenuous conflict, to enjoy the society of his friends, d'Argens, Mitchell and Guichard, to take pleasure in the company of his nephews, who were keen on dancing and the other amusements which Leipzig could afford.

Countess von Voss, who was living at Magdeburg at this time, and indeed had to give up her house for the accommodation of the widowed Princess of Prussia, writes, Jan. 12, 1761 : "The Princes are back again, all very pleased, and delighted with their visit to the King."

Her diary at this time is a record of festivities, of games of Pharaoh and Blind Man's Buff, comedies and masquerades, as well as of the dinners and suppers which she found so wearisome.

The centre of social attraction was always Princess Henry, the wife of the King's now eldest surviving brother. She was a daughter of the house of Hesse Darmstadt, remarkable for her beauty and wit, and she seems to have won all hearts, even for a time that of her husband.

Prince Henry had been very unwilling to marry, "to leave behind him a race of useless princes," [1] but it offered the only way to freedom from the strict state of discipline in which the unmarried princes were kept at Potsdam.

The first seven years of their marriage were to all appearances happy enough; Kalkreuth, the Prince's adjutant, is credited with the slanderous stories about her, afterwards refuted, which brought about their complete separation. Henry, it is said, never forgave him for this.

Countess von Voss cannot find words enthusiastic enough to describe the charm and amiability of this

---

[1] Thiébault, II, 18.

Princess, who distinguished her with special favour; she writes of her as "*die Divina*," "*la belle fée*," "*l'incomparable*," and so on. Her mind is much exercised about the attentions of a certain Prince of Nassau, one of the prisoners of war whom Frederick allowed to live in Magdeburg on parole, who was "*zum Todtschiessen*" in love with the Princess, and the anxious Countess dreads the trouble which the possible discovery of this attachment by the Princess Amelia might cause.

The young Prince of Prussia is occasionally mentioned in her pages; doubtless she took a special interest in the son of the man she had so dearly loved.

The round of gaieties in which the Court indulged during this war has been much censured; and indeed it does appear somewhat heartless when one realises how Prussia at the time was fighting for its very existence, and how great was the misery in the country. In Berlin itself, in 1761, the poverty was so great that by the King's orders almost one-third of the population (thirty thousand out of a hundred thousand) received bread as alms.[1]

Frederick-William is described at this time as tall and of fine proportions, resembling his father in his agreeable and friendly manners. D'Argens wrote of him to the King—

"You must have been very pleased with the Prince of Prussia; every one who saw him in Magdeburg has innumerable nice things to say of him."

[1] Nicolai: *Anekdoten*, p. 88.

YOUTH AND FIRST MARRIAGE

The next winter Frederick again had his nephew with him at Breslau; in May took place his confirmation, on which occasion he was girded with his father's sword; and in the summer he was allowed to join his uncle and take part in the campaign.

During this summer Frederick wrote of him to Prince Henry—

"Your nephew is out to-day with us foraging. A spirit of activity is awakening within him. We are mere pygmies in comparison with him."

But already he was beginning to find that Frederick-William did not possess the qualities he most desired in his successor. The younger brother Henry became his favourite, and his dislike to the other increased. The young Prince must have been well aware of it, for his letters of this time state that the contempt with which his uncle treated him made him sometimes wish himself dead.[1] In personal bravery the Prince was never lacking; it is possible that what Frederick detected in him thus early was that love of pleasure and lack of resolution which marred his later life.

Meanwhile the long, embittered contest was drawing to a close. Russia, on the accession of Peter for his brief reign, had at once ceased hostilities; France, and after her the German States, withdrew from the coalition, and at last Austria herself was willing to conclude the peace of which Frederick had long been desirous, no one knowing better than he did the exhausted condition of the country. The Peace of Hubertsburg in February 1763

---

[1] Philippson: *Geschichte des preussischen Staatswesens*, 29.

brought none too soon an end of the long and weary conflict.

A little incident in this campaign is worth relating, if only for the way in which it has been travestied. The King and his nephew were riding along the lines exposed to the enemy's fire, when a cannon-ball struck down the horse of von Pirch, a page who was riding close to the Prince, whose own horse at the same moment plunged wildly, unseating his rider. Von Pirch, disentangling himself from the fallen steed, was looking about for a safer spot, when the King, who had probably seen exactly what had happened, called out to him not to forget to remove the saddle from the dying horse. The boy turned at once, and, regardless of the fire, unfastened the saddle and brought it with him.

The same story, as afterwards circulated, ran thus: A cannon-ball struck the ground close to where the Prince of Prussia was riding; he was seen to fall from his horse, and every one thought he was killed. Amid the universal horror the King's voice was heard calmly ordering that the saddle should not be forgotten; and this was quoted as a proof of his cold-hearted and niggardly temperament!

Great preparations were made in Berlin for welcoming the King on his return after the Peace of Hubertsburg, but Frederick was in no mood for festivities. The war had indeed ended so far in his favour that he retained Silesia, and he had won himself an imperishable name; but he was a worn-out man who believed himself to be near death, and

78

he realised how the life-blood of the nation had been drained in the long struggle.

A mile along the road to the city decorations had been prepared, and crowds awaited him in vain all day. It was not till after nightfall that he appeared, and after a brief visit to his family in the Berlin palace, went off alone to Charlottenburg.

After the peace the Prince was kept very strictly to his duties at Potsdam under his uncle's stern eye, and was no longer allowed to take part in those festivities at Court, in which he had taken such pleasure.

His qualities, it now appeared, were the very opposite of those desired by Frederick. Even his virtues were contemptible in his uncle's eyes. He was generous to a fault, ready to give way to others, easily kindled to enthusiasm, with even some chivalry about him; but of the stern self-denying devotion to duty and his country necessary to a ruler of Prussia at this time, there was in his easy, pleasure-loving, sensual nature not a trace.

At first after the peace he was for a time in better favour with Frederick, and was taken by him, in the spring of 1763, on his journey of inspection into Pomerania and the Westphalian provinces. The next year, however, there came storms.

Frederick's hopes of training a successor after his own pattern had failed, and on failure Frederick was always mercilessly severe. Von Borcke, the military governor, was suddenly sent into retirement to Pomerania, and Beguelin, the tutor, was ordered to Berlin, where he was kept practically in confinement.

A MYSTIC ON THE PRUSSIAN THRONE

From this time, though there were occasional reconciliations, uncle and nephew were never really on good terms. Frederick had suffered severely in his own youth from a father's dislike and displeasure; he had known blows and imprisonment, and had even been compelled to see the passing to his death of his friend and confidant. It is said he was determined not to treat any one else with such severity. But when we realise Frederick's strong personality; how, in the verdict of his contemporaries, when he set himself to win and persuade he was absolutely irresistible, and how by a glance and a few disdainful words he could quell the rashest opponent, we can imagine that Frederick-William, living under the cold, disapproving eye of his uncle, and bearing his dry sarcasms and biting taunts, might possibly even have preferred the blows and imprisonment.

And as the sycophants and flatterers, never lacking to a young Prince likely soon to occupy a throne, told him a very different tale about his gifts and merits, it is not strange that he should hate the uncle who so often humiliated him. He knew, too, that his uncle set spies on him, his own body-servant being among the number who carried tales of him to the King.

The rift between them had for its worst consequence that the young Prince took more and more to society of a socially and morally lower class. When admitted to his uncle's table he was silent, awkward and constrained, but he made up for it in the society of his boon companions. Of these there were plenty ready to indemnify a handsome and generously minded young Prince for his uncle's severity; and he gave himself up more and more to the company of unworthy favourites.

Frederick had recourse to the usual remedy for an over-gay young Prince. He looked about for a wife for him, and found one in Elizabeth, the daughter of Duke Carl of Brunswick-Wolfenbüttel. This family was already closely allied to the Hohenzollerns, Duke Carl being the brother of Frederick's wife, while his wife was Frederick's sister Charlotte, so that the young couple were doubly cousins.

She was beautiful and high-spirited, a favourite with Frederick, who, though never allowing a woman to influence his life, yet took considerable pleasure in the society of clever and intelligent women.

The marriage took place on the 4th of July, 1765, in Charlottenburg. An old custom, that formed a part of the festivities on this occasion, dates back from the early days of the Brandenburgs, and belongs to their position as First Chamberlains of the Empire.

This was the *Danse des Flambeaux*, thus described by Thiébault. The ministers of state, each armed with a lighted torch, make the round of the ballroom in slow steps and according to the rank of their office. The newly-married Princess follows at the same pace, giving her hand to him who is chosen for the honour of accompanying her. Her first chamberlain has a list, and tells each man

<hr />

[1] Thiébault: *Mes Souvenirs*, III. 309.

in turn : " Her Royal Highness invites you to give her your hand." He accordingly goes up to her, makes a profound bow, and, while his predecessor likewise bows and then retires, he offers his hand to the bride, and walks with her till he is replaced by the next.

M. de Guines was French ambassador at this time, and was much annoyed to find that not only Austria —which was natural—but also Russia, had precedence of him. He therefore pleaded that a wound received in the late war had so lamed him that dancing was impossible for him. The next evening the dancing was renewed at Prince Henry's house, and de Guines took care not to arrive till the ceremonial dances were over. But he himself gave a *fête* on the following night, when the grace and agility of his dancing showed clearly that his lameness was of a purely diplomatic character, due only to his jealousy for the honour of his country!

After the wedding the relations between uncle and nephew were for a time better. The young people were welcomed occasionally to Sans Souci, bringing some life and gaiety into the lonely dwelling.

One of the conquests the bride made at Court was that of the Princess Wilhelmina, Frederick-William's only sister. She was then a girl of thirteen, just at an age to be flattered by the friendship of a new and charming sister-in-law, and she worshipped her with girlish enthusiasm.

There are still extant some recollections of her early life at the Prussian Court written by this

Princess, and the simple, naïve narrative gives us a glimpse of the family life from the inside.

She was never closely associated with Frederick-William in her childhood. He was seven years older, and had, as we have already seen, a separate establishment under masculine control. She writes of him as "naturally reserved and timid."[1] He was not at his ease with the King, a fact scarcely to be wondered at if it be true, as she relates, that his uncle, Prince Henry, made the boy read all the embittered correspondence that had passed between the King and his father from the time of the disastrous retreat from Zittau till the latter's death.

As to Wilhelmina herself ("Filmina" she was called in the family circle), she had refused to be inspired by her governess with a dread of her uncle, and she found, as so often happens, the bolder course a much more successful one.

She was allowed to be often with her sister-in-law, and she notes the extraordinary influence Elizabeth had over the King. Not that he was blind to her faults, but that she had a wonderful knack of talking him round and getting him to see them in a favourable light. We find mention of frolicsome evenings when the ladies of the Court were allowed to assume for the time the functions of the King and his ministers, drawing lots for the different positions; of another time when they were all invested with sovereignty, Frederick having ordered a sugar crown

[1] *Erinnerungen der Prinzessin Wilhelm von Oranien*, edited by Prof. Volze.

and sceptre to be placed beside each lady's plate at table.

In May of 1767 a daughter was born to Frederick-William, that Frederika who afterwards came to England as the wife of the Duke of York, second son of George III.

But the same month brought a great loss to the Hohenzollern family, and to Frederick a grief that saddened the rest of his days.

This was the death of the promising young prince, Henry, Frederick-William's only brother. The preference Frederick had shown for this nephew was, as has been already mentioned, very marked, and his hopes for the future were centred on the boy. At the age of fourteen Prince Henry had begged to be allowed to accompany his uncle in the field, a request that naturally was not granted. It delighted Frederick to find that the boy occupied the time when he was left at Magdeburg by diligent study, taking of his own accord an extra course of lessons on fortification, in which he believed himself weak. He shared his uncle's love of philosophy, and by the time he was eighteen had mastered the systems of Descartes, Leibnitz, Malebranche and Locke, not merely retaining in his memory their reasoning, but bringing a clear judgment to bear on the matter.

At the close of the war he had been summoned with his brother to Potsdam, where he carried on his military training in a regiment of Guards, and it was noticed that the younger brother was much more frequently invited to the royal table than the elder.

YOUTH AND FIRST MARRIAGE

Early in 1767 he was in the Kyritz garrison, and was ordered to bring his regiment from thence to Potsdam for the spring review. On the march thither he halted in the village of Protzen, and took up his abode for the night in the house of the widow of General von Kleist. When he should have continued the march next day it was found that small-pox had developed, and he was obliged to remain. Doctors from Ruppin and Berlin were brought as soon as possible, but on the 26th of May the young Prince died. The room of that country mansion in which he breathed his last is still called "the Prince's room."

To Frederick the loss was irreparable. In a letter to his brother Henry he wrote: "I loved the child as if he had been my own." He wrote a eulogy of the young Prince, that was read at a Meeting of the Royal Academy of Science, in which he exalted his precocious talents and admirable character in a manner that conveyed a barely concealed censure of the elder brother.

Princess Wilhelmina, too, felt the loss deeply. Only three years older than herself, Prince Henry had been her playfellow and companion. In her *Recollections* she counts it for righteousness in Frederick-William that he had never resented her open preference for his younger brother.

Meanwhile, in the domestic affairs of Frederick-William the horizon had not long remained serene and unclouded. His marriage did not put a stop to his numerous other amours, and among these latter there was one connection he made which, seemingly insignificant at first, was destined to influence his whole life.

Wilhelmina Encke, afterwards known as Mme. Rietz and finally as Countess Lichtenau, was the daughter of a poor musician, and Frederick-William first saw her when, as a child of twelve, she went to and fro carrying parcels for her elder sister who, as singer at the Italian Opera, had attracted the fugitive admiration of the Prince.

Some say he first noticed her through interfering to save her from her sister's harsh treatment, but at any rate he soon became interested in her. It was a time when Rousseau's *Emile* was popular, and theories of education were much in the air. The young Prince began by educating the girl, finding her a French governess, and himself instructing her in music, geography and history!

Without being beautiful, Wilhelmina Encke was possessed of a fine figure and undoubted powers of attraction. The royal tutor merged later into the royal lover. Never, she wrote in her biography, was so poor a girl the beloved of a prince; she sometimes had to starve one day in order to entertain him the next.

Elizabeth of Brunswick was not the one to put up patiently with a husband's infidelity. Frederick's own description of the affair is this: "The husband, given up to a licentious life from which the efforts of his relations could not wean him, was constantly guilty of infidelity towards his spouse; the Princess, who was in the bloom of her beauty, felt herself much injured by such a neglect of her charms; her lively temperament and the good opinion she had of herself brought her to the determination of revenging her wrongs by paying him out in the same coin. She fell into excesses that were little inferior to his. Family quarrels broke out and soon became publicly known." [1]

Frederick's personal liking for Elizabeth was not allowed to weigh in the balance when the interests of Prussia were at stake.

Princess Wilhelmina had in the meanwhile married the Prince of Orange, Stattholder of Holland, and had removed to her new home before the crisis came in the matrimonial relations of Frederick-William and his wife. From her *Recollections* it is easy to see that her sympathies were with her sister-in-law. Rightly or wrongly, she lays much of the blame on the two younger brothers of this Princess for blackening the Prince of Prussia in his wife's eyes and making ridicule of him in her presence. The King certainly was angry with one of them, William, for he was sent back to his regiment at Frankfort on the Oder. According to Thiébault, his fault was not enlightening the King as to what was going on, although he was in his sister's confidence. But Thiébault is not always correct in his surmises.

Family councils were held; the welfare of the country demanded that there should be no difficulties about the succession to the throne, and a divorce was decided on. In Carlyle's words, it was "done in a beautifully private manner." Elizabeth—her

[1] *Œuvres de Frédéric*, VI, 23.

own family agreeing to the measure—was sent to Schloss Jasenitz, near Stettin, where she lived for seventy-one years, dying in 1840 at the age of ninety-four. And except for one very characteristic incident, to be told in due course, history is silent about her doings all those years.

CHAPTER V

HIS SECOND MARRIAGE

THE death of young Prince Henry left Frederick-William the only male Hohenzollern of the younger generation, and when Elizabeth of Brunswick was divorced, Frederick lost no time in finding another wife for his nephew. Count Schulenburg was sent round to some of the German Courts on a "Brautschau," *i.e.* a tour of inspection of all the likely brides.

At Hesse Darmstadt, where the Landgrave had four unmarried daughters, he was very well received. He wrote of them to Frederick: "The Princesses have nothing brilliant to offer. They are not beautiful, not even pretty, but they are not lacking in engaging qualities. Princess Frederica seems specially worthy of the Crown Prince's consideration. She has sound health, a good heart and much vivacity."

Frederick, in his letter to the bride's father, added some fictitious warmth to this not very enthusiastic description—

"My nephew and I have heard such high praise of the amiable qualities of your Highness's daughter, Princess Frederica, that his ardent desire is for a royal marriage that should bind her to him for life."

The Prince won his uncle's approbation by the

readiness with which he agreed to this union. But an objection to matrimony could never be reckoned among Frederick-William's failings. He wrote to the young lady's mother, urging her to forward his suit to her daughter, while to the Princess herself he wrote—

"Most gracious Princess! My circumstances require that I should marry again. Judging from all the good that I have heard of your Royal High-ness, I am convinced that on your person alone my choice can fall. I have not the happiness to be known to you, nevertheless I hope that you will not reject my petition, and that you will be assured of my doing everything in the world to be worthy of your esteem and your friendship." [1]

The Princess's consent was not difficult to obtain, nor was that of her parents, whose own marriage had been a singularly happy one. Her mother was that Landgravine of Hesse Darmstadt whom Frederick delighted to extol as far superior to most of her sex; he described her as "a man of merit."

Frederick wrote with his own hand to his future niece as follows—

"Your letter gave me great pleasure. Its con-tents are quite in accordance with the wishes of my dear nephew, in whom I always take a lively and tender interest. Your Highness has given him your heart and your hand; and with such distinguished merits at his, your union with him can only be accompanied by happiness of every kind. I shall take pleasure in seizing every opportunity of show-

[1] Paulig: *Friedrich Wilhelm II*, 65.

FREDERICA LOUISA, WIFE OF FREDERICK-WILLIAM II.

ing you the feelings of tenderest esteem with which
I am my dear Cousin's most affectionate cousin
"Frédéric."

Not much time was lost over the matter, for the
wedding took place at Charlottenburg on the 14th
of July, 1769, not quite three months after the first
wife's divorce. A few days later the young couple,
with the bride's mother, Princes Henry and Ferdinand and Princess Amelia, paid a visit to Potsdam.

An incident in connection with this ceremony is
mentioned by Herr Paulig. It being customary for
all who took part in a royal wedding to receive
presents, Frederick asked one of his ministers what
amount was usually spent in this manner. On the
minister mentioning a sum, Frederick at once halved
it, declaring that this amount must be made to do.
The probability is quite in favour of the story being
true. Frederick needed money so badly for schemes
of practical utility, for draining marshes and cutting
canals, for fostering commerce and agriculture, that
he hated parting with it for mere Court functions.

It was the rarest thing for him to entertain royal
visitors at Potsdam in those days. Only one
instance after this do we find of his inviting a party
that included ladies, and this was in the following
year, when the widowed Electress Antonia of
Saxony, a princess whom he specially delighted to
honour, was travelling through Prussia.

He received her in the new palace of Potsdam,
and invited a select company of princesses and
ladies from Berlin (not including his wife) to meet

her. Knowing her love of music, on the first evening of her visit a concert was organised in the palace.

Not often, we imagine, was there a royal family
whose musical gifts and talents were of such a high
order. Frederick so hated mediocrity and ineffici-
ency that we may feel assured no one was allowed
to take part in this performance who did not come
up to his high standard of merit. The Electress
Antonia contributed her share by songs and piano-
forte solos; the King played the flute, the Prince of
Prussia the 'cello, and the Hereditary Prince of
Brunswick the first violin.

Frederick-William's musical gifts would have
been remarkable in any sphere of life. He had in
Duport the best violinist of the day for a master,
and in this direction he displayed not only talent,
but a steady perseverance. His 'cello, like Frederick's beloved flute, accompanied him on all
journeys and campaigns. He had a cultivated
taste, and appreciated old Italian music as well as
the modern German. Of Hadyn's orchestral music
he was particularly fond.

Soon after his marriage Frederick-William
accompanied his uncle to a meeting at Neisse with
Joseph II, who had been elected Emperor on his
father's death, and was associated with his mother
in the government of Austria and Hungary.

Personal interviews between sovereigns were in
those days events of rare occurrence even in the case
of such a near neighbour as Austria, whose possessions not only adjoined the Prussian territory, but
partially encircled it.

HIS SECOND MARRIAGE

Joseph had long wanted to see his mother's life-long enemy, the King of Prussia, who aroused his admiration as the most skilful general and the foremost man of his day. Already in 1766 he had made a pilgrimage to the battlefields of the Seven Years' War, and had then sent an intimation through the Austrian minister at Berlin of his desire for a meeting.

Frederick willingly consented, but Maria-Theresa and her all-powerful minister Kaunitz had scruples as to the advisability of the measure. Joseph gave way on this occasion, but did not abandon the idea, and when in August 1769 Frederick went to Silesia for the usual summer reviews, he again offered a visit.

It came opportunely for Frederick, who was now fearing the too great aggrandisement of Russia; and though bound by a recent treaty to help Catherine with either men or money in any war, he hoped by a *rapprochement* with Austria to put a limit to the Russian schemes in Poland. The same jealousy of Russia had probably led Maria-Theresa and her advisers to consent to the interview they had protested against before.

The meeting was to be of an unceremonious character. Joseph travelled as the *Graf von Falkenstein*, and Neisse, a town close to the frontier, was the place chosen.

The Emperor had especially requested that the Prince of Prussia should also be present, and the two young men seem to have been mutually attracted to one another.

A MYSTIC ON THE PRUSSIAN THRONE

Joseph was one of the most interesting characters of the period. In advance of his age, with large ideas and grand aims, he was full of energy and ardour for reform, but lacked the necessary prudence and judgment to recognise that the times were not ripe for the changes he contemplated. He has been called "a French Revolution on the throne." In his own country he loved to go about incognito, like a Haroun Alraschid, playing the part of a little Providence in rewarding the virtuous and punishing (somewhat arbitrarily) the guilty. Had he lived when the times were less out of joint, he might have achieved a great deal; as it was he only succeeded in gaining for himself the name of a disturber of the public peace, and in arousing the anxiety and distress of his neighbours.

"He had a frankness of manner which seemed natural to him," wrote Frederick in his *Memoirs;* "in his amiable character gaiety and great vivacity were prominent features." [1]

The greatest cordiality prevailed at this meeting. Frederick remarked that he regarded it as the happiest day of his life, since it marked the union of two houses that had too long been enemies; and Joseph replied that for Austria Silesia no longer existed.

The courtesy was returned by Frederick in the following year, when he paid a four days' visit to Joseph at Neustadt in Moravia. He was again accompanied by Frederick-William. It was remarked of the latter at this time that he was embar-

[1] *Œuvres de Frédéric*, VI, 25.

rassed and ill at ease in conversation and in too great subjection to his uncle.

Prince Albert of Teschen in his *Memoirs* wrote of him as follows: "The Prince unites with an almost gigantic figure and a breath and embonpoint which threaten to become colossal, an expression of good humour which impresses one in his favour, but he displays no remarkable talent." It should be remembered, however, that a man would need to be a good deal above the average to shine in the company of a Frederick, a Prince Henry, a Joseph II, a Kaunitz and a Prince de Ligne.

Some of those Austrian generals were present on one or other of these occasions with whom Frederick had only spoken hitherto through the roar of cannon. No one could be more tactful and charming when he chose, and a pretty anecdote is told of him in this connection. When Loudon entered to take his place at the table, Frederick called out to him: "Come and sit near me, M. Loudon; I much prefer having you by my side to facing you!"

At the first meeting nothing of any political importance seems to have passed, beyond a mutual promise to remain neutral in case of war breaking out between England and France, as seemed probable at the time.

At the second interview Kaunitz was present and had long conferences with Frederick. There was anxiety in both their minds lest the war between Russia and Turkey should lead to a general conflagration. Austria could not permit of the cession

95

of Moldavia and Wallachia to Russia, and both were at one in desiring to keep the Russian power within limits.

While they were still at Neustadt a courier from Constantinople brought the Sultan's request for the mediation of their two Courts in making peace with Russia; and the problem before them now was how to induce Russia to conclude a peace that should not, by dismembering Turkey, destroy the balance of power and make herself a menace to the rest of Europe. We shall see presently how, by throwing a weaker neighbour to the wolves, their own safety and the peace of Europe were assured.

In spite of all the compliments exchanged and the friendly demeanour of both parties at this meeting, Frederick came back from it with a profound distrust of the Emperor, in whose mind he discovered the germs of many ambitious projects. He had several busts of him in Sans Souci, and was wont to remark concerning them: "That is a young man on whom I must keep an eye." Another time he expressed himself thus: "The Emperor Joseph has a head; he is capable of much. It is a pity he always takes the second step before he has made the first."

Just previously to this meeting of the sovereigns at Neustadt, in August 1770, a son had been born to the Prince of Prussia; the son who was afterwards to succeed him as Frederick-William III.

And thus Frederick had at last the satisfaction of seeing the succession assured. He visited the Prince's house on the day of the birth and took the newly-born infant into his arms. To a friend he wrote—

"An event of the greatest importance to me and the whole royal house has filled me with the liveliest satisfaction, and what deepens my joy all the more is that it is shared by the whole Fatherland. Could it but one day share with me the further joy of seeing this young Prince treading in the paths that led his forefathers to renown!"

This second marriage of Frederick-William brought no domestic happiness to either of the pair. Letters, still extant, that were written during his absence soon after their marriage are full of affection on his part; but it soon became evident that she had not succeeded in gaining an empire over his heart and weaning him from the bondage into which he had fallen.

Her own moral conduct was without reproach, but she is described as being somewhat unamiable, neglectful of her dress and appearance, and taking no pains to please, yet gentle and much given to works of benevolence.

Outward respect and consideration Frederick-William always showed her; indeed, intentional unkindness to a woman would have been almost impossible to his kind heart and indulgent temperament. She brought him many children, to whom she was a devoted mother.

The negotiations between Russia and Turkey, in which Prussian and Austrian interests were so much involved, went on for a long time before any satisfactory settlement could be reached; and that

H 97

solution of the problem which they found in the First Partition of Poland needs to be touched on, however slightly here, since when Frederick-William came to the throne his participation in the later partitions forms a blot on his name, and the greatest excuse to be found for his conduct in those after years is the fact that he saw similar transactions carried out now without any effective protest being raised against the crying injustice.

There was a time not so very long since when Poland had been the most important power in northern Europe. Her outlying position made her, with Hungary and Venice, the bulwark of Christendom against the Turks, while on the north-east she interposed a strong barrier to keep off the hordes of what were then looked upon as the obscure barbarians of Muscovy. But as Russia began to realise something of its great strength; as the reform of the army, which preceded all other reforms in that country, put into the hands of its sovereign the control of an immense machine, powerful by reason of its numerical strength and the blind obedience and stolid endurance of the peasants who composed it, there began that interference in Polish affairs which never ceased till Polish independence was a thing of the past.

The constitution of Poland bore no resemblance to any other, ancient or modern, and was almost fantastic enough for a Gilbertian comic opera. It was styled a republic, yet they had a king, not hereditary, but elected. There was a Diet, but it was really only a meeting of delegates, whose duty

98

consisted in declaring the will of their respective communities. Any one of these could at once stop the passing of a public measure simply by declaring his dissent from it, and this privilege—called the *liberum veto*, and highly valued as a fundamental part of their constitution—sometimes rendered any legislation whatever impossible. There was a time, at the beginning of the reign of Augustus III, when a pacific anarchy lasted for thirty years, no measure of government or legislation being passed!

At other times violent measures were resorted to for forcibly preventing the attendance of a member likely to dissent. One of the most extraordinary incidents related in connection with this is that of a member who, finding the doors closed to prevent his entrance, managed to make his way down the chimney, and at the critical moment thrust out his head and shouted out his protest. Whereupon an incensed neighbour drew his sword and severed the head from the trunk.[1]

The real power was in the hands of the nobility, who were practically absolute in their own dominions; the peasants were in the greatest degradation, compelled to work so many days a week for their lord that they had no chance of raising themselves out of their abject poverty. There was no Polish middle-class; all the trade was in the hands of Germans or Jews. In the days of her glory Poland was foremost of all European nations in the way of religious toleration; Protestants,

---

[1] Koppen: *Die Hohenzollern*, II, 502.

A MYSTIC ON THE PRUSSIAN THRONE

Anabaptists and sectaries of all kinds, driven out from other countries, found a refuge there, and to the Jews it became a second home. But of late years the Jesuits had gained an ascendancy, and measures had been passed to prevent the Dissidents—as all were called who were not orthodox Catholics—from any share in the government.

Unfortunately for Poland she had neighbours whose interest it was to keep up this miserable state of anarchy, which passed by the name of liberty; and all attempts at unification of the State in the hands of a more powerful sovereign were thwarted by Russia on the one hand and Prussia on the other.

Unfortunately, too, in the factions into which Poland was divided, the party that wished for reform played into the hands of the foreign aggressors, while the national party strove to keep up the old impossible methods.

The fact that the sovereigns were elected by the Diet gave great openings for foreign interference; by bribery and intimidation Russia could generally get her puppets on the throne, though Sweden, France and Austria all tried to have a finger in the Polish pie. Thus when Augustus II died in 1733 there had nearly been a general European war over his successor. France wanted the restoration of Stanislaus Leczynski, whose daughter was the wife of Louis XV. But Russia and Austria upheld the late King's son, who succeeded him in Saxony; and Russia, under the Empress Anne, solemnly guaranteed the Polish constitution, and on this pretext marched 60,000 men into Poland and compelled the election of her candidate under the name of Augustus III.

Unhappy Poland soon learned what it meant when a so-called foreign ally guaranteed her constitution or her integrity; it became the recognised formula as a preliminary of invasion.

On the death of Augustus III in 1763, it was again a Russian Empress who virtually decided the succession. Catherine bestowed the crown on a discarded lover, who had enjoyed her favour before she came to the throne, Stanislaus Poniatowski. The next year she and Frederick made an alliance to oppose the strengthening of the royal power by making the crown hereditary, and to support the Dissidents. These two powers and Austria all declared their firm determination to maintain the integrity of Poland, which, however, meant in plain words that none of them would allow the others to increase their territory at Poland's expense unless allowed a share in the spoil. The language of diplomacy has much the same meaning to-day.

Frederick claimed for himself the first project of a partition, which fell, he says, on deaf ears. It was Austria who actually took the first step, and that in the same year which saw the meeting of the two sovereigns at Neustadt, by quietly marching over the frontier and taking possession of the district of Zips, which had indeed once formed part of Hungary, but had been in Poland's possession for 350 years. But it was Russia who gave the impulse, for it was evident to the other countries that if they took no steps to interfere, the whole of

Poland would fall into her power, and who could tell whether it might not be their turn next?

The project was started—all authorities seem to agree in that—during a visit that Prince Henry paid to St. Petersburg at the Czarina's request. A remark of Catherine's has come down to posterity as pregnant of result. Hearing of the aggressive action of Austria in Zips, she said to Prince Henry : " It seems that in Poland all one has to do is to stoop and take what one wants." Some say that Prince Henry, on seeing a roast capon brought to table that was overdone and theatened to fall in pieces, so that it was necessary to divide it and put it on separate dishes, remarked significantly : " See ! the fate of Poland ! "

But at any rate Henry came back with a definite proposal, and at the same time Russia's demands before she would consent to make peace with Turkey were so enormous that Frederick grasped at the idea of sacrificing Poland, so as to induce her to give up the other acquisitions that would infallibly have driven Austria to take arms. So the three proceeded calmly to the cutting up of the weaker neighbour. Frederick contented himself with very much the smallest portion, but it was one that filled up the awkward gap between East Prussia and Pomerania, and thus was of the greatest use to him.

All his diplomatic efforts, however, failed to induce Catherine to let him make his possession complete by the acquisition of the two towns of Dantzig and Thorn. The Vistula was his, and the harbour of Dantzig, but Catherine declared that she had guaranteed the liberty of this little republic. Frederick attributed her firmness in this instance to the malign English influence; but he finally yielded the point. His minister, Hertzberg, was always most anxious for the acquisition of these two towns; and in Frederick-William's reign we shall see how greatly his policy was governed by this ruling idea.

Austria's consent was obtained after long negotiations, Maria-Theresa's scruples being with difficulty overcome. She was not too much blinded by zeal for the political interests of her country to see the matter from the point of view of international morality. With true prophetic instinct she saw what a precedent this made. When in the beginning of the next century Napoleon "indemnified" one country, whose aid he might momentarily require, by slices out of another, he was after all only following an example that the three partitioning nations now set.

But Maria-Theresa, though she wrote to Kaunitz that " public right shrieked to heaven " against them, felt herself no longer able to enforce her personal desires against the judgment of her counsellors. She consented under protest.

An incident in this connection, mentioned by Sir James Mackintosh, is not without interest. The conferences about the partition were supposed to be carried on with the greatest secrecy, yet Prince Louis de Rohan (of diamond necklace fame), who had been sent to Vienna as the ornamental part of the French Embassy, got an inkling of what was going on. He was not believed when he sent word of it, since Durand, who was supposed to be the working member, knew nothing of it.

In a private letter he wrote—

"I have seen Maria-Theresa weep over the misfortunes of oppressed Poland; but that Princess, practised in the art of concealing her designs, has tears at command. With one hand she wipes away her tears, with the other she wields the sword for the Partition of Poland." [1]

This rather spiteful account fell by some means into the hands of Mme. du Barri, who read it aloud at one of her supper-parties. It happened that one of her guests was an enemy of de Rohan's, and he carried the story to the Dauphiness, Marie Antoinette. Her natural indignation at this insulting mention of her mother was increased by the erroneous belief that the letter had been written to the Du Barri herself. Marie Antoinette never forgave de Rohan, and it was his anxiety to make peace with her and regain her favour that was his incentive to the scheme of the diamond necklace.

Frederick had no scruples of the sort, and consequently he did not much believe in those of Maria-Theresa. "She is always in tears," he said, "yet she is always ready to take her share." Russia, as the strongest, got the largest portion of the spoil, though whether the partition was actually such as Catherine marked out, when she dipped her finger in the ink and divided Poland on the map in one of her conferences with Prince Henry, history does not say.

[1] Sir James Mackintosh, p. 357.

HIS SECOND MARRIAGE

Frederick, at any rate, was well satisfied with his acquisition. Carlyle, always ready to believe that any successful action is by reason of its success proved to be righteous and in accordance with the Divine Will, writes thus of him: "Nobody seems more contented in conscience, or radiant with heartfelt satisfaction, and certainty of thanks from all wise and impartial men, than the King of Prussia, now and afterwards, in regard to this Polish atrocity!"[1]

If anything could justify the action it was the zeal, the energy and capacity he displayed in bringing law, order and prosperity into a land where such things had been of late unknown; where the villages were little better than groups of dunghills, where the towns were mostly in ruins, and where no man knew what was his own.

[1] Carlyle: *Frederick the Great*, X, 31.

CHAPTER VI

ONE of the steps taken by Frederick-William with
a view to gaining the favour of his uncle was that
of entering into a correspondence with Voltaire.
For in spite of the well-known quarrel between
these two remarkable men, who never seemed able
to discover whether they most admired or detested
one another, a correspondence still went on, and
Frederick's nephew might well have thought to
gratify him by showing deference to the philosopher
whom he had once so delighted to honour.

Certainly of his own initiative Frederick-William
would never have desired any intercourse with the
witty sceptic, for in religious matters his point of
view was as different from that of his uncle as in
political. His father had not, like Frederick and
Henry, been influenced by the wave of rationalism
that spread over Europe in the eighteenth century.
He had been accustomed to take Frederick's place
at any ceremony of a religious character. Queen
Elizabeth-Christine left behind her several pious
dissertations, and it is evident that the family influences surrounding Frederick-William in his childhood were of a nature to make him view with
repugnance Frederick's alienation from the orthodox
faith. It is true that Frederick-William's religious

teacher, Sack, had tried to imbue him with a spirit
of toleration towards all creeds, that there stood
in his dressing-room a bust of Moses Mendelssohn,
the enlightened Jew, to whom even Frederick had
refused admission to the Berlin Academy; but
towards the rational deism of Frederick or the
materialism of his French friends, the young Prince
had not the slightest leaning. Indeed his impres-
sionable mind already showed symptoms of that
inclination to the marvellous, which afterwards
made him the dupe of unscrupulous schemers.

The question as to what should be the subject of
his discussions with Voltaire was a difficult one; he
asked the advice of his old tutor Beguelin, stipulat-
ing that it must be neither poetry, metaphysics nor
his Uncle Frederick! The immortality of the soul
was the topic finally chosen; but the correspondence
did not come to much. Frederick-William's interest
in it was purely perfunctory. He contented himself with slightly altering the letters that his tutor
sketched out for him, and after a few months
(November 1770 to March 1771) the correspondence
flickered out.

In 1772 Frederick took his nephew with him to
the review in West Prussia, and when that was over,
sent him to superintend a similar function in East
Prussia, a province in which the King himself had
never set foot since 1758, being unable to forgive
the inhabitants for not having, as he considered,
offered a sufficiently firm resistance to the Russian
invasion.

Glimpses of life in Berlin at this time are to be

found in the *Diary* and *Letters* of the first Earl of Malmesbury, who as James Harris, and afterwards as Sir James Harris, was there in 1767 and again from 1772 to 1776.

He found it an over-built town with more fine and large houses than could well be occupied. Both Frederick and his predecessor had wished to see their capital adorned with fine residences, and Frederick-William I had set about it by the simple autocratic method of issuing orders to many of his nobility to build themselves town houses, careless as to whether it left them with means sufficient to occupy the houses when built.

Frederick, with his large way of seeing things, was concerned for the appearance of the town as a whole. When the new opera-house, the Catholic Church and Prince Henry's palace were built, he found that the latter faced some property belonging to the Margrave of Schwedt, that was partly stable and partly garden. He therefore desired the Margrave to erect a building of at least two storeys high, so that the frontage should be more in keeping with the surrounding buildings. The Margrave accordingly continued his stables to the end of the frontage, raised a wall to the height of two storeys, had it pierced with windows and built a great portico in front through which carriages could pass, but did nothing further. Now it so happened that Prince Henry's palace, which was opposite, had a large façade but only a small and insignificant door. An Italian architect, happening to stand between the two buildings and noticing these features, remarked :

" Extraordinary ! Here is a house without a door, and there is a door without a house ! "

Lord Malmesbury himself had a house so large that he could only occupy a quarter of it. He wrote of the new palace at Potsdam, which Frederick had begun to build soon after the close of the Seven Years' War, as very magnificent, superior to Versailles, the Escurial or any palace he had seen, but as tasteless and tawdry in spite of its magnificence. Carlyle called it very happily "a stone apotheosis of an old French beau."

J. G. Förster in his *Correspondence with Jacobi* writes of the town—

" Berlin is certainly one of the finest towns in Europe. But the inhabitants ! Hospitality and a tasteful enjoyment of life have degenerated into luxuriousness, riotous living—one might almost say gluttony ! " [1]

And Lord Malmesbury describes Frederick's subjects as poor, vain and without principles, the women utterly corrupt.[2]

A change had come over the capital since the days when Frederick-William I watched over its morals with the eye of a stern parent. His methods were despotic and peculiar. He would stop passers-by in the street and interrogate them as to their calling and manner of life. It is said that he once doubted the word of a dancing-master, and the unfortunate man had to dance a saraband in the public street to convince the King that he had stated his

---

[1] J. G. Förster : *Briefwechsel*, I, 201.
[2] *Malmesbury Diary*, I, 83.

profession truly. Despotic and peculiar as his methods were, they were also effectual; and Frederick the philosopher was heard to say in his old age that he only wished he were leaving behind him such an industrious, frugal, God-fearing nation as he had found on his accession.

Frederick had appointed as Governor of the city Lieutenant-General von Ramin, the severest of martinets, with the idea that he would maintain good discipline. His surliness and truculence made him unpopular in the city, but nevertheless he had enough of the courtier in him not to risk incurring the displeasure of a Prince who must before very long succeed to the throne. Thiébault tells of an occasion when the Prince, being in disgrace with his uncle, was ordered to return to Potsdam and not to visit Berlin next day, although a ball was to be given at his Uncle Henry's palace. The Prince, however, disobeyed and came in, as he hoped, secretly. But Frederick had knowledge of it and ordered General Ramin to arrest the Prince.

The General was seated at the supper-table when the order came in, which he had no desire to carry out. He found a way out of the difficulty by pretending he could not see to read it; asking one of his aides-de-camp to hold a light, he carefully held the letter so that the officer could not fail to see the contents. The latter readily understood what was expected of him, and while nominally obeying the command by assembling a squadron for the arrest, he hurried off to the ball-room, which he entered in disguise, warning the Prince so that he got off in safety.

The King himself could not certainly be accused of setting an example in extravagance. In contrast to most sovereigns of his time he looked upon the funds of the nation as a deposit to be used solely for the public benefit. His own personal expenses were of the smallest, and he saw to it that there was no extravagant outlay in Court functions or even in royal hospitality. A satirical Frenchman once remarked that he thought there must be some festivity going on in the Queen's palace, for he had seen an old lantern being lit above the grand staircase! Frederick would cut short the stay of his royal visitors by a politely expressed regret that they were obliged to leave on a certain day, this being the first they had heard of the obligation! Indeed he carried frugality to an excess; and his ministers when sent abroad were allowed so little that such an appointment sometimes meant financial ruin.

The extravagant tastes of the Prince of Prussia were one cause of his great disfavour with the King. Malmesbury wrote of him: "In dressing, whenever he can venture to lay aside his uniform, he is refined and delicate to a degree." He kept a valet travelling between Potsdam and Paris to keep him informed of alterations in the fashion.

Between the expensive tastes and prodigal generosity of the Prince and the parsimony with which Frederick doled out money to his heir, it is not surprising to hear that heavy debts were incurred. Malmesbury wrote in March 1775—

"It is impossible to describe the pecuniary distress of the Prince of Prussia. On his marshal's death a debt on the kitchen establishment of £15,000 and on the others in proportion. His credit is entirely exhausted, and this, joined to the state of subjection in which he lives, affects, in a very sensible manner, his spirits."

Indeed a person in his confidence had even approached Malmesbury with a view to borrowing money from the English Government. To this request the envoy turned a deaf ear. In the youth of Frederick England had been more complaisant, and had advanced him money, which on his accession had been punctually repaid. Frederick-William's efforts at other courts were also fruitless; but a business house in Holland lent him large amounts, which he also at the beginning of his reign repaid with interest.

Meanwhile his relations with Wilhelmina Encke had received a sort of sanction from his uncle, who believed her to be a harmless person not likely to attempt interference in public affairs. What Frederick most dreaded was lest some clever, scheming Frenchwoman might gain an influence over the too easily led Prince. At one time he had suspected the favourite of trying to obtain official posts for her friends, and ordered his officials not to accept the recommendations of "a certain exalted person." She had been banished to Hamburg on one occasion, but after an absence of only a few months she returned to Berlin.

Frederick warned her that she would do well to marry some suitable person, and promised her a dowry. Such an one was found in Rietz, who had attracted Frederick-William's notice as a gardener, and had been attached to his person as a body-servant. He is said to have been the usual scape-goat on the occasions of those sudden outbursts of anger, to which Frederick-William, like most of the Hohenzollern family, was subject. Even the philosophic Frederick, according to Malmesbury, broke his favourite fiddle on the head of a valet. Rietz found it worth his while to put up with these infrequent outbursts, for which, when the storm was over, he was more than amply recompensed. He was also quite willing to accept the position of nominal husband to the favourite; and he not only now found means to gratify his taste for luxury and revelry, but actually began to fancy himself a genius.

Goethe writes of a meeting with him later on in Mannheim—

" I sat at one end of the long, well-filled inn table, while at the other sat Rietz—a tall, well-built, broad-shouldered figure of a man, such as one might have expected to find a body-servant of Frederick-William II. He and his companions had been very noisy, and rose from the table in excellent spirits. I saw Herr Rietz coming towards me. He greeted me in a most confidential manner, expressed his pleasure at making, after long desire, my acquaint-ance, added some flattering remarks, and then said:

I must excuse him. He had also a personal reason for desiring to see me. People had always assured him that men of genius and intellect were invariably small and lean, sickly-looking and frowsy (*vermüfft*), like many specimens that had been pointed out to him. That had always annoyed him. He did not believe himself to be quite an idiot (*auf den Kopf gefallen zu sein*), though he was healthy and strong and possessed of sound limbs. But now he was delighted to find in me also a man of fine appearance, who was nevertheless held to be a genius. It pleased him greatly, and he wished us both long enjoyment of our good health."

On condition that the favourite, now bearing the title of Madame Rietz, should live outside of Berlin and keep the Prince from possibly more dangerous acquaintances, Frederick permitted the latter to buy a house for her. Charlottenburg was chosen as her residence, and Frederick gave him 20,000 thalers for the purpose. One can fancy with what a wry face the King, with so many useful projects crying out for assistance, would dole out money for this purpose.

But another influence than that of the new Madame Rietz was soon to make itself felt. Before, however, we come to Bischoffswerder and the Secret Orders that played such a large part in the life-history of Frederick-William, there are events of greater public importance that must not be overlooked.

Foremost among these was the Bavarian war. The friendly relations between the House of Austria and the Prussian King, displayed at the meetings in Neisse and Neustadt, were not to remain long untroubled. Posterity exonerates Frederick the Great from any suspicion of an ambitious motive or any lust of conquest in this war, which he undertook solely to prevent the encroachments of Austria in Bavaria. This time he appeared as an upholder of the rights of those States of the Empire which had put him under their ban during the Seven Years' War; and by so doing he gained for Prussia a position and a *prestige* among them, which prepared the way for the leading part that was to be hers in later days.

The "Holy Roman Empire of German Nations" is to us readers of to-day a high-sounding name of little import; a vague and shadowy organisation whose functions we fail to grasp. Austria and Prussia, Saxony and Bavaria are comprehensible entities, had actual boundaries and could be seen on the map. But of this Empire, to which three hundred States owned a titular allegiance, it is—as Seeley remarks in his *Life of Stein*—as difficult for us to understand the true nature, as it is for those who know nothing of Oxford and Cambridge to conceive what the University is as distinct from the colleges.

For so many years—except for the brief and troubled interval when Charles VII nominally held it—had the Imperial Crown been in the possession of the reigning family of Austria, that it had almost begun to be looked upon as an appanage of the Habsburgs.

A MYSTIC ON THE PRUSSIAN THRONE

Though tottering to its decay, the Empire was still all that held together the numerous self-governing States large and small, and, scattered among them, the Imperial towns, the domains of the Imperial Knights and of religious foundations that owned no allegiance except that to the Head of the Empire.

Loyalty to the Emperor was still a feeling that influenced the policy of German princes; though in the case of many, during this transition period, it was complicated by a distrust and a jealous suspicion of the Austrian holders of the title.

The Habsburg Emperors were often credited with a desire to augment Austria at the expense of the rest of the Empire. Bavaria, especially Lower Bavaria, had long been coveted to round off the Austrian possessions, and attempts had already been made to get it by exchange. The Chancellor, Kaunitz, who was all-powerful in Maria-Theresa's time, made it the business of his life to acquire this province, and at the beginning of 1778 he believed the opportune moment had come.

On the 30th of December, 1777 the Elector Maximilian Joseph died, and with him was extinguished one branch (the Wilhelmische) of the family to which had belonged Upper and Lower Bavaria and the Palatinate. By one of those Family Compacts, so common in Germany, dating from centuries back, Bavaria now fell to the representative of another branch, Charles Theodore, Elector of the Palatinate. Austria had some slight grounds on which to lay a claim to part of this heritage, and to better these she had, before the death of Maximilian, made a bargain with Charles Theodore, a Prince without either ambition or a sense of honour, who had no legitimate sons and was glad to sell his claim to Bavaria so as to be able to provide for his numerous illegitimate descendants.

On the death of the Elector the prime minister had duly proclaimed Charles Theodore as his successor, but the Emperor Joseph sent troops into Lower Bavaria, and Charles Theodore at once made public his resignation of his claim. Thus, three days after the Elector's death, Bavaria, to its own surprise, found itself Austrian.

But Charles Theodore had a nephew, who as next heir certainly had an interest in the matter. This nephew, Charles Augustus, Duke of Zweibrücken (or Deux-Ponts), had been approached by Austria; and, conscious of his powerlessness, he was on the point of agreeing to the transaction, when an envoy from Berlin gave him to understand that Frederick, with the world-famed Prussian army behind him, would support his resistance.

This materially altered the aspect of affairs. The Duke of Zweibrücken refused the Austrian offers, and announced his opposition to the cession of Bavaria both in Vienna and at the Imperial Diet, where Saxony and Mecklenburg also asserted claims. For three months the matter was contested, but Austria would listen to no representations, and Frederick was compelled to have recourse to arms, though he hoped to the last that a demonstration in force would be sufficient.

A MYSTIC ON THE PRUSSIAN THRONE

His speech to his generals at the review before setting out shows that he went to war in a very different spirit from that of former days. He made touching allusions to the knowledge they had of one another through the many hardships they had shared. Like himself they had grown grey in the service of their country, and though he did not doubt their sharing his horror of bloodshed, he exhorted them to show humanity to a conquered foe and to keep a strict discipline among their own troops.

It was throughout a half-hearted war. Each side hoped that the other would give way rather than come to a decisive conflict.

Malmesbury wrote on April 11th, 1778—

"The garrison left us yesterday morning. The Prince of Prussia marched the same day out of Potsdam at the head of the Guards."

But it was not till the end of June that Frederick abandoned all hope of getting Austria to renounce her project by peaceful means, and marched, with Frederick-William in command of a corps, into Bohemia, while Prince Henry and Count Solms advanced through Saxony.

Prince Henry was again an unwilling combatant. He would have preferred coming to an arrangement with Austria, whereby Prussia might have been compensated by some other acquisition of territory for permitting the swallowing up of Bavaria. His success in the Polish business had perhaps given him a liking for arrangements of this kind. The Duke of Brunswick, his nephew, designated him as "that partitioning Prince."

118

THE BAVARIAN WAR

The Austrians had an army of about 250,000 in the field, one part under Loudon awaiting Prince Henry, while the main body under Joseph himself and Lacy held a very strong position near Königgrätz.

There was consternation in Vienna at finding the redoubtable Frederick again actually in the field, and Maria-Theresa, in motherly anxiety for her two sons, wrote, without their knowledge, an autograph letter to him, trying to start a renewed negotiation.

But though this failed, the two great armies standing opposite to one another in Bohemia never came to a decisive combat. Frederick was getting old and knew that his powers were no longer what they were; he was also aware that a great deterioration in his army had taken place. Its *prestige* was still, however, very great; and he had no desire to risk his hard-won laurels. He was not aggressive in his policy and sought no aggrandisement. To save Bavaria from the clutch of Austria with as little bloodshed as possible was his aim.

The Austrians, too, preferred remaining entrenched in an almost impregnable position to risking a battle in the open, and nothing but skirmishing and reconnoitring took place. Most of the engagements were between foraging parties; the provisioning of the armies was the greatest difficulty of this campaign. In spite of the best endeavours of the Silesian minister, von Hoym, the Prussian army suffered much privation; and sickness and desertion wrought more havoc among their ranks than a battle would have done. A " Potato-war " was the name given by the Prussian soldiers to this seven months' eventless campaign; the Austrians called it a "Zwetschken-rummel" (plum-scrimmage), while their officers, chafing at the inactivity in which they were kept, nicknamed it "the Bavarian law-suit."

With the approach of winter came the necessity for a Prussian withdrawal into winter quarters, and this in a difficult country and in the face of a powerful enemy was a movement that demanded much skill.

This was the only opportunity of distinguishing himself that Frederick-William had in this campaign. He would probably have remembered that it was through failure in a somewhat similar, if possibly more dangerous task that his father's life had been wrecked; at any rate his own dispositions were acknowledged on all sides to have been masterly.

Frederick, the chary of praise, wrote in his account of this war—

"This Prince distinguished himself on various occasions by his vigilance and by his excellent arrangements." [1]

His post, when the retrograde movement began, was on St. Katharinenberg, and he had to leave it at a most unfavourable moment; but his resolution and discretion enabled him to bring his troops safely to camp on the heights of Pilnikau.

Count Schmettau wrote: "When I had the honour of reporting to the King on the execution

[1] *Œuvres de Frédéric*, V, 253.

of this retreat, his face lit up with interest and pleasure, significant of extreme satisfaction. He inquired into every detail, if the firing had been hot, if the march was carried on steadily and in unbroken order; indeed in the whole campaign this was the only moment in which the King appeared satisfied, because this trial effort, which was a masterly one, showed him what he might hope from his successor."

And Frederick further wrote: "M. de Wurmser made several attempts to attack the Prince of Prussia's post, but was always repulsed; a result of the activity and the good disposition of this Prince, whose conduct would have done honour to any officer in like circumstances."

When Frederick met him at Breslau with the contingent he had thus brought safely through, he embraced him in the presence of the troops, with the words: "I no longer consider you as my nephew, but look on you as my son. You have done all that I could have done in your place." At the close of the war he was raised to the rank of lieutenant-general.

In November the whole of the Prussian army had withdrawn into winter quarters, and only a few isolated skirmishes occurred.

Meanwhile Russia and France were endeavouring to bring about a conclusion of this unsatisfactory war, and at a conference at Teschen, Austria at length consented to relinquish her claims to all save a very small portion of Bavaria, that linked the Tyrol with her other possessions.

The war had cost Prussia twenty-nine million

thalers and 20,000 men, and brought it no material gain; but its moral effect had been great in display- ing Prussia as the champion of the integrity of the States of the Empire against an aggressive Austria. Frederick was a hero in the eyes of the Bavarian people. In peasants' huts his portrait now gained an honoured place next to that of the national Saint Corbinian.

After this war the relations between Frederick- William and his uncle were more friendly, or at any rate appeared to be so, for we find Lord Malmesbury writing, under the date of June 5th, 1779—

" H(is) M(ajesty)'s affection and complaisance to the Prince of Prussia daily increases, and the Prince's attention and deference for the King keeps pace. The Prince's character continues to rise in the public estimation. His military reputation particularly is fixed beyond a doubt in the opinion of every officer." [1]

[1] Lord Malmesbury's *Letters*, p. 417.

CHAPTER VII

THE ROSICRUCIANS

Soon after this ineffective Bavarian campaign Frederick-William had a bad illness, during which he was very carefully nursed and tended by the man who was later to exert such a powerful influence over Prussia's sovereign and consequently over the destinies of the nation. This was the "sombre and visionary Bischoffswerder," as Mirabeau described him.

Of Saxon nationality, Johann Rudolf Bischoffswerder had yet served with the Prussian army in the last campaigns of the Seven Years' War. An injury due to a fall from his horse led him to retire when peace was declared, and he entered the service of the titular Duke of Courland, a Saxon prince and member of one of those secret societies whose nebulous doctrines and marvellous promises attracted so many adherents in the latter part of the eighteenth century.

The outbreak of the Bavarian war had offered Bischoffswerder another chance of military service, which he eagerly seized, serving as a captain under Prince Henry in Bohemia. The end of the campaign found him a major and attached to the suite of the Prince of Prussia. The illness of the latter gave him a grand opportunity of acquiring a hold

123

over the mind of a Prince so susceptible to kindness, so open to influence.

Bischoffswerder was a man of imposing size, yet agile and of great prowess in most bodily exercises. Brought up in the artistic, intellectual and luxurious Court of Saxony, his manners had a dignity and refinement, enhanced by an almost mysterious solemnity, not ill adapted to impress the credulous with the idea that behind him stood some powerful, unseen force. He had by this time won a high position among the Rosicrucian fraternity, and was a firm believer in the healing power of an elixir known to the Order, to which he and Frederick-William attributed the latter's recovery.

There was in the eighteenth century, especially in Germany, a great vogue for secret societies. To a great extent it was a reaction against the dry rationalism of the movement known as the "Aufklärung."

It is impossible to understand aright Frederick-William's relations with his uncle, his actions in private life or his edicts when he came to the throne without some idea of the contending influences that swayed the minds of men at this period.

We had nothing in England that corresponded to the "Aufklärung." We have not even an adequate translation for the name of this movement—a name that had its origin in the illustrations on the title-page of some of Christian Wolff's works: a rising sun breaking through the mist.

Though Rationalism had its pioneers among English thinkers, it made no way among the people

JOHANN RUDOLF BISCHOFFSWERDER.

at large. It was different in Germany, where the new opinions, introduced mainly by Wolff, were spread abroad not in philosophical treatises only, but in publications simple enough to be "understanded of the people"; and where the dogmatism of the orthodox was particularly rigid, meticulous in detail and out of touch with nature and humanity.

Beginning with an attempt to reconcile reason and revelation, the movement gradually took on a more anti-religious character. Frederick himself, like Voltaire, shrank from a bald atheism; but Voltaire's followers in France and their German imitators (for everything French was fashionable in Berlin) did not stop short of a scepticism that mocked at all religion and a materialism that acknowledged no bonds of morality. Religion was considered good only for the masses.

The new opinions found adherents of very varied types: from sensualists who asked nothing better than to be freed from all moral obligations and restrictions up to men of lofty character and high ideals who welcomed a religious philosophy that saw more of God in nature than in theological arguments, and set reason above ecclesiastical authority.

The "Aufklärung" was preached from many Lutheran pulpits. Even within the Roman Church a strong feeling arose against the despotic forms of Church government, against superstition and love of the miraculous. The Emperor Joseph II, head of the Holy Roman Empire, was deeply influenced by the *Aufklärung*.

Naturally the movement had its opponents. It aroused a new zeal, born of opposition, in the minds of the strictly orthodox; and a reaction against its dry utilitarianism causing the pendulum to swing in the opposite direction, a wave of mysticism, of wild credulity and belief in the marvellous and supernatural spread over the land.

To those who longed for the regeneration of mankind and for improvements in the existing order of things, but found no outlet for their zeal in the conditions of public service at the time, the idea of a society of noble and enlightened spirits, linked by secret ties and working together for the general good, made a powerful appeal. The two Societies of Jesuits and Freemasons already existed to point out the way.

Frederick himself had founded a Bayard Order, and after the Seven Years' War a secret society of Friends of the Fatherland. The students at the various universities had their own secret societies, one of which was the nucleus of the famous Order of the Illuminati.

The Jesuits had been suppressed by Clement XIV in 1773, but in the secret societies they found a means of carrying on their activities unopposed.

From the lap of Freemasonry arose the Order of "Strict Observance," which had its origin in France, but was afterwards called Scottish, since part of its programme was the restoration of the Stuarts in Great Britain. It offered grades of rank with high-sounding titles, and numbered many German princes among its adherents. Among these was Ferdinand,

THE ROSICRUCIANS

Duke of Brunswick, of fame in the Seven Years'
War; a man held in such high esteem for probity
and sincerity that his appointment as Grand Master
of the German Lodges doubtless did much for the
increase of the Order. The Leipsic Lodge of this
Order was much influenced by a man named
Schrepfer, who laid claims to supernatural wisdom
and more than mortal powers; and among those
taken in by his deceptions were the Duke of Courland, Bischoffswerder's patron, and Bischoffswerder
himself. Schrepfer, whose suicide on account of
debts did not suffice to open the eyes of his victims,
called himself a Rosicrucian.

The origin of the Rosicrucian fraternity, which
first became known to the public in 1614, is still a
disputed point; the works that are supposed to throw
light on the subject only serve to make the darkness
visible; and to get a solid fact out of the maze of
supposition and hypothesis is difficult. It is probable that, beside the original society of that name,
there were other associations that adopted its title
and emblems. There is also a Rose-cross degree
in Freemasonry, which tends still further to increase
the confusion. Not only is the authorship of the
manifestoes issued by the society still a disputed
point, but in the one case where this has practically
been settled, the *Chymical Marriage of Christian
Rosenkreuz*, published by Andreæ in 1616, it is
doubtful whether the work was intended seriously,
or as a satire on the prevailing taste for the occult
and the marvellous! [1]

[1] This quaint allegorical romance may be read by the curious
in A. E. Wayte's *Real History of the Rosicrucians*.

A MYSTIC ON THE PRUSSIAN THRONE

The particular fraternity of Rosicrucians that came to the front in Germany in the beginning of the latter half of the eighteenth century boldly laid claim to occult powers, to understand the Hermetic mysteries and magical signatures, and to have authority over elemental spirits. They held out all the old hopes: the discovery of the secret of the transmutation of metals, of a universal elixir, of the Philosopher's Stone. Medical and chemical secrets were to be discovered that should greatly benefit the world. There were some, like the surgeon Theden, who tried to catch falling stars, believing that from their substance might be distilled the "prima materia," a tincture for universal use; and others who hoped to find a means of making living animals or finding metals in putrid rain-water!

The mania for these societies even penetrated into the domain of feminine fashions. Large white muffs *à la franc-maçons* became the vogue.

The real leaders of the society worked in secrecy; each member received a new name by which alone he was known to all save his immediate superior; he was completely in the dark as to whence came the mysterious orders he received, and yet this unknown higher authority must be implicitly obeyed. Naturally, such a society would soon become a happy hunting-ground for clever impostors and swindlers, who could exploit for their own purposes the simplicity of the credulous.

Bischoffswerder was already a member of the Rosicrucian fraternity when he first came to Berlin in 1773, and he bore the magnificent title of

THE ROSICRUCIANS

FARFERUS PHOCUS VIBRON DE HUDLOHN; but it was not till after the Bavarian war and the illness through which he nursed Frederick-William that his persuasion induced the latter to join the Rosicrucians.

It was with Freemasonry that Frederick-William began. Frederick the Great had been initiated into the Order as a young man, but had soon lost interest in it. Nevertheless, during his reign the number of Lodges had increased, so that in 1777 there were thirteen in Berlin alone. Zinnendorf, the head of the whole medical staff of the Prussian army, was a zealous supporter of the Swedish branch of Freemasons, and had united with it the Lodge of the Golden Keys, to which Frederick-William belonged.

Now, however, won over by Bischoffswerder's imposing personality, impressed by his knowledge and the high moral principles he professed, the Prince desired to join the Rosicrucian fraternity, whose secret leaders were naturally delighted to have such a distinguished recruit; though, in order to impress him more deeply with the sanctity and seriousness of their authority, they made him undergo a year's probation and exhorted him to a stricter morality in his life before admitting him into the society.

The name of ORMESUS MAGNUS was bestowed upon him, and only a few of the confraternity had any idea who it was that passed under this title. In an account of a meeting of the Order at Hamburg, the circle-director is described as closing his dissertation as follows: "Since our highest Superiors recognise and foresee that a newly joined Brother of the name of ORMESUS MAGNUS may be able to do much for the spread of Christ's kingdom and our Order, they have enjoined on us to pray for him. Which we do as follows——"

Bischoffswerder was, at any rate at this time, sincere in his beliefs, and his enthusiasm and zeal were honest. The same can scarcely be said of the man who through him was now brought into contact with Frederick-William, and became, one might almost say, his evil genius—Johann Christoph Wöllner.

Wöllner, the son of a pastor, had belonged to the rationalistic party, the *Aufklärers*, and had been an ardent admirer—or at any rate a lavish flatterer— of Frederick the Great. He had studied agriculture and written about it, advocating various reforms adapted from the English system, whereby he had attracted Frederick's notice and favour. But by his marriage he had incurred the King's displeasure. Having been tutor to the son of General von Itzenplitz, he so ingratiated himself with the widow and sister of his pupil that he was permitted to marry the latter, a great heiress. Frederick had a great dislike to see members of the nobility marry out of their own class; he refused Wöllner's petition to be raised to his wife's rank, calling him "a deceitful, intriguing priest." Wöllner appears never to have forgotten his rebuff from the King, and when his hand was at the helm of public affairs, it was always in the opposite direction from that which Frederick had guided it that he sought to steer the ship of State.

THE ROSICRUCIANS

For fifteen years Wöllner had written—though mainly on agricultural subjects—for the *Allgemeiner deutscher Bibliothek*, the chief organ of the *Aufklärung*, and he was closely befriended with Nicolai and other leaders of that movement. In 1770 Prince Henry gave him a post in the management of his estates. He owned a good house in Berlin, in which he lived, and he was now forty years of age.

Judging from his history and his previous opinions, one would not have suspected him of a tendency to religious mysticism; and it seems more probable that he joined the Order of Strict Observance among the Freemasons and afterwards the Rosicrucians less from conviction than with the hope of furthering thereby his ambitious schemes.

If so, his desires were to some extent realised. He displayed such zeal and energy in working for the Order that he soon became an adept, and founded a Rosicrucian Lodge of which he was first orator and then circle-director. CHRYSOPHIRON was the name he was known by in the Order generally, while to the secret superiors he was HELIOCONUS.

We find the former rationalist addressing his followers thus : " Oh, my brethren ! the time is not far off when we may hope that the long-expected Wise Ones from the East will teach us and bring us into communion with High and Invisible Beings."

After the Bavarian war the next important duty that devolved upon Frederick-William was one that he did not bring to a successful issue, but its failure was due mainly to outward causes for which he was not responsible.

Of late years, and especially during the reign of that remarkable woman the Czarina Catherine, Russia had emerged from its position of outer barbarism and begun to play an important part in European politics, a keen rivalry existing among the other nations, especially Austria and Prussia, to have her as an ally.

As a girl in her home at Cüstrin, Sophie-Frederike of Anhalt-Zerbst (for the name of Catherine was only taken on her marriage) showed no signs of the remarkable qualities she was afterwards to display. Her governess found her "serious, thoughtful, cold," and little dreamed of the forces hidden beneath that outward calm, or of the great *rôle* in the world her pupil was to play.

When her marriage with the heir to the Russian throne brought her to the St. Petersburg Court, she set herself quietly to work to gather information and to gain an insight into the affairs of the country, which stood her in good stead when the brutal murder of her husband by the Orloffs put an end to the brief struggle for supremacy between the pair, and placed absolute, despotic power in her hands.

In her youth she was described as remarkably beautiful, with dark hair and blue eyes, a slim figure, graceful carriage, and a most melodious voice. But her talents and force of character were more remarkable than any beauty. Brought up in the narrow, restricted atmosphere of a petty German principality, she proved herself, when at the head of the greatest Empire in Europe, fully equal to her position. Without good generals or capable statesmen, she yet managed to effect considerable reforms, to organise the internal administration and greatly to improve her army.

Her worst enemies, wrote Malmesbury, were her accessibility to flattery and her own strong passions. The long succession of her favourites made her reign scandalous even at that period in Russian society, when morality was at a very low ebb, though the greatest luxury prevailed, and a slight though brilliant outward polish concealed the vacuity of illiterate and uninformed minds.[1]

Frederick had at one time possessed great influence over Catherine. She shared his admiration of Voltaire and the Encyclopædists, and French models were as much imitated in St. Petersburg as in Berlin. Count Panin was long in Frederick's pay, and he represented at the Russian Court the influence of Prussia, which, however, was at this time decidedly waning before that of Austria.

Frederick used every diplomatic art within his power to regain his position with Catherine and her heir, the Grand-duke Paul. During Prince Henry's second visit to Russia, when his mission was to smooth any friction that had been caused by the wranglings and discussions incidental to the partition of Poland, the Grand-duchess had died in childbirth. She was a Darmstadt Princess, and sister to Frederick-William's second wife. Prince

---

[1] *Malmesbury Diary*, p. 201.

Henry ingratiated himself with the sorrowing husband by his sympathy on this occasion, and suggested for his consolation a second union, this time with a Princess of the house of Würtemberg.

In July 1776 the Grand-duke had visited Berlin, and the family of his intended bride were invited to meet him. Preuss tells us that on this occasion an unusual effort was made at display. Old rusted chariots, once glorious with gilding, that had not seen the light of day since Frederick's grandfather, the first King of Prussia, had given place to his Spartan successor, were brought out and furbished up.

If the attempted revival of old splendours did not impress the Grand-duke, the personality of the Hohenzollern family certainly did. Malmesbury acknowledges that he never knew any one so persuasive as Frederick could be when he chose to put forth his powers; both Grand-duke Paul and General Romanzoff went back more thoroughly Prussian than ever. With the amiable character of Frederick-William Paul seems to have been particularly impressed; both he and his new wife not only liked him, but thought him talented and likely to play a great *rôle*.

The Czarina, however, was at this time much under the influence of Prince Potemkin, who had been impervious to all Frederick's efforts to win him over to his side. It was he who inspired Catherine with jealousy and distrust of her son Paul with his Prussian leanings, and who dazzled her mind with those glorious visions of a new Greek Empire under the sway of her descendants, when the Crescent was to be finally swept away by the Cross. The realisation of these visions was the goal of all her later policy. Her grandson, in anticipation of his Eastern empire, was named Constantine.

Catherine was clear-sighted enough to recognise that, for all Frederick's friendliness, he did not favour her Eastern policy, and would rather see the strengthening of Turkey than the further aggrandisement of Russia. From Austria far more than from Prussia was there hope of assistance in her schemes. The Emperor Joseph was quite willing to further her plans in the East in return for friendly assistance in the West. An interview she had with him at Mohileff in May 1780 strengthened the friendship between them, and on her return to Russia he stayed with her till the end of July.

This friendship greatly disquieted Frederick, and as a counter-move he decided to send his nephew to St. Petersburg in the autumn.

As a diplomatic move the measure was foredoomed to failure. Catherine and Potemkin were too deeply committed to the Austrian alliance and the Eastern scheme for it to have a chance of success, and Frederick's efforts to renew the old friendship only annoyed her.

She kept his envoy waiting three days before even signifying her consent to the visit. By a confusion between the Old and the New styles of reckoning time, Frederick-William had been dispatched too soon; but Catherine refused to return from the country in time to receive him at the earlier date, so that he was compelled to linger on the way. Count Görtz, the Prussian ambassador at St. Petersburg, took advantage of this delay to meet him at Narva and give him a masterly description of the state of affairs at the Russian capital, and an insight into the character of the most prominent people at that remarkable Court.

The thrifty Frederick had only allowed his nephew 30,000 thalers for the expenses of this visit, a sum very far from adequate considering the lavish splendour of the Russian Court and the presents it would be necessary to give. Frederick-William was compelled to meet the extra costs by borrowing 100,000 thalers on his own account.

Frederick may have hoped that his nephew's personality might make a favourable impression on Catherine, who was notoriously susceptible to masculine charms; but this was far from being the case. Count Panin and many of the Russian courtiers were much impressed with Frederick-William's fine figure, manly bearing and gracious manners, but the Czarina seems to have taken a personal dislike to him and to have made no effort to conceal it. Apparently she also desired to show Frederick, by his treatment of his nephew, how little she cared just then for his friendship.

Malmesbury, then Sir James Harris, was in Petersburg at this time, busy as usual in opposition to Frederick, mining and counter-mining, each trying to predispose Catherine in favour of his own country. Malmesbury found that Frederick, who was very bitter at that moment against our "Goddam government," as he called it, had warned the Prussian minister against our ambassador's evil machinations, and Malmesbury was rather flattered than otherwise to find himself of so much importance in the great Frederick's sight.

His diary is full of Frederick-William's visit and of the Czarina's rudeness to him, made all the more marked by the friendship she showed to the Austrian and English ambassadors.

"In public," he wrote, "she treats him with a coolness and reserve quite foreign to her character, and never speaks to any of his suite. At the Masquerade on Friday and at Court on Sunday he did not play at cards with her; it is the more remarkable as, to make room for me on my coming after she was set down, she made Prince Bariatinsky give me his place. While she is behaving with this very unusual neglect to the Prussian party, she is paying the most marked attention to everything which regards the Court of Vienna. She told Count Cobenzel, before the Prince of Prussia and all his attendants, that a day never passed that she did not recollect and regret Count Falkenstein (the name under which Joseph II travelled); and is profuse to the Prince de Ligne in her expressions of regard and admiration for the Emperor.

"This conduct, so different from what the Prince of Prussia expected, and which he is sure will expose him to the ill-will and anger of his uncle on his return, has so far affected him that he is still less at his ease than at Berlin."

And again: "I have been for these three days

witness to such slights and inattention she has shown
him that I have been amazed at his patience and
temper. Tuesday at Mons. Nariskin's, Master of
the Horse, she neither played, nor asked him to sup
at her table, to which she admitted none but myself,
her favourite and Prince Potemkin. Yesterday at
the masquerade she appeared under the mask, and
immediately on her coming in took me to accompany
her through the apartments, saying (in French):
'Do not leave me all the evening; I have made you
my cavalier, and I want you to protect me against
bores.' She stayed from seven till ten, and took
not the smallest notice of the Prince, or any of his
followers; nor, indeed, scarce of any one but Lady
Harris and myself."

Under the date of September 22nd, 1780, he
wrote to Lord Stormount—

"H.R.H. is endeavouring to bring over Prince
Potemkin, and, if possible, to obtain through him a
more favourable reception at the latter end of his
residence; I, however, do not believe he is likely to
succeed, neither, if he did, that even P. Potemkin
has influence enough to overcome the aversion the
Empress has conceived for him. After insinuating
by every kind of means that it would be agreeable
to her if he would fix his departure for an early day,
she at last has ordered her private secretary to tell
Count Panin very plainly that he must contrive to
get him away soon, as she felt if he stayed much
longer she might say something rude to him. However strange this may appear, I can assure your
Lordship it is fact."

THE ROSICRUCIANS

From contemporary German sources comes a story of a last interview Catherine had with her royal visitor, whom she received although a temporary illness had confined her to bed, and "while shedding floods of tears she gave him the most lively assurances of her friendship for the King and himself, so that he left the imperial chamber quite moved." [1]

Malmesbury, however, after the Prince's departure wrote—

"There was not the smallest change in the Empress's behaviour to the last. She expressed a uniform disgust and *ennui* whenever her illustrious visitor was present, and in speaking of him ever rated his talents and abilities at the lowest pitch. . . . In short, he is gone away displeased and disgusted."

The amity between Frederick-William and the Grand-duke Paul was, however, further confirmed by this visit; they swore an eternal friendship. Paul's second marriage had proved to be a very happy one. His first wife had kept him in the same state of subjection to which his mother had accustomed him, so that during her lifetime he had appeared spiritless and lethargic. But Sophia Dorothea of Würtemberg was of a mild and gentle disposition; for the first time his character was able naturally to expand; he was cheerful and happy, and the dissolute Russian Court was surprised to see in the household of the heir to the throne an example

[1] Dohm's *Denkwürdigkeiten*, II, x. He gives the Prussian Ambassador Görtz as his authority.

of simple, virtuous married life, such as they, unhappily, were little inclined to follow.

Prince Potemkin and his clique treated the Grand-duke as of very little consequence. This extra-ordinary man was then at the height of his power. He is described as being far from handsome, indeed almost repellent in appearance, but with a powerful and impressive personality. He was vain of his one beauty—a splendid head of hair, and was in the habit of having it combed while he gave audiences. He was strongly opposed to the Prussian influence at Court, and we have seen that Frederick-William's efforts to win him over were as unavailing as his uncle's bribes. Count Panin was already in the Prussian interest, but at this time his star was not in the ascendant. It seems then, that, except for cementing his friendship with the future Czar, the Prince's visit to Russia was a failure.

But Frederick was too wily to advertise the fact. On the contrary, he feigned to be delighted with the success of the mission. He not only came to meet his nephew and greeted him with an embrace, but he also ordered the officers of the garrison to congratulate him on his return, which from him was an unusual and very flattering distinction.

"I have now tried him in war and tried him in peace," he said; "in Russia he rendered me good service with the greatest skill possible."

CHAPTER VIII

THE END OF FREDERICK'S REIGN

FREDERICK-WILLIAM himself can have been under no delusion as to the result of his mission to Russia. The consciousness of this failure, added to his disappointment in not having, after the Bavarian war, been given some honourable and important post, tended greatly to depress his spirits.

His military duties at Potsdam were irksome and monotonous. More and more attention was given to a punctilious exactness in small matters of drill and exercise. Princes and princelings at Potsdam had no easy time. Prince William of Brunswick, in answer to a question as to his occupation, said it consisted mainly in conjugating the verb to be bored.

With his uncle, of whose disapproval he was always conscious, Frederick-William was never at ease; and he turned more and more for comfort to the little coterie of wonder-workers, whose hold over him strengthened daily.

Mme. Rietz had from early youth, and especially when in Paris with her sister, dabbled in such forms of so-called spiritualism as were then in vogue—table-turning, mesmeric trances and the rest. The Prince's inclination to belief in the marvellous made him an easy dupe.

141

A MYSTIC ON THE PRUSSIAN THRONE

There were strange doings in the house Wöllner occupied in Berlin, where a regular stage was prepared for "manifestations." Words of counsel and warning were supposed to reach the Prince from the lips of departed sages and heroes, notably Marcus Aurelius and the recently departed philosopher Leibnitz, Julius Cæsar and Frederick-William's own ancestor, the Great Elector of Brandenburg. When we find that a ventriloquist of the name of Steinert was paid a yearly salary for his services, and that mirrors, gauze curtains and darkened rooms formed part of the *mise en scène* of these manifestations, it is easy to conjecture how the marvels were effected. It is less easy to discover who among the coterie were conscious deceivers, and who, besides Frederick-William, were the deceived.

What with his belief in Bischoffswerder's mental attainments and lofty moral character, his trust in Wöllner as an oracle of practical wisdom, and the powerful attraction that Wilhelmine Rietz still held for him, Frederick William fell deeper and deeper into the power of these three.

Bischoffswerder apparently at first made efforts to wean the Prince from his attachment to Mme. Rietz, and was partially successful, since the relations between them became merely those of friendship and confidence. But she had the gift of keeping her admirers charmed and entertained; she was not exacting in the matter of constancy, and she kept her empire over the mind of Frederick-William to the end of his life.

She tells a curious story of how once, in the early

142

days of her poverty, she had expressed to the Prince her fears lest he might be persuaded some day to desert her. He was correcting her writing exercise at the time, and had a penknife in his hand, with which he cut into the ball of his left thumb and wrote with the blood: "By my princely word of honour I promise you never to forsake you. F. W." Wilhelmine was not to be outdone, and she declares that she plunged the knife so recklessly into her own thumb that she could have written reams with the blood, and carried about a lasting scar as a memento.

But in spite of her ascendancy over him and the pleasure he took in her society, it was not Wilhelmine Rietz, but Wöllner, Bischoffswerder and—in the first part of his reign—Hertzberg, whose counsels really dictated the policy of Frederick-William II.

Count von Hertzberg was one of the few ministers employed by Frederick the Great who had energy, character and a decided policy of his own. Though even of him Thiébault says that "He was very valuable under Frederick's directions, but would infallibly lead into error those who trusted to his guidance." His own opinion of his talents was a high one; he even flattered himself so far as to think that Frederick adopted his suggestions. But he was a sincere, zealous and hard-working statesman, having his country's welfare strongly at heart, and he was probably the best of all those who influenced Frederick-William. He loved to have the threads of an elaborate and involved diplomacy between his fingers, but sometimes his schemes miscarried through their very subtlety.

In the latter part of Frederick's reign, annoyed by a preference that he fancied the King had shown to Finckenstein over himself, he set himself to win the favour of the heir to the throne, and tried to inoculate him with his own far-reaching and ambitious political views. He believed Prussia to be capable of still further increase in size and power. Ever since the partition of Poland the fact that Dantzic and Thorn had not been included in Prussia's share had been an unceasing vexation, and he determined not to rest till this was rectified. He complained to the Prince of his uncle's obstinacy in adhering to principles that were now outworn and out of date, and Frederick-William replied by counselling him to " look on his present position as a campaign in which something must be suffered for the public good, and to be strong in patience." [1]

The old King was meanwhile well aware that for many of those about him he had lived too long, but that was not a matter that would greatly distress him. He once wrote to Voltaire : " I go my own way, do nothing against the inner voice of my conscience, and trouble myself very little what opinion of my actions is formed in the minds of featherless bipeds, very few of whom ever think."

While the republican J. G. Förster, who came to Berlin in 1779, complained in a letter to Jacobi of his annoyance in finding " how every one, even the most sensible and intelligent, deifies the King and

[1] Heigel, *Deutsche Geschichte*, I, 65.

worships him in such a foolish manner that even what is wrong or bad or unreasonable in him is at once acclaimed as something excellent and super-human," there were others to whom the little, withered old man with the brilliant eyes and the sharp tongue was the one hindrance that stood in the way of the happy times that were to come in with the next sovereign, whose chief desire was to earn the title of the Well-beloved.

What Frederick called the "toys of his old age" were his schemes for the amelioration of the land. Neither his inherited domains nor his newly acquired provinces were rich, fertile lands that easily yielded a good harvest. Much labour was needed to wring a subsistence from the thankless soil. There were swamps to be cleared, marsh lands to be reclaimed, canals dug, new methods of agriculture, new breeds of sheep to be introduced. "In such things," he wrote to Voltaire, "the mind can still take pleasure, even when the imagination is deadened."

But for all such schemes money was wanted, and the methods he employed for increasing the revenue did more than anything else to render him unpopular with his subjects. With his prejudice in favour of most things French, he had been led to believe that by borrowing his Gallic neighbour's system of excise a much greater revenue could be obtained through indirect taxation than had hitherto been available.

He borrowed not only the system, but also the officials to carry it out, and a disgusted German populace found itself exposed to inquisitorial visits from French Customs officers to "smell out" if coffee had been roasted. For tobacco and coffee had been made Government monopoly, and to prevent the smuggling of the latter, no roasting of it was allowed save at the places where it was authorised to be sold.

Frederick, though he liked coffee for his own drinking, believed it had a debilitating effect; he declared that beer-soup, on which he himself had been brought up, was much more wholesome for the people. Moreover, he did not like to see so much money go out of the country for a foreign produce. It was taxed up to 250 per cent. of its value, and the hated French officials—"cellar-rats," as they were nicknamed—were permitted to make people's lives a burden by the privilege they had of entering and searching houses at any hour of the day or night.

The plan was not very successful in bringing in a larger revenue; the salaries of the highest officials were nearly four times as great as those of Prussian ministers; it led to a great increase of smuggling, rendered easy by the scattered position of the Prussian provinces, with the frontier of a neighbouring State always close at hand; and it became a fruitful cause of crime and disorder.

Frederick's idea had been that as coffee, cocoa, tea and tobacco were not actual necessaries of life, the tax would tell more on the rich than on the poor; but on the contrary, it was especially to the lower classes that the *régie* became a hateful thing, and it caused a revulsion of feeling against the ruler who had introduced and protected the "foreign swindlers."

THE END OF FREDERICK'S REIGN

The story of the poster is well known—how Frederick, seeing a crowd assembled and gazing at something hung high on a wall, stopped to see what it was, and finding it was a caricature of himself sitting doubled up, grinding away at a coffee-mill between his knees, he gave orders that it should be hung lower down, "so that people could see it without getting a crick in their necks."

It was a happy touch, in the true style of the "Alter Fritz" who had talked familiarly to "his children" as they bivouacked round the fire in the old days of the war. He still retained the magnetism of his personality. The muttering changed to applause, and the offending poster was pulled down and torn into a thousand pieces.

Another very characteristic example of Frederick's summary, but sometimes good-humoured dealings, will be familiar to readers of Carlyle. Goods from abroad, and especially articles of luxury, were very heavily taxed, and when through the Custom-house of Stettin there passed a dress of very rich silk coming from Lyons and addressed to the Princess Elizabeth of Brunswick, the divorced wife of Frederick-William, who was living in compulsory retirement close by, the charge to be made upon it was so high that the Customs officer considered it advisable to detain the goods until payment was made.

A "high and peremptory kind of lady" like this Princess was not to be treated in this fashion. She sent word that the dress was to be brought immediately, and that she would pay what was due. But no sooner had the official appeared before her than the Princess seized her Lyons dress and paid the "dues" in the shape of two good slaps on his face, ordering the poor man instantly out of the house!

Much wounded in his official dignity, the officer wrote out a long account of the transaction, which he sent to the King with a formal complaint of the "dishonour done to him while carrying out his duty." Frederick had always a liking for this Princess, whose banishment had been a necessity for the country's sake. He wrote back that he would himself pay the charges due; the dress was to remain with the Princess, the slaps with him who had received them, and as for the dishonour—never, he declared, could the application of a beautiful hand dishonour the face of an officer of customs![1]

It was rarely indeed that Frederick—autocratic as he was in all else—meddled with the administration of justice, which was, he prided himself, carried out in Prussia with absolute fairness and without respect of persons. Though always upholding the privileges of the nobility and liking to keep a sharp and definite line between the different classes of the population, he considered himself particularly the guardian of the interests of the poor, and nothing angered him so much as the idea of oppression of them in his name.

In the one notorious case in which he did summarily interfere, the Miller Arnold lawsuit, it was his mistaken belief that the rich litigant had been

Carlyle, *Frederick the Great*, IX, 272.

favoured, the poor suitor disregarded, that led him to an arbitrary and most unjust action.

A miller and his wife, living at Pommerzig in the Neumark district, fell into arrears with their rent, and pleaded as an excuse to their landlord, a certain Count von Schmettau, that the brook which turned their mill had been partly diverted to make a fishpond by a landowner living higher up the stream. The landlord suggested their prosecuting the owner of the fishpond, Freiherr von Gersdorf, but he declared he must have his rent or they must go. He allowed them time, but after four or five years they were summoned for arrears, and the mill was sold.

Frau Arnold, who seems to have been the predominating partner, had before this presented a petition to the King, when in 1775 he was at Crossen in the neighbourhood, but without result. Now she made various appeals, to the College of Justice for Neumark, to Grand-chancellor Fürst when he made an official examination at Cüstrin, and finally to the King again, who this time sent down an officer, Colonel Heucking, who, together with a member of the Cüstrin law-court, was to investigate the matter thoroughly. Not unnaturally, considering that the one approached it from the side of strict legality, and the other was conscious that the King was already prejudiced in the poor miller's favour, their conclusions differed.

The Colonel's report reached the King first, confirming his former impression that justice had been perverted in favour of the powerful landowner. He then ordered the whole case to be gone into by the highest Berlin tribunal of justice, and when this confirmed in every particular the decree of the Cüstrin court, his anger knew no bounds. He summoned Chancellor Fürst and the three councillors who had drawn up the judgment to his room, where he was laid up with the gout, and made short work of the affair. Fürst was summarily dismissed from his office; the councillors both of Berlin and Cüstrin not only lost their posts, but were condemned to a year's imprisonment in a fortress, and to repay the Arnolds all they had lost in the matter. His minister Zedlitz had the courage to refuse to pass such a sentence on men who had but done their duty according to the letter of the law, but Frederick proceeded without his assistance, determined that a striking example should be made, and all men should be convinced that in his kingdom the poor man was not to be oppressed with impunity. The case made a great sensation in Berlin, and indeed all over Europe; for this taking of the law into a monarch's own hands was a notable act even in those days.

It had one consequence that he probably had not foreseen. Every peasant who had a grievance— and few had not—thought he had but to apply to "Alter Fritz" in person, and all he wanted would be obtained. In a letter of Lord Malmesbury's he wrote—

"The peasants set out for Berlin by dozens and by scores, loaded with memorials, petitions, complaints, persuaded that they were to receive the money they had spent, perhaps in an obstinate quarrel or a malicious prosecution. They landed opposite the Palace and held up their papers towards the apartments where they supposed the King to be."

Frederick, when aware of their presence, would send a hussar to receive their memorials, and at first made an effort to investigate the cases, till they multiplied so that it became impossible, and he then lost patience and "threw one whole lot of papers, *pièces justificatives* and all, into the fire." The tree at Potsdam still stands under which these petitioners waited patiently, always in the hopes that Frederick's personal intervention would bring them all that they desired.

The most important political measure of the last few years of Frederick's reign was one in which uncle and nephew were for once cordially agreed. This was the League of Germanic Princes, formed as a bulwark against the threatened encroachments of Austria, which though it achieved little at first and appeared to have existed in vain, yet had a far-reaching influence on the future of Germany.

Carlyle, writing in 1865, dismissed it in half a page as a "feat that is obsolete now," "fallen silent everywhere," that "left not even a ghost behind." A few years later, and the seed that had seemed dead burst into vigorous life. This short-lived league of German princes was in reality the first step in Prussia's road to the headship of the German nations.

Frederick was too clear-sighted not to have seen long ago the rottenness of the Imperial constitution; and its "phantom army," the endless formalities of its outworn system, the pompous insignificance of its numerous petty courts had not escaped the shafts of his keen wit.

He was aware that a plan had been mooted among some of the smaller States to combine in defence against their more powerful neighbours. But these efforts had been thwarted by mutual jealousy.

What decided Frederick to attempt a combination under Prussian leadership was the aggressive policy of Joseph II, who, probably also conscious that the Empire as such was near to its collapse, had concentrated his attention on rounding off and consolidating his hereditary dominions. Towards Bavaria, that Naboth's Vineyard to Vienna, he again stretched forth his hand, thinking the time favourable to bring about the exchange he desired, since Frederick had now neither Russia not France as an ally.

Catherine was all on his side, not only on account of her great personal liking for him, but because she needed his help for her Eastern schemes. When, in 1782, the Grand-duke and his wife were allowed to travel in Europe, she forbade their going to Berlin, the one place they were most anxious to visit, but insisted on their including Vienna in their tour. The understanding she had with Joseph enabled her to carry out her scheme of annexing the Crimea.

To gain Bavaria Joseph was ready to give in exchange the Austrian Netherlands, which were to be made into a kingdom of Burgundy. Charles Theodore was again willing to consent if it were made worth his while; but the Duke of Zweibrücken, though Catherine sent her own ambassador, Romanzoff, to win him over by promises or threats, stood out firmly and laid the case before the Diet, claiming Prussia's help.

Frederick took up his cause with alacrity. He and Hertzberg set to work at once on a scheme for a constitutional League of Princes of the Empire, to which Frederick-William gave his willing agreement and co-operation. The old King, who had always command of forcible phrases and apt illustrations, reminded those whose adhesion he wanted of the fable of the horse's tail, that no one could pull out as a whole, while if the hairs were taken separately it was easy enough. And he further warned them that those who stood by to see their neighbours devoured would only have, after all, the privilege of the Grotto of Polyphemus, that of being devoured last.

Frederick seemed to renew his youth over this business. His ministers proceeded too slowly for him. "*Feuer, meine Herren, Feuer!*" he cried to urge them on. He forgot his contempt for the minor states, for the "wigs" of Hanover and the "pedants" of Regensburg. Hanover and Saxony were the first to join, and they were followed by most of the others.

One of the first political missions entrusted to Stein, afterwards to play so conspicuous a part in the regeneration of Germany, was that of visiting the various rulers to induce them to join, and the story of his efforts throws a good deal of light on the peculiarities of the petty German courts of that time. Some of them were models in miniature of the French Court under Louis XV; in one case he could get no business done because the Landgrave had disappeared from public gaze and was not to be found! His greatest triumph was in procuring the adhesion of the Elector of Mainz, whose position in the Empire was only second to that of the Emperor.

Joseph and Kaunitz had again to own themselves defeated and to abandon their project.

It was in 1783, three years before Frederick-William's accession, that the influence over him of Mme. Rietz was more closely threatened than at any other period. This was due to an attachment between him and one of the ladies-in-waiting of the Queen, an attachment that had many points in common with his father's unhappy love-affair of nearly forty years ago.

The heroine of this old story, Countess Voss, had now returned to Berlin, and was constantly in attendance on Elizabeth-Christine in Schönhausen. Her husband was now First Chamberlain of the Queen's household.

Frederick-William knew all the story of his father's unhappy attachment, and had always shown —and continued to show till the end of his days— a great esteem and affection for Countess Voss. He had known her well when he was a boy of sixteen at Magdeburg, and she, then a beautiful woman of thirty, had a special affection for the son of the Prince who had loved her.

154

THE END OF FREDERICK'S REIGN

Her brother had a daughter, Julie, whom he had sent, at Elizabeth-Christine's request, to be one of her attendant ladies at Schönhausen. At her very first appearance at Court it was evident that she attracted the attention and admiration of the Prince of Prussia.

She is described as being of the type that Titian painted, with red-gold hair and a skin of dazzling fairness. At Court they called her Ceres, and portraits were painted representing her as the goddess. Count Mirabeau, who visited Berlin in the last days of Frederick, had a good deal to say of Mlle. Voss. He was no admirer of her beauty, and not even a believer in the sincerity of her long resistance to her royal lover. He wrote of her as "*la belle, qui, selon moi, est fort laide.*" His cynical eyes saw nothing but calculation in her struggle against her feelings, and he jealously watched and counted the words and glances exchanged between the pair. He dreaded her influence, for she was credited with Anglomania, chiefly because she spoke German or English in preference to French, and did not share the popular proclivity for the latter nation.

In Countess Voss's Diary there is frequent mention made of the Prince's attachment to her niece, which soon began to cause the good lady much anxiety.

In January 1784 she wrote—

"The Prince admires Julie more than I quite like. He talks to her a great deal; I am afraid she is not insensible to his admiration, and nothing but unhappiness can come of such an affair."

155

And later—

"I had a long talk with the Prince alone. I told him it was wrong of him to pursue Julie with his passion, I said it could only make her unhappy, indeed I gave him my plain opinion and told him the whole truth in great seriousness. He promised to alter his conduct and do all that I desired. He had another explanation with Julie afterwards, and I know that she reproached him (and rightly) with the injury that he was doing to her reputation thereby. He came away very sad and depressed; I told him again seriously that there must be an end of the matter, and he promised me it should be so."

This promise he appears to have kept for some time, and in January of 1785 we hear of offers of marriage made to Julie, notably of one from Count Dohna, but nothing came of it. Rumour whispered that the Prince had contrived to prevent the marriage.

The old Countess's kind heart made her find excuses for the infatuated man. "The Prince has a very unpleasant life in his own household," she wrote; "the Princess is not at all nice to him (*sehr unartig mit ihm*)."

Evidently his feelings had been too much for him, and his promises were forgotten, for she wrote again—

"The Prince again talks much with Julie; this must be stopped. Worst of all I am afraid that she cannot get him out of her mind."

"The Prince is always going to Schönhausen to the old Queen, and I know that it is only on Julie's account. I am afraid he has not given her up completely, but is trying to think if there is not some hope for him. If only this may not lead to harm in spite of all his promises!"

And in January 1786: "The Prince's passion is still the same; he tries more than he did to conceal it, and he is very cautious, but he does not deceive me. My loved Julie, on the contrary, behaves excellently."

A few weeks later: "The Prince would not play this evening. I saw it was only that he might snatch a moment to speak to my niece. God knows what he said to her, she seemed to be much moved and unhappy about it, and then suddenly he lost his composure and grew very excited; but they were too far off for me to hear what they said."

"March 1786.—I am sorry for the Prince, but in spite of his passion for Julie, he does not break off his connection with his so-called friend. To-day he was very much depressed and out of spirits, I think it was the result of some serious words Julie had said to him."

The Countess seems to have made great efforts to get Julie sent away from Berlin and the proximity of the infatuated Prince, but Julie's own family apparently did not realise the danger, and she remained. There were moments when Countess Voss's fears subsided, and then again her anxiety would be keenly aroused.

"March 28.—The Prince begins again to speak to Julie whenever he can, and these eternal conversations and discussions are not good for her."

"May 5.—I reminded the Prince of what he seemed for some time to have forgotten, and he renewed his promise. He is so good after all! (*Er ist doch sehr gut!*) God grant he may remain so when he is King!"

Once she succeeded in getting her niece away on three months' leave, whereupon she wrote—

"May 15, 1786.—The Prince is dreadfully unhappy, but I hope this absence will put an end to the matter, and bring him to reason."

But in the beginning of July this entry appears—

"It terrifies me to discover that apparently the Prince writes to Julie and she answers him!"

"July 15.—He was very gentle and kind to-day, and in talking about my poor niece and his duty to her, spoke reasonably and submissively and with the best resolutions."

"July 21.—The Prince is very quiet and shut up in himself (*in sich gekehrt*); he talked to me a great deal about her to-day, and is more than ever resolved to do his duty."

But by the middle of August Julie was back in Berlin; and all the Countess's hopes of a gradual weakening of this infatuation were doomed to disappointment.

"August 15.—Julie came back to-day, and this very evening the Prince came in, and all the old story has begun again—it is too wrong!"

This entry is dated only two days before the death of Frederick the Great placed the royal lover on the throne.

CHAPTER IX

ON THE THRONE

THE long-expected death of Frederick the Great took place on the 17th of August 1786. The Prince of Prussia had been in the neighbouring palace of Potsdam for some time before the end in expectation of being summoned to his uncle's deathbed, but neither he nor any other of the family received any summons. Frederick's country was his family; and beyond that he had of late years no interest.

Hertzberg had been sleeping at Sans Souci for more than a month past. He sent news of the demise at once to Frederick-William, who dressed himself hastily and was in the death-chamber by three o'clock in the morning.

His eldest son, afterwards Frederick-William III, was also summoned, and he has left in his diary the following artless account of that momentous morning—

"Potsdam, 17 August 1786. I awoke at half-past three hearing some one talking to Herr Behnisch (his tutor). I was told that Major von Bischoffs-werder's servant had brought me the news of the King's death. I got up at once, the horses were saddled, and I rode with Captain Schenkendorff to General Bachoff's. We rode at a trot towards the Nauenschen Gate, but it was closed. It was opened for us, and we rode quickly to my Father's palace. When we arrived, the huntsman Schröder told us my Papa was already at Sans Souci. We rode at full gallop there, dismounted and went up to the first floor. I went up to my Father, the present King, and congratulated him. He went with me into a side-room where he told me of various things I had to do now, and then allowed me to see the dead King.

"He lay in the Concert room, stretched out on his camp bed, with a small hat on his head that was tied round by a bandage under the chin. He had an old blue silk cloak round him, under which he had on a fur waistcoat. His legs were in large, loose boots; the right leg was very much swollen, and one still saw signs of the discharge. Two lacqueys were standing there with green boughs, keeping off the flies. Dr. Selle was there too. The hussar servants told me about the King's last moments.

"Then my brother Louis came. We had not yet eaten anything and were very hungry. They brought us some fruit and Hungarian wine, of which we were very glad."

It had been Frederick's desire to be buried at night, without any ceremony, in a tomb he had prepared in the garden of Sans Souci, visible from the window of his writing-room. But on visiting it Frederick-William decided it would be unbecoming to allow the great King to sleep there, where several of his dogs had been already buried. And he saw to it that the obsequies were carried out with

such stately and fitting ceremonial as was a due
tribute to the King who had made Prussia what it
was.

That same evening the body, dressed in the
uniform of the first battalion of Guards, was carried
in a hearse drawn by eight horses through the streets
of Potsdam in the midst of a silent and sympathetic
crowd, and placed in the audience chamber of the
palace, where it was watched during the night.
Throughout the next day the public were admitted
to see the dead King as he lay under a baldachin.
They say the shrunken and wasted form was almost
like that of a child, but that the worn face looked
beautiful in death.

Prussia could scarcely believe that its great ruler
was no more. The recorded naïve remark of a
peasant boy put into words what many were probably thinking: "Who is going to rule the world
now?"

And if the people who were near enough to see
the blemishes as well as the grandeur of his
character, had forgotten much that he had done for
them, in foreign countries and remote places of the
earth his name had become a household word.
Goethe tells us what a place he filled in his own
boyish imagination ("We were all Fritzisch"); and
in his accounts of his travels in Sicily, he wrote that
he and his companions were urged by their hosts in
some Sicilian village to tell them all they could
about the great King, and that they concealed the
news of his death, not wishing to spoil the heartiness
of their welcome by being the bearers of such bad

tidings! This was in April of the following year. News did not travel fast in those days!

Frederick-William's first acts on coming to the throne were in accordance with the best anticipations that had been formed of him. That he particularly distinguished Count Hertzberg by bestowing on him the Order of the Black Eagle caused some astonishment to the people who did not know of the friendly relations that had subsisted for some time between this minister and the heir.

At his public appearances to receive the oaths of fidelity and the acclamations of his people, the impression he made was altogether favourable. The prevalent feeling was pretty well summed up in the phrase in Schlözer's *Staatsanzeiger:* "The kindly King will perhaps never attain to the dread heights of his uncle's greatness, but in kindness of heart and character, in earnest care for the happiness of his subjects he far surpasses him."

His gracious manners, and particularly his use of the polite pronoun "Sie" instead of the derogatory "Er," went a great way towards winning him the place he desired in the public esteem.

In the introductory chapter has been given the description of him penned by H. von Boyen, a gallant soldier and an ardent admirer of the great Frederick, whose memoirs are good reading, displaying, as they unconsciously do, the fine, simple character of the man. He had no particular cause to love Frederick-William, who did not give him the promotion his friends tried to obtain for him.

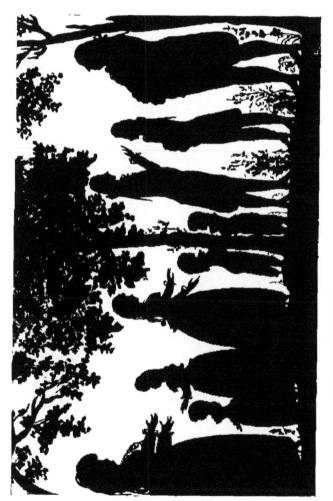

SILHOUETTE GROUP OF FREDERICK-WILLIAM II AND FAMILY.

ON THE THRONE

Prince Reuss, the Imperial ambassador, gave as his view—

"So far as I can venture to judge the mental qualities of the Crown Prince from the opportunities I have had, honesty and benevolence seem to be the salient points of his character. Whether he really has a firm and steadfast character and can maintain it in these circumstances remains to be seen."[1]

There was hovering round the Prussian Court at the time of his accession, actively engaged in taking notes, a French busybody who, without being formally accredited to the Court or given any regular diplomatic position, was employed by the French Government to watch the conduct of the new ruler and the influences at work around him, to see what France had to hope for from him and what to fear.

Count Honoré de Mirabeau had much knowledge of human nature and a sharp scent especially for its weaker side. His political insight was keen. He saw that to bring Prussia to its present position every nerve had been so strained that a relaxation was inevitable. Of the new ruler he prophesied that he would become the tool of petty intriguers, of the small officials about his person and particularly of the mystics. He saw weakness of character in Frederick-William's great anxiety not to be ruled by others. A strong man has no need to fortify himself with resolutions against being led. Mirabeau wrote of him—referring to the mistake that had been made in not lending him money when

---

[1] G. Wolff: *Oesterreich und Preussen*, 223.

he was Crown Prince—as follows : " A Prince who had not much in him, perhaps, but who was grateful, and who was certainly an honest man if he would never be a great King, so that it was rather to his heart than to his mind that one should appeal."

Mirabeau's views of the king grew more and more unfavourable as it became more evident that the French influence was no longer to predominate. The accounts he sent home of the King's private life, exaggerated as such gossip usually is, were found by Talleyrand to be much more piquant reading than the reports of the accredited ambassador. (Mirabeau had himself tried to induct a French lady into the position of favourite, but in vain.) The French influence at Court was altogether on the wane. Prince Henry, its ostensible head, had lost favour with the King through betraying an over anxiety to rule him. Mirabeau considered him more a hindrance than a help, and declared that the best hope for the country lay in the possibility of the reigning Duke of Brunswick attaining to the virtual management of affairs.

On the very day of his accession Mirabeau handed the King a letter containing a suggested programme of reforms and a scheme of government. Some of the measures advocated were excellent in themselves; a few were even carried out; in the main they were sweeping reforms that only a revolution could bring about; and in the suggestions regarding the army it was evident that the leading idea was to make Prussia harmless to France.

The one feature of the new reign that most disconcerted Mirabeau, the same that contributed greatly to Frederick-William's early popularity, was the cultivation of a national feeling, and the encouragement of national art and literature in the place of a servile imitation of all things French.

"We are German, and German we will remain," said the King before his ministers in council; and the phrase was caught up and quoted with delight throughout the land.

The victory of Hertzberg's influence over that of the French-minded Prince Henry was highly popular. The citizens of Berlin seemed to have found in Frederick-William a King after their own heart. Frederick had favoured the nobility; the only class, he thought, from whom a sense of honour could be expected. He liked, too, to consider himself the father and protector of the poor. But he was never able to conceal his scorn for the ordinary citizen, "the man in the street."

It was as a "citizen-King" that Frederick-William was at the beginning of his reign so popular. In a simple blue coat with brass buttons, accompanied only by a huntsman, he would take a morning walk in the Tiergarten and watch with interest the games of the children about him, or chat with the elders. He often gave the townspeople admittance to watch the festivities of the Court, and would not mind if, with ladies on his arm, he was compelled to push his way through a crowd.

His first acts on coming into power were directed to rewarding those who had befriended him, and to redressing some injustices that had been inflicted by his predecessor. He paid off the debts that he had contracted as Prince of Prussia. His old tutor, Beguelin, was ennobled and given a property that brought him in a good yearly income, and these benefits were made doubly valuable through being accompanied by a gracious and grateful letter. His military Governor, Count von Borcke, was given promotion and the Order of the Black Eagle. Officers who had suffered through their attachment to him—in the case of Wartensleben, because he had refused to act as a spy—were recalled and promoted.

His benevolence extended to his first wife, Elizabeth of Brunswick, who received the welcome and astounding news that she was free to live where she pleased, and that her income was increased. The poor woman was transported with joy. No longer would she be reduced to dancing quadrilles with chairs for partners! Though she had not been on horseback for eighteen years, she rode out that very day, in order to taste the sweets of liberty.

Another instance of reversal of his uncle's judgments was the case of the swashbuckler, Baron Trenck, who was now permitted to return to Prussia and resume possession of what was left of his estates. Countess Voss relates how he thus saw once again, in her old age and ill health, the Princes Amelia whom he had loved when they were young, and how she promised to take his daughter into her care, a promise, however, that death prevented her from carrying out.

ON THE THRONE

And Prussia's after-history might have been differently written had not Frederick-William re-instated in the army a young officer, who afterwards as Marshal Blücher gained a world-wide fame. He had been passed over in promotion owing to his gay manner of life and some particular act of violence, and had written to Frederick himself, complaining that the man who had been raised over his head had no other merit than that of being the son of the Margrave of Schwedt, and asking leave to retire. Frederick made short work of his appeal. He noted on the margin: "Captain Blücher may go to the devil!"

Another instance in which generosity proved the best policy was that of Hans von Yorck, who had been cashiered and ordered a year's imprisonment for expressing openly on parade his indignation at some unworthy conduct on the part of a superior officer. Frederick would not be persuaded to lessen the punishment, but Frederick-William gave him at the time a recommendation to his sister, the Princess of Orange, and on coming to the throne made him a Captain of Fusiliers.

That glaring act of injustice that Frederick, out of very zeal for pure and impartial justice, had committed in the case of the miller Arnold, was now set right as far as it was possible after so long a time. At the request of the injured councillors their conduct was thoroughly inquired into, with the result that their innocence was established, and those who still survived were readmitted into the public service. The law-suit was resumed at the point where

Frederick had arbitrarily interrupted it, and the Arnolds were condemned to pay a large sum in restitution; but as they were quite unable to do this, the King generously put an end to the matter by paying it out of his own purse.

The first measures of the new reign, mostly the outcome of Wöllner's suggestions, were undoubtedly well meant, and in many directions considerable improvements were made; but all too soon there was felt in every department the lack of the one master-mind' that had directed all with unity of purpose and a firm, unswerving policy.

The two last kings had treated the nation like a child that had to be kept in leading-strings; and now the guiding hand had been withdrawn before it had learned to stand alone. Ministers in every department had looked to Frederick for direction; he had suffered no independent action; and now they were nonplussed at finding themselves under a master who looked to others for guidance.

It is true that Prussia, now so increased in size and importance, had outgrown a one-man rule. Changes were inevitable, for it had not moved with the times. A clear head, a keen judgment and a firm hand were specially necessary at this critical period; and it was fatal to Prussia that the reins should at this moment come into the hands of a well-intentioned Prince who had no strength of character, but let his best-meant projects fall when they encountered serious opposition.

It was easy to see the failings of Frederick's system and to set right a few injustices here and there; it was a very different thing to originate a new constructive policy that should be more in accordance with the spirit of the age.

Wöllner's policy was based to a great extent on opposition to everything that Frederick had introduced; and it accorded very well with the new King's own desires to go back in many respects to the more collegiate system of his grandfather, the first Frederick-William.

This system, with its numerous ministers having each their separate department, though they had to meet in conference over every important measure, had been still retained in form; but Frederick had practically disregarded his ministers and ruled the country from his cabinet without consulting them, merely charging them to carry out his orders. The men of inferior ability whom he employed in his cabinet (who were called cabinet councillors, but were in effect nothing more than secretaries) were the only officials with whom he came into personal contact, and the only ones who were sometimes able to influence him, through their knowledge of his character, by the turn they could give to the matter brought before him.

One of Frederick-William's first acts was to reconstruct the General Directory on something like its former lines, and to settle the principles on which it was to work.

His first desire was to lighten somewhat the excessive burden of taxation; and a sigh of relief rose from the whole country when the hated " Régie " was abolished, and the abhorred " cellar-rats " were no longer able to make inquisition when and where they chose. It was not without some injustice to individuals that the change was made; de Launay, the head of the institution, though acquitted of the malpractices with which he was charged, was made the scapegoat of the public hatred, and was practically driven back to France a ruined man.

Tobacco, as well as coffee, ceased to be a Government monopoly, and a short-lived attempt was made to establish free-trade in corn; but unfortunately no means were taken to provide in other ways for the loss to the revenue that was entailed by these measures of relief. The shrinkage of income was bound to be felt, especially by so open-handed a sovereign; and before long new and equally vexatious systems of taxation had to be introduced.

In the department of education great improvements were made. It is remarkable that Frederick should have paid so little attention to this matter, but he was something of a mental aristocrat, and thought that culture was only for the elect few. Zedlitz, the minister of education, was one of the ablest of his officials, and he did as much as it was possible to do for higher learning, considering the difficulty he had in obtaining money for the purpose. In spite of his being a sharer of Frederick's freethinking views, he was maintained by Frederick-William in his position, and he even obtained the King's consent to the educational measure of January 1787, which gave the whole direction of education into the hands of a professional collegium.

But this was before Wöllner began to meddle with this matter.

Until now the pay of teachers had been so poor that in small districts the work was frequently combined with that of shepherd or night-watchman. Frederick had given the post of teacher to many of his disabled soldiers, some of whom were not even able to read and write. Now strenuous efforts were made to build more schools and to bring about improvement in the quality of the teachers as well as in their pay.

One most praiseworthy concession that Frederick-William made at the instance of the Chancellor Carmer was the acknowledgment that no member of the public service could be dismissed arbitrarily and without sufficient cause. This was practically a restriction of absolute power, since it recognised the principle that public officials were servants of the State and not of the monarch solely.

In the army some much-needed amelioration was brought about; not so much with regard to its efficiency as a fighting-machine—Frederick had said the last word on that point—but to the humaner treatment of the individuals composing it. It is marvellous to consider what work he got out of that army, considering the way they were brought together and the conditions under which they lived.

Though recruiting in foreign countries was not quite so vigorously and unscrupulously carried out as in the days of Frederick William I's "lange Kerls," when no man of unusual stature—not even the very priest before the altar—was safe if he were

within reach of a recruiter for the King's Potsdam
Guards, still more than one-third of the rank and
file were other than native Prussians, and all kinds
of tricks were permissible to induce men to join the
army. Rakes and scapegraces were offered bogus
commissions, and on joining found themselves under
the sergeant and his stick, in that service from which
there was no escape short of disablement or death.
Desertion entailed severe penalties on all who even
remotely assisted.

Frederick's idea of discipline was that the soldier
must fear his superior officer far more than he
dreaded the foe before him; and the fearful punishment of "running the gauntlet" was still kept
up. And yet Frederick, when he shared their
hardships and led them to victory, was the idol of
his men.

The period of home and foreign service was now
legally fixed, and forcible as well as deceptive
recruiting methods stopped. Improvements in
clothing were made, and a daily ration of bread was
allowed. Measures were taken to provide for the
care of invalided officers and men, and some pro-
vision was made for the children of those in service.

Frederick-William did not attempt to keep, as his
uncle had done, the whole administration of the
army in his own hands, but formed a ministry, with
seven departments under the presidency of two war
ministers. And the two branches of the service that
Frederick had neither understood nor properly
valued, the artillery and engineers, came in now for
some much-needed attention. An artillery school

was founded in Berlin, and an engineer academy at Potsdam.

But against all these ameliorations must be set the fact that the zeal and earnestness, with which the service had been carried out, began to slumber; the fear of blame for duty disregarded or not exactly fulfilled decreased first in the upper and then in the subordinate ranks.

Frederick-William, as Mirabeau noted, would attend the military exercises, make the troops march, and after saying a word or two, would go off. While Frederick, in his old age, on the coldest of winter days, would scold and storm for hours, and rarely give a word of praise. Yet the harried troops, kept in continual activity and anxiety, were proud to see "le vieux" at their head.

Moreover, the good-natured Frederick-William had not the heart to dismiss those old officers who were past their work, and were unable to adapt themselves to the inevitable changes that time made necessary.

In regard to learning, literature and the fine arts generally it was a most welcome change that Frederick-William leaned to the encouragement of native talent. No longer could it be said, as it was bitterly remarked in Frederick's time, that in the King's eyes it was a crime to have drawn one's first breath on German soil!

It is true that Frederick-William had no more appreciation than his uncle of the new light that dawned on German literature with the appearance of Goethe and Schiller. Frederick had read *Götz von Berlichingen*, and condemned it as "a detestable imitation of those bad English pieces," meaning probably Shakespeare; and Frederick-William made no attempt to draw either Goethe or Schiller to Berlin. But according to his lights he did his best for German literature.

Ramler was then considered the first of living Prussian poets, though his reputation has not lasted to our times. Frederick's neglect of him had been much resented. Frederick-William allowed him a pension and entrusted to him the management of the new National Theatre.

In vain had Anna Louisa Karschin sent laudatory verses again and again to Frederick. She was a woman of peasant birth, who had grasped at every opportunity of educating herself and early began to write poetry. A certain Baron von Kottnitz interested himself in her and enabled her to come to Berlin, where she was encouraged by some of the foremost writers and became for a time the vogue in Berlin society. She was once taken to Sans Souci, when Frederick gave her a little monetary help, but for her further complimentary verses she could get no recognition until at last he sent her a present of —two thalers! which the poetess returned with indignant and decidedly doggrel verses.

The tales of Frederick-William's generosity to others led her to apply to him; and he made the poor woman happy by giving her what she had long desired, a house of her own. A fête was organised, in which Wöllner, clad in black velvet, greeted her with verses no better than her own, and informed her of the intended gift. No wonder that she sang of "the golden days of good Frederick-William!"

The Berlin Academy of Science now ceased to be an entirely French institution. Lectures were given in the vernacular, and many German authors and *savants* were admitted as members.

The German theatre, in spite of the valiant efforts of Döbbelin, had been unable to hold its own against the French troupe favoured by Frederick and the nobility; now, translated into the new house in the Gendarmenmarkt, it blossomed out into vigorous life. It was principally here that Shakespeare was made known to the German public, and the influence he has had on German literature is simply incalculable.

In architecture, too, Frederick-William found employment for native artists, much to the public satisfaction. When in the former reign the newly-built tower of the church in the Gendarmenmarkt fell, there was great indignation expressed against the French architects who "built with gingerbread instead of stone." The Brandenburg Thor and the marble palace at Potsdam were among the great works entrusted to German architects and sculptors.

The year 1786 was long known as the year of presents and honours, which the King dealt out with only too lavish a hand, if he did not quite deserve Mirabeau's sneer: "that it would soon be easier to find a noble than a man in Prussia." But such liberality could not always be maintained, and high expectations were aroused on all sides, whose non-fulfilment naturally produced bitterness.

A MYSTIC ON THE PRUSSIAN THRONE

One of the objects the King had much at heart —and it was on this string that Wöllner harped in order to ingratiate himself—was the return from the rationalism introduced by Frederick to the fervent practice of the orthodox religion. To a great extent he had his people behind him, for a reaction had set in, and it pained many to find preachers denying from the very pulpit the doctrines they had undertaken to teach.

Though his piety sat oddly on a man of Frederick-William's extraordinarily relaxed morals, we have no reason to doubt his sincerity. He saw the beauty of virtue, though he had not strength of mind to resist his own passions. Unfortunately he entirely lacked a sense of humour, or he could never have banished the troupe of French comedians as harmful to the morals of the people, while his own example did more than anything else to encourage the laxity and licentiousness already so prevalent in Berlin society. As a French writer puts it: "He was pious with sincerity and immoral with candour."[1]

The royal piety soon found imitators. The Bible once more became "hoffähig" (admissible at Court); the empty churches filled again. In Frederick's time it had been said: "You need not believe in a God, but you must obey a corporal." In Frederick-William's time no rigid adherence to duty was expected, but those who wanted his favour assumed a religion if they had it not; and if they could lay claims to supernatural powers, to holding

[1] E. Hennet de Goutel, in *La Revue*, Feb. 15, 1911.

communion with beings in a higher sphere, their advancement was fairly certain.

Thus if not a hypocrite himself, he was undoubtedly the cause of hypocrisy in others. Men like Wöllner saw that the way to power lay in affecting a zeal for the furtherance of religion, and the King was not keen-sighted enough to distinguish between the real and the false.

ORMESUS MAGNUS daily became more a tool in the hands of his fellow Rosicrucians. The cleverer among them gauged his character successfully. Bischoffswerder, for instance, studiously avoided any display of his influence over his royal master; "to be all, but to appear nothing," was his motto. "Not Bischoffswerder, but I desire this," was the King's answer to complaints, and doubtless he believed it true.

In the commencement of his reign Hertzberg's advice, especially as to foreign politics, was mostly followed. But a time was to come when the secret brotherhood had it all their own way.

CHAPTER X

For three years before the death of his uncle Frederick-William had been, as we have seen, greatly attached to Fräulein Julie von Voss, and now that he had attained to power it became a matter of absorbing interest to those about him whether her influence or that of Mme. Rietz would predominate. Mme. Rietz's letters to her mother betray much anxiety and alarm. She had long ceased to be anything more to Frederick-William than adviser and confidant, purveyor alike of ghostly counsel and worldly amusement, but she was clever enough to make herself indispensable to him. The Court had great hopes that the influence of Julie von Voss would overcome that of this low-born adventuress.

Countess Voss wrote in her diary a few days after the death of Frederick—

"Aug. 22nd.—The new King does nothing but good, gives with both hands to the poor; it is incredible how much he is beloved."

But on the next day she qualifies her praise with the remark—

". . . But unfortunately his conduct to my niece was the same as before."

And on August 25th: " The King comes as often

MME. RIETZ, AFTERWARDS COUNTESS LICHTENAU.

as he can, and then he walks with Julie in the garden. But she is as quiet and reserved with him as possible, which somewhat reassures me."

From this time her anxiety and consternation continually increase.

"Oct. 1.—The King came and wanted to talk to me; but he is so taken up by the one thought that he neither sees nor hears anything else. I confess that I have lost all patience with him, and find the situation impossible and unpardonable.

"I see now plainly that she loves the King, in spite of all her denials. . . .

"My poor niece has opened her whole heart to me. . . . Ah! I am afraid that the matter is not to be stopped. . . .

"The King seems only to be happy when he can see her. When she is there he sees no one but her, talks to no one but her, and has nothing else in his mind but his passion.

"The King complained to me that my niece treated him badly; he has almost quarrelled with her; yet he still continues to talk to her. . . .

"He sat alone with her in the old Queen's cabinet; truly she no longer seems to be cruel to him. . . . God only knows how unhappy I am over this matter."

"30 December.—To-day that happened which I have dreaded for a long time: my niece threw herself into my arms and told me that her fate was decided. . . . I confess I find her so much to be pitied that I have no words to condemn her."

It appears that Julie could resist the King's

entreaties and reproaches; but the idea that his affection for her might cool was too much for her resolution.

"Poor Julie," wrote the Countess, "was in despair this evening; she loves the King, and her conscientious scruples have at last wearied and depressed him. She says she is too weak to give him up now, and he will not agree to the conditions she made. . . .

"The King came to supper; he was quiet and depressed, poor Julie was restless and unhappy. When he pursued her with his passionate love, she was firm and steadfast; now that he is cooling towards her she cannot hold out, and she will not let him go. . . .

"He is visibly cooler to Julie, and the poor girl is wretched at the change in him. For the rest, he is more amiable than ever with every one, even his wife and children. Every one is devoted to him, and quite delighted by his kindness and friendliness."

The conditions that Julie had imposed were that the Queen should give her written consent to the union, that though of necessity it must be a left-handed marriage there should be a religious ceremony, and that Mme. Rietz and her children should leave Berlin. Against the two first the obstacles might well have appeared insuperable; nevertheless, it was only in the third that the King did not give way.

The Queen was always in money difficulties; a sum of money that would pay off her debts was one inducement, the hopes of undermining the influence of the Rietz was another, and her consent was obtained.

And for the religious ceremony an historical precedent was found by the Consistorium. In 1540 Philip the Magnanimous, Landgrave of Hesse, had wished to marry a lady of the Court, Margaretha von der Saal, during the life of his consort, Christina of Saxony, and brought forward the example of the Old Testament patriarchs. The Reformers were at first shocked at the idea, but gave way rather than lose such a powerful supporter of their cause. Luther and Melancthon both gave a qualified consent, which Luther afterwards retracted, and when the marriage actually took place and was made public Melancthon's remorse was so great as to bring on an illness that very nearly proved fatal.

Such as it was, this precedent was made to serve, and the ceremony was performed in the chapel of the Charlottenburg Palace in May 1787.

At first it was kept a secret, and Fräulein Voss continued in her post at Court. The following further extracts regarding her niece are from the Countess's diary—

"She held out for a long time, but she was passionately attached to the King, and after she had given him her heart she allowed herself to be over-persuaded. In spite of this grave mistake of hers she remains a noble creature, still worthy of esteem, and I know that she is too right-minded ever to feel happy again after such a fall."

After a few months Julie found the position and the concealment too painful and awkward, and she took advantage of the King's absence in Silesia to visit her relations in the country, and from there she wrote for permission to retire from her post at Court. The widowed Queen, who as yet had no idea of what had happened, granted her request.

But in September, when the King returned, he wanted to establish her in Potsdam. On the 4th of September the Countess wrote—

"My niece writes to me from Brandenburg that she is going on the 9th to Potsdam, and she prays God to support her in the new life that awaits her. May God help her! it is a difficult step that she must take now in braving it out before the world."

"28 Sept.—Princess Frederika was at the hunt in Wusterhausen; the King was also there, and for the first time my niece was with him. They tell me, to comfort me, that she seems to be happy."

"6 Nov.—Julie has been given the title of Countess von Ingenheim. The poor girl writes to me that she is very unhappy; how sorry I am for her! The Encke (Mme. Rietz) does a hundred things to annoy her, and has just as much influence over the King as before."

The position had its awkward side, as the following extracts show—

"1 Dec. —Princess Frederika will not see Julie. The King has commanded her to do so. I think he is wrong to compel her."

"11 Jan., 1788.—A ball at the King's, where the Crown Prince for the first time saw Julie as Countess Ingenheim, which was a very unpleasant moment

for both of them. Unhappy girl! what a painful
position for her!"

There came a time when the Countess was
evidently annoyed with her niece. She figures in
the diary as "the Ingenheim"—

"22 Feb.—The old Queen had a big dinner-party,
and she asked the King whether she should invite
the Ingenheim; of course he said yes, and so she
came to the dinner. I think it was very wrong of
the Queen to invite her in order to please the King.
In the evening she did not play lotto with the company, but with the household in the ante-room. At
dinner she was placed opposite to the King."

"4 March.—A big dinner at Minister Arnim's, at
which the King and the Ingenheim were present.
But in spite of all this she is sad, for the King still
sups every night as before with the Rietz, and that
is very annoying for her."

The Countess's heart, however, softened again
when her niece was in trouble—

"21 Dec.—The Ingenheim entreated me to stand
by her in the time that was coming; the King also
begged it of me on the following day, and I could
not bring myself to say no."

—and she was evidently taken to her heart again.

"2 Jan., 1789.—Julie gave birth to a son to-day;
the King was there and was very delighted."

"4 Jan.—The child was baptised. The King
himself held it at the font; it is called Gustav
Adolph Wilhelm. Julie's brother, Bischoffswerder
and I were the godparents. The King was nearly
all day with the invalid. It is the fact that he is

183

really the best Prince that one could find in the whole world; the pity is that he has so little strength of will, that he is without energy and at times so violent."

At first Countess Ingenheim appeared to be making a good recovery, but it unfortunately happened that the King at this time slipped and injured his foot. Not only did the accident give her a fright, but as it prevented the King visiting her bedside and he was unhappy at not seeing her, she disregarded the warnings of doctor and nurse and the severity of the weather, and went to his room long before she was in a fit state to take such a step.

On the 20th of January the Countess wrote—

" Poor Julie is very anxious and uneasy about the King, which is not good for her."

" 22 Jan.—Julie is seriously ill; she has taken a very bad cold, but above all it is the excitement and the anxiety about the King that does her harm."

" 25 Jan.—To-day the King could come down and be with her again; he can just manage to take a few steps. . . . There were also several guests at dinner, and they played in the evening."

" 29 Jan.—Although the King is nearly all day with her, that does not set her at rest; she is so afraid of the malignant influence of the Rietz that might turn his heart against her."

" 5 Feb.—To-day there was a big Court, and Julie too went again for the first time (since her illness), although she has not yet recovered from that fright about the King. She will not give way, but I am afraid she is doing herself harm. The King gave her a little *étui* with 50,000 thalers inside and his portrait set with brilliants—the stones are very fine."

"Feb. 24th.—Julie has fever and a cough; she is up and goes out, but I am not happy about her."

"March 5.—There are fears of a galloping consumption for poor Julie. I cannot say how unhappy this makes me. The King is beside himself; he does not know of the danger, but he is very anxious about her."

"March 25.—What a day of misfortune. Quite suddenly, at eight o'clock this evening, poor Julie died. It came upon her like an attack of suffocation. No one dreamed of any immediate danger. The King went to Potsdam in the afternoon. I went to see her towards evening, but Princess Frederika, who was with her, advised me not to go in, because she had had an attack, and so I never saw her again. I grieve for her with all my heart, and every one grieves with me. It came with dreadful suddenness; I cannot yet believe it. She died in the palace, in the same room in which her child was born."

The King was in despair and inconsolable at this loss, and the regret in the Court seems to have been universal. Even the Queen seems to have sincerely lamented the death of her successful rival, and to have repeatedly exclaimed: "I have lost my best friend!"

There were rumours of poison administered in a glass of lemonade, but an autopsy proved the state of her lungs to have been a sufficient cause of death.

A MYSTIC ON THE PRUSSIAN THRONE

Much had been hoped for from Julie's influence as against that of the Rietz and the Rosicrucians. Hers was a finer nature than most of those whom the King delighted to honour; but she had not succeeded in doing much to counteract the influence of the circle that surrounded the King. She was no match for them in intrigue.

For a long time the King could not bear even to meet Countess von Voss. The very sight of her recalled his past happiness and present desolation. Coming across her unexpectedly one day in Schönhausen, he utterly lost his composure and could not restrain his tears.

For a year he grieved as inconsolable, and then —a new passion took possession of him.

But we have already gone chronologically too far ahead in order to tell Julie's story as a whole. To return to public affairs—in which the King's matrimonial aberrations made no appreciable difference —the two first measures dealing with outside politics were both laudable.

On the death of the Count of Lippe-Bückeburg his powerful neighbour, the Landgrave of Hesse-Cassel, sent troops to take possession. His plea was that the ruling family had no legitimate right, since they descended from an unequal marriage, though this marriage had been legalised by imperial decree and acknowledged by the Landgrave's own predecessor.

The Landgrave was an influential member of the League of Princes, whom it was not desirable to offend. Still, the action was quite contrary to the spirit of the League, whose object was the defence of the smaller principalities.

Frederick-William wrote to the Landgrave a friendly but strongly worded remonstrance, which had the effect of inducing him to remove his troops, but did not so offend him as to imperil his adhesion to the League.

The other was an injustice of old date that Frederick-William rectified. Prussia, in its capacity as State of the Empire, had once quartered troops in Mecklenburg-Schwerin in order to ensure the execution of an imperial decree. It had been found convenient for recruiting purposes to retain them there, and though the dukes had repeatedly offered payment of the sum due, both the last two Prussian kings had put obstacles in the way of a settlement. Frederick-William put an end to the long friction by the removal of the Prussian troops.

The first event of European importance in his reign was the brief campaign in Holland, where a too facile success greatly increased the *prestige* of Prussia in Europe, and made the disasters of the following French campaign seem at the time so utterly inexplicable.

The disturbances in Holland were of long standing. Ever since the seven northern provinces had separated themselves from the Catholic southern provinces in 1679, the republican-minded burghers had always looked with suspicion on the house of Orange-Nassau, to one of whose valiant sons, however, they always turned for a leader in times of war, though in peace they dreaded their encroachments on the civil liberties of the land.

Holland, as the richest province, had the most influence in the confederation, represented it in diplomacy and had the control over its finances, standing as civil head opposed to the Stattholder as military chief.

It was not here, as in France, the outbreak of an oppressed people against an insupportable tyranny; the self-styled "patriots" of Holland represented the commercial element; the poorer classes for the most part held to the Stattholder. It was the rich burghers of Amsterdam and other large towns who were anxious to diminish his powers and abolish the hereditary nature of his office.

In foreign politics Holland had usually followed England's lead; but of late years the French influence had prevailed, and in the War of Independence, which reacted so strongly on monarchical Europe, the States had taken the side of the American colonies. All the blame for their non-success was laid by the "patriots" on the Stattholder William V, who was accused of purposely neglecting the fleet out of sympathy with the English. From secret conspiracy the patriots went on to open attack. The house of the French ambassador at the Hague was their meeting-place, for they received every encouragement from France; while the Stattholder's party looked to England for assistance, and found a strong rallying-point in the ambassador who had been sent over to deal with this difficult crisis, Lord Malmesbury, then Sir James Harris.

THE CAMPAIGN IN HOLLAND

William V was a Prince of no great character, but his wife, Frederick-William's only sister—that Wilhelmina into whose girlish diary we have already had a peep—was a Princess of great judgment and strong resolution. But the niece of Frederick the Great, brought up in the traditions of an absolute monarchy, was little likely to exert a reconciling influence upon the contending factions; on the contrary, she was recognised as the masculine element at the Stattholder's Court, and it was in her more than in her husband that Malmesbury found a firm and energetic ally.

In the time of Frederick the Great she had appealed for his help against the contumacious citizens, but beyond reminding the States of what they owed to William V's famous ancestors, and counselling moderation to both parties, he declined to interfere.

When Frederick-William came to the throne she saw more hope of assistance. But naturally anxious as the King was to help his sister, encouraged thereto by Hertzberg, who had long looked upon Prussian interference in Holland as a duty, he wanted to act in conjunction with France and not risk a breach with that country, having the dread of Austrian aggression always before his eyes.

In June of 1787 he wrote to Hertzberg—

" I shall remain firm in the resolution I have taken to restrict myself to negotiations in an affair which only affects me indirectly, though the welfare of my sister and her children interests me, but not to the extent to lead me to risk the welfare of my State in order to repair the mistakes of the Prince of Orange."

He sent Count Görtz to Holland to attempt a reconciliation between the adverse parties, but hostilities had actually broken out when he got there.

Malmesbury had made a hurried journey to London, where he had gained over the Cabinet to his views, assuring them that active intervention would be unnecessary; money would suffice. He did not believe, in spite of French promises, that they would really take action in the patriots' favour.

The first outbreak of hostilities was at Utrecht between the troops of the Stattholder and the free corps, whereupon the burghers ordered the Rhine-grave of Salm, who was the general in command of their forces, to occupy Utrecht.

Even in Holland itself there was a party for the Stattholder; the dock-workers in Amsterdam had planned a rising in his favour, which, however, failed for want of unity.

The patriots now appointed a commission of five for the defence of the country, giving them powers of dictatorship.

They had the advantage over the Stattholder's troops in number, but it seemed likely that in the States-General a majority for the Orange party might be obtained; and Princess Wilhelmina believed that if she went to the Hague her presence might bring over some waverers.

But on her way there (in June 1787), with only four persons in her suite, she was stopped by the enemy, made to turn back and spend the night at Schonhooven, where she was so closely guarded that a sentinel with a drawn sword was even placed in her bedroom. In vain she remonstrated with the Defence Committee; she was not allowed to continue her journey, though they permitted her to return to Nimeguen without further molestation.

Such treatment of a royal Princess caused naturally a great sensation. Malmesbury, who had agreed somewhat unwillingly to the Princess's journey, was dismayed. "Check to the Queen," he wrote to Lord Caermarthen, "and I am afraid in one or two moves, checkmate." But he received a consoling reply that perhaps "the knight would come to the Queen's rescue, and all be saved."

And so it was. Frederick-William was naturally incensed at this treatment of his sister; nevertheless, he tried at first to get personal satisfaction without embroiling Prussia in the civil war. But the patriots refused all apologies; England promised assistance, and when the attention of Austria was occupied by the outbreak of war between Turkey and her Russian ally, the Duke of Brunswick [1] was placed in command of the troops, and the order to march was given.

The policy of France at this juncture can only be explained by the critical condition of her own affairs. She neither counselled moderation to her allies, nor helped them effectively when they stood obdurate.

[1] This was Charles William Ferdinand, mentioned before as the Hereditary Duke, and nephew of Ferdinand, brother to Queen Elizabeth-Christine.

A MYSTIC ON THE PRUSSIAN THRONE

After replying to the Prussian ultimatum, which demanded within four days due reparation to the Princess, with a refusal coupled with an offer to send an explanatory mission to Berlin, the patriots confidently looked for French assistance; all they got, however, was 200 gunners and a few officers. Vague hopes were held out of help in the spring.·

The very day on which the answer to the ultimatum was received, September 12, 1787, the Duke of Brunswick crossed the frontier. At the same time he issued a proclamation to the effect that he was not waging war with the United Provinces, but that from Holland satisfaction must be obtained.

Two centuries before Holland had heroically defended herself against the might of Spain. A hundred and fifty years before she had repulsed a French invasion of much more formidable dimensions under Condé and Turenne; and the present advance with so small a force was considered by experts a rash act.

But many causes helped to favour the invaders; first and foremost, the want of unity among the defenders. It was a "house divided against itself." The Duke's measures were taken with the greatest forethought and the most exact precision. The time of new moon was chosen, when the ebb and flow of the tide is slightest, so that though Holland's defences, the sluices, were opened, the flooding did not reach the point when it would have been disastrous to the Prussians till after the decisive blow against Amsterdam had been struck.

He was always well informed of the enemy's

movements, for partisans of the Stattholder were everywhere to be found. In Gueldres the invaders were welcomed as deliverers of the people; children ₋ollowed them singing folk-songs about William of Nassau that had been forbidden by the patriots.

The strongly fortified Gorkum surrendered at the first cannon-shot. In Hague itself the authorities completely lost their heads; the popular feeling swung round violently in the Stattholder's favour. Orange tokens were visible everywhere. The leaders of the rising fled to Amsterdam, and on the 20th of September the royal party returned in triumph to the town.

Only in isolated instances was there serious resistance to the Prussian forces. Whole divisions, deserted by their leaders, gave themselves up without firing a shot; fortresses that could have stood long against storm and siege hung out the Orange flag on the first appearance of the Prussians. A frigate-of-war with ten cannon that had struck on a sandbank actually surrendered to a battalion of grenadiers and a squadron of hussars!

Only Amsterdam itself still stood out; and the Duke of Brunswick was not without anxiety about the result of an attack, considering the approach of winter and the rising of the water. He offered terms to the enemy, which were refused.

A council of war was held in the room of the Princess Wilhelmina at the Hague. As the Duke of Brunswick declared that in speedy action lay the best chance of success, and Malmesbury was of the same opinion, it was decided to storm the place.

A MYSTIC ON THE PRUSSIAN THRONE

The Prussian leader had discovered the one weak point in the defence, the Haarlem Lake, which had been neglected, while men-of-war lay in the Zuydersee and the Y river. He sent there a division of Prussian troops in boats, which assailed the besieged in the rear at the same time that the attack on the forward entrenchments began, and contributed much to the victory.

The first storm was unsuccessful and cost many lives, but the Prussians renewed the attack, taking one redoubt after the other, till they were able to direct a fire on the city from three sides, when it capitulated, and the resistance of Holland was at an end.

The Duke of Brunswick spared the feelings of the conquered by refraining from making a triumphal entry. Frederick-William even forebore to claim an indemnity for the expenses of the campaign—a magnanimity that greatly helped in reconciling the contending factions, but was less favourably received by the tax-payers at home. Later on he was induced by his advisers to demand half a million gulden, which he distributed among the returning soldiers.

In Holland itself medals were actually struck in commemoration of the victory, and one was presented to the Duke of Brunswick in token of "inextinguishable gratitude."

This Prince was now at the height of his fame, having added to the laurels gained in the Seven Years' War by this rapid, decisive and well-planned campaign. The reputation of the Prussian troops was also greatly enhanced, and the idea of their invincibility spread abroad.

The Duke himself, however, knew better. He told Custrin some years later that in this campaign his army had run terrible risks, and that with common prudence the Dutch could have utterly destroyed it.

Not only in military matters did the Duke's reputation stand high. His administration of his own Duchy was admirable, and among his fellow-princes in the Empire he took such a high place that when the League was first mooted there was no question about his being chosen as the head. With characteristic hesitation, however, he refused to do anything till he knew what Frederick the Great thought on the subject.

His youth had been passed under the influence of his two renowned uncles, the Prussian King and Ferdinand, Duke of Brunswick; and though said to have been naturally of an impetuous disposition, he had so schooled himself to submission that the habit became ingrained, and he never in all his life learned to be really self-reliant. Prince Henry, the mocker, declared that the Duke was still afraid of his two uncles, though they were dead! It seems almost as if a very strong personality like that of the great Frederick had a blighting effect on the resolution of those around him.

At this time, however, he had not shown that fatal irresolution which afterwards made all his courage and skill and great merits of so little avail. His European reputation was immense. He had been warmly received in England when he came over to marry Princess Augusta, the sister of George III. It will be remembered that the second daughter from this union was the unhappy Queen Caroline, the wife of George IV.

A biographer of his remarks very truly that had he died now, before the French campaign, historians would have said that if only the Duke of Brunswick had lived Europe would have been saved from the Napoleonic domination.

An unfortunate result of this campaign was the overweening confidence in their own capability that it engendered in the Prussian soldiers, together with a contempt for a citizen army, both of which beliefs were to receive a rude shock in the next campaign.

Prussia gained nothing save in reputation by this enterprise. To France it was a great defeat. Its long-cherished schemes of ascendancy in Holland had failed; it is even said that the pitiful rôle played by the French Government in this matter was one of the causes of its downfall.

England was really the greatest gainer; her influence in Holland now became paramount. Lord Malmesbury gained his peerage by his skilful conduct of the affair; Frederick-William gave him the Prussian eagle for his coat-of-arms, and the Stattholder the Orange device: " Je maintiendrai."

The French actually accused him of engineering the affair of the Princess's detention in order to induce Frederick-William to take up arms. Though this has been abundantly disproved, the fact that while Prussia bore the brunt of the campaign, England won the fruits of the victory, is of a kind to give colour to the theory, still so ineradicably implanted in the Continental mind, that in all foreign disturbances "perfide Albion" secretly urges on the combatants, who find at the close, to their disgust, that it is for her that they have pulled the chestnuts out of the fire.

CHAPTER XI

AFTER the successful intervention of Prussia in Holland, Duke Charles Augustus of Weimar, who was the leading spirit of the League of Princes, was anxious that the Republic should be induced to join their protective alliance, and out of its riches contribute something towards the maintenance of a defensive army. This patriotic and high-spirited Prince, memorable for his long and close friendship with Goethe, had great schemes in his head—doubtless many of them inspired by the poet—for the reorganisation of the dying Empire through this League of the Germanic Princes.

Alarm at Austria's aggressive and disturbing policy had brought many of the States into one camp and made them temporarily forget their mutual animosities; he hoped to make of the League a lasting institution, he had ideas of a tariff union, a universal and reformed code of laws and a standing imperial army. He had been unceasing in his patriotic efforts, travelling from petty court to petty court, trying to awaken interest in his plans of reform.

But he could not make the dry bones live. The dead weight of custom was against him. Nothing but the immediate dread of Austria's aggression kept the smaller States united among themselves and with Prussia; no sooner was the alarm asuaged than their particular interests again divided them.

And Hertzberg, who had co-operated in its foundation, was no longer in favour of the League now that it had fulfilled its temporary purpose. He gave no further encouragement to the Duke of Weimar's plan than polite good wishes. At the time when the Duke was working hard at the project and in constant communication with the King, Hertzberg complained to his colleague Finckenstein in a letter : " It appears that we have a third minister among us," and he pointed out to Frederick-William dangers that might ensue from carrying out the Duke of Weimar's plans.

Frederick-William's own interest in the League had cooled as time went on. He still revered the outworn forms of the old Imperial institution too much to approve of a root and branch reorganisation such as was necessary. And his unfortunate tendency to drop, after a time, the designs he welcomed at first with great enthusiasm came here into play.

So died the last chance of reform from within for the Holy Roman Empire. It now only needed a shake from without to bring down the whole tottering fabric.

The personal attraction that had drawn together Joseph II and Frederick-William at their meeting in their youth had been powerless against the conflicting interests of the two nations and the bitter opposition of their ministers of foreign affairs.

A MYSTIC ON THE PRUSSIAN THRONE

Kaunitz and Hertzberg each saw in the neighbouring country only a natural and unappeasable rival, to thwart whose plans and hinder whose advancement was their first duty.

Kaunitz had advised the Emperor to meet Catherine's advances. In 1787 he had joined her in that remarkable journey that seemed to Count Ségur, who also was of the party, like a succession of scenes out of the *Arabian Nights;* where a wilderness was temporarily made to blossom with villages swarming with enthusiastic inhabitants (who were then moved on to appear again at the next halting-place); and in a desolate spot a prosperous harbour was called into being as if by magic.

Though Joseph saw through Prince Potemkin's magnificent comedy of illusion, he yet greatly overrated the real strength of Russia, being amazed at her riches and the stolid fidelity of her soldiers, who, whether they received their food and payment duly or not, were always ready to lay down their lives for their sovereign without a murmur.

The treaty between them, in which he promised help to Catherine's schemes in the East in return for her assistance towards his in the West, had serious consequences for Austria; for Turkey's declaration of war, forced on her by Catherine's policy, compelled him in honour to assist Russia, as the party attacked, just at the time when Hungary was seething with discontent and the Austrian Netherlands were in revolt in consequence of his too hasty and arbitrary plans of reform. And he had the further mortification of finding that Russia did not put out half her strength, but left him to bear the brunt of the campaign, which began most unfortunately for Austria.

Though he was destined to get no benefit from this Russian alliance, it caused great consternation in Europe, especially as it was feared that France and Poland might join it, and that the result of the war would be a partition of the Balkan provinces between the two Empires.

This fear led to the Triple Alliance between England, Prussia and Holland, in which Lord Malmesbury was an active agent. He took advantage of a visit that Frederick-William paid to his sister at Loo, in the spring of 1788, to urge his views upon him personally. He had learned on reaching the Hague that a strong party in Berlin was trying to instil into the King's mind a suspicion of England and a distrust of Malmesbury himself as an artful and dangerous man; and he set himself to counteract these opinions.

Frederick - William had come attended by Bischoffswerder, Brühl, Gensau and Stein. Malmesbury confided in none of them, but contrived to talk to the King without his *entourage*. The first interview was at seven in the morning, when Frederick-William listened to the ambassador's arguments and promised to reflect upon them.

That same evening there was a ball, and while the guests of the royal party were amusing themselves, Frederick-William and Malmesbury had a long conference in the garden behind the pavilion where dancing was going on, which resulted in the signing of a provisional agreement, followed by the definitive treaty signed in Berlin in August.

It met with much disapprobation from the French party in Berlin; even Hertzberg was displeased. According to Ewart's account, he was furious at what he called a plot to entrap the King, and the English ambassador had great difficulty in soothing him and inducing him to see the advantages of the treaty. A secret article agreed to the admission of Holland and Sweden to the league. Another secret adherent was no other than Grand-Duke Paul, the heir to the Russian throne. Frederick-William had suggested to him, through Goertz, the advisability of a connection with England, to which his reply was: "All that I can say at the moment is that my devotion to the system which unites me with the King of Prussia is unalterable, and that I agree to his views with all my heart."

Sweden did not wait to be invited to join the alliance, but declared war against Russia (in June 1788) in the hopes of regaining her conquered provinces.

Meanwhile Turkey had proved a much more formidable opponent than had been expected, and Joseph, who was himself in the field, saw one disaster after another overtake his troops, while a serious illness increased the depression caused by the news of the formidable alliance directed against him and his ally. Though the campaign of 1788 ended with the fall of several Turkish fortresses, and the storming of Oczakoff—where no quarter was given on either side and 10,000 Turks and 4,000

Russians were killed in one murderous hour of combat—was considered a brilliant victory for Russia, Joseph came back to Vienna a sick and broken man.

It was in accordance with the anti-Austrian policy still pursued that Prussia entered into friendly negotiations with the Pope, endeavouring to mediate between the Holy See and the refractory archbishops within the Empire.

The Pope addressed a letter to Frederick-William, which marked a change of sentiment inasmuch as it addressed him as " Majesty " and contained the following passage : " You will see from our thus sending to you, most illustrious and mighty King, what confidence we place in you and how much we hope from your humanity "; while as late as Frederick's time the Holy See had refused to recognise the Prussian ruler as a sovereign, and characterised the assumption of that title as "unpardonable presumption."

In the end, however, Prussia declined further interference in the difficult and complicated questions between the archbishops and the Nuncio, beyond promising to aid in a settlement when both parties desired it.

Meanwhile this year 1788 was memorable in Prussia for the passing of the much-abused Religious Edict.

The original intention was laudable enough. The "Aufklärers," the rationalist party, had too long been uncontrolled, and had run to extremes that called for some moderating action. To profess religion was to expose oneself to scorn and contempt. To intervene and take steps to ensure that preachers should not denounce from their pulpits the very doctrines they had undertaken to teach, was a measure that the times demanded.

It was a measure that Frederick-William had personally very much at heart, for he himself spurred Wöllner on to activity; and Wöllner soon discovered that a show of zeal in religious matters was the nearest way to the realisation of his ambitious projects.

This crafty schemer understood his royal master's character only too well, and knew how to turn its weaknesses to his own advantage. He played on both the dominating strings, the overmastering sensuality and the emotional piety which led him to regret and repent his excesses. Before Frederick-William's accession to the throne, when the more sincere among the Rosicrucians were trying to induce him to separate himself entirely from Mme. Rietz, in whose "Satanical fetters" he was held, Wöllner overrode the suggestion, and doubtless endeared himself to the Prince by this defence of the favourite.

His opportunities of influence were great, for all the King's letters and petitions were sent to him in the morning, and later in the day he gave in his report concerning them, so that it was easy for him to keep back anything he chose. He was nicknamed the "Little King" and the "Vice-King." But for all this he did not get promotion as rapidly as he hoped, and Frederick-William was deaf to some of

JOHANN CHRISTOPH WÖLLNER.

his hints as to offices he would not object to hold. It needed the aid of his fellow mystics and the mysterious power of the Secret Order behind him to bring him at last to his goal.

The Minister of Education, Zedlitz, an honest and capable man whose schemes for the improvement of schools and colleges had at first met with the King's approval (in spite of his being an "Aufklärer"), was finally driven by Wöllner's intrigues to resignation. Frederick-William, always more inclined to justice and benevolence than the men by whom he allowed himself to be led, consoled him with the Order of the Black Eagle and some minor appointment. And in July 1788 Wöllner was made a Minister of Justice and head of the spiritual department in all the Lutheran churches, schools and charitable foundations.

Only a few days later was passed the Religious Edict. The ostensible object was the' restoration of the Christian religion in its original purity; to put bounds to unbelief, superstition and the falsification of the fundamental doctrines of the faith, together with the lax morality that these induced. It spoke much of toleration, and freedom of conscience; of putting constraint on no man's opinions so long as he fulfilled his duties as a citizen and refrained from interfering with the faith of others.

But as interpreted by its real author, Wöllner, it was very much more than that. It was an attempt to enforce a strict and rigid adherence to the tenets of the "symbolical books" of the Lutheran and reformed churches; it forbade the formation of new religious communities; it put a restriction on freedom of discussion, and permitted an inquisitorial prying into the facts taught in schoolroom and lecture-hall. Church and educational appointments were given only to those who were glib with their professions of rigid orthodoxy; while others were dismissed, in some cases without inquiry and in others even when the inquiry had proved their innocence.

This retrograde step in a country that had been accustomed to the toleration of a Frederick aroused a violent outburst of indignation, such as is almost without parallel in the history of the country. Numberless protests were made against it, among them one signed by five out of the counsellors of the Upper Consistory.

The result, however, of this storm of protest, and the publication of so many pamphlets directed against it was unfortunate. It gave Wöllner a handle for the introduction of his next retrograde measure, a restriction of the freedom of the Press.

An edict of the 19th of December of the same year was intended to prevent press freedom from degenerating into licence. As Carmer had a hand in the framing of it, it was moderate in tone, and modern historians compare it favourably with later as well as earlier press edicts.

But it met with intense opposition. Frederick had accustomed his people to a large freedom in this respect. "Gazettes," he said, "if they are to be interesting, must not be interfered with," and in his time the existing restrictions were not enforced.

RELIGION AND PRESS EDICTS

Moreover, Wöllner could make use of this, as he did of the religious edict, for the gratification of his personal rancours and enmities. It mattered little that the King's intentions in both these attempts to force men to orthodoxy and virtue by royal edict were good, when the carrying out of them was entrusted to such men as the *camarilla* who had his confidence, and at a time, moreover, when scandal-mongers were busy with stories of the performances that went on in the Rietz establishment.

In the indignation against these two measures the King's popularity declined to vanishing-point. A flood of the most scurrilous pamphlets were poured forth, mostly published outside the frontier, in which vulgarity took the place of wit, and the wildest stories of royal revels were eagerly read and believed by the credulous.

Mirabeau's pamphlet had led the way. In the summer of 1787 a French edition had appeared anonymously of the *Letters of a Travelling French-man*, better known as the *Secret History of the Court of Berlin*, which, though disowned by Mira-beau, was known to be founded on the letters he sent from Berlin to Talleyrand and the Duc de Lauzun.

The first part, written in the last days of Fred-erick's life, gave a good description of the way all parties were striving for the favour of the coming ruler. But as time went on and his hopes of estab-lishing a preponderating French influence at the Berlin Court failed, his desire to regale his corre-spondents with scandal increased, till—in Heigel's

207

words: "He distorts and disfigures, falsifies and besmirches," and his portraits became cruel caricatures. "A nation that is rotten before it is ripe," was his sweeping condemnation of the Prussian people.

Injured as the King felt by the appearance of this work, he took no steps against the author. In Paris the book was indeed ordered to be burned by the hangman, but against Mirabeau, though well known to be its author, no attack was made. Prince Henry, who had been the cause of Mirabeau's coming to Prussia and had the most right to be aggrieved at this abuse of his friendship, treated the matter with a good-humoured contempt that Frederick might have displayed. He sent the book to his friends and asked them if they recognised his portrait.

Several refutations were issued; one by the historian Posselt, who found the key to this "record of lies, abuse, contradictions and spitefulness of all kinds" in the author's failure to insinuate himself into the King's favour; another by Baron Trenck was not of a character to do much good, since it contained more abuse of Mirabeau than serious attempts to refute his statements.

And now one scurrilous pamphlet followed another. No longer was Frederick-William the "well-beloved." Under slightly disguised, but easily recognisable titles, he was held up to ridicule and abuse.

But the heaviest vials of wrath and hatred were outpoured upon the two advisers, Wöllner and Bischoffswerder.

RELIGION AND PRESS EDICTS

Still, with all this indignation and dissatisfaction, there was no disposition in Germany to follow the example of its French neighbour, whose internal troubles were becoming acute. In July of this year (1789) was the storming of the Bastille.

Intellectually the fundamental ideas that were at the bottom of the French Revolution had made great progress in Germany. But the assent that thinkers and writers gave to doctrines of the rights of man, the sovereignty of the people, and so forth, was purely academical, and they never dreamed of carrying their theories into practice. They merely watched with sympathy the attempts of the French to rid themselves of the intolerable weights that had been hung on their necks by the Court, the clergy and the aristocracy.

To be a little revolutionary was the fashion. Ladies wore the tricolour and headdresses *à la Carmagnole*, and officers of the guard in Potsdam allowed the tune "Ça ira" to be played on the bugles. Even Hertzberg, most loyal servant of the Prussian monarchy, applauded a speech made in the Joachimsthaler Gymnasium on the King's birthday, in which the victory of the new ideas was greeted with enthusiasm. Frederick-William himself was supposed to look with no ill favour on a movement that curtailed the privileges of the nobility.

In connection with the taking of the Bastille an incident (related by Philippson) is very characteristic of Wöllner's methods in dealing with the King.

On the 28th of September he handed to Frederick-William, with impressive solemnity, a communication from the unknown Superior of the Rosicrucian Order, as a token of gratitude for the issue of the Religious Edict. This communication was supposed to have been written in the previous April, three months before the fall of the Bastille, of which it contained a literal prophecy.

Wöllner's letter on the subject, in the royal archives in Berlin, contains the following sentence: "It struck me particularly in the part concerning France that this decree was written on the 21st of April, and the revolution did not take place till the 14th of July. Your Majesty will see that I am not wrong in always maintaining that the S[acred] O[rder] has not forsaken us, and your Majesty may be sure that this strong protection neither can nor will desert you either in war or peace. God be praised, for He knoweth His own!"

A more suspicious nature than Frederick-William's might not have laid much store upon a prophecy that was not brought to his notice till ten weeks after the event.

One event in this year that should not pass unchronicled was the visit of Mozart to Berlin.

To the musical world of Germany the accession to the throne of Frederick-William brought a very welcome change through the appreciation of native talent that he showed, and the efforts he made for its encouragement.

Frederick's taste had been all for Italian music, and neither Handel, Gluck nor Hadyn found favour with him.

RELIGION AND PRESS EDICTS

With Frederick-William music was a life-long passion. The band that he maintained was considered the best in Europe. He still played the violoncello in Court concerts, attended rehearsals and practised—say the chroniclers—with as much diligence as if his bread depended upon it.

To musicians, both native and foreign, he showed great personal kindness as well as liberality. Hadyn wrote quartettes for him; Boccherini received a pension, in return for which he sent the King yearly one of his compositions.

In Mozart's music he took especial delight, and when in the spring of 1789 Prince Lichnowsky persuaded the great musician, then in very straitened circumstances, to visit Berlin, he was very graciously received. He attended the Court concerts of chamber music and received a commission for several quartettes. In three of these, which he completed in the following year, the 'cello, Frederick-William's instrument, is awarded an important part.

The King tried to keep the great musician in his capital by the offer of a very well-paid post, but Mozart's love for Vienna was too great for him to accept such an offer.

Nevertheless Frederick-William insisted on having Mozart's operas played in the National Theatre in Berlin, where they gradually won their way with a public long accustomed to the lighter Italian music. After the great composer's death, his opera *Titus* was played at the King's command (in 1796) for the benefit of Mozart's widow, who was then on a visit to Berlin.

CHAPTER XII

For a whole year the King had been inconsolable for the loss of Countess Ingenheim. And then there appeared a new lady-in-waiting at the Court, a Countess von Dönhof, whose beauty was of a striking and uncommon order.

In the Diary of the elder Countess von Voss the first mention of this lady, who was to be her niece's successor in the King's affection, appears strangely enough on the very day of that niece's funeral.

"April 4 [1789].—To-day the new lady-in-waiting, Countess Sophie Dönhof, who has already been appointed, arrived and was presented at Court."

Not till the beginning of the next year is the lady mentioned again.

"27 Jan. [1790].—I came to-day back to Berlin, from Rudenhausen, where I was staying with my daughter, and went in the evening to the Queen Dowager's Court. The King and Queen were there. The company overwhelmed me with kindness, the King especially was touchingly kind and friendly; but it struck me that he takes a great deal of notice of the new lady-in-waiting, Dönhof."

"30 Jan.—They say here that the intimacy between the King and the Dönhof came on and developed rapidly. I can see that he is very much in love with her, but a renewed guilt of the kind would be too dreadful. I cannot believe that it will happen."

"31 Jan.—The King talked to me a good deal, and I noticed all the time that he did not lose sight of his fair one."

"18 Feb.—I played whist with the King; he was in good spirits and most amiable. Ah! if only he were not so indolent and so weak in will, what happiness it would be for us all, and for himself too!"

"March 6.—There was a party at Countess Eichstadt's; the King was there, and was much occupied with his fair one, whose behaviour does not please me. She is very pretty, but I do not think she has a good character."

"10 April.—The Dönhof has sent in her resignation, and has suddenly gone away. Some people say she has gone to the King at Potsdam."

"13 April.—People talk of nothing but the Dönhof. She is with the King at Potsdam, and he gives parties and concerts in her honour. Ah, the poor King!—how can all this be excused?"

"15 May.—Bengersky is in disgrace, and Lindenau and Bischoffswerder are threatened with the same through the influence of the Dönhof, who does not like them. She is still in Potsdam; the King is said to call her openly: 'My dear wife.'"

And indeed to this title she had as much right as the poor Countess Ingenheim, who had been her predecessor. The King had written to her—

A MYSTIC ON THE PRUSSIAN THRONE

" I am separated from my wife; I am widowed of Mme. Ingenheim. I offer you my heart and my hand."[1]

The Consistory had again been summoned, and having a precedent before them in the case of Fräulein Voss, had no difficulty in permitting this union. In April 1790 the Court preacher Zollner performed the religious rite which gave the King another left-handed partner.

The same struggle against the machinations of Mme. Rietz and the intriguers who had the King's confidence, that had been too much for the gentler Julie, made Sophie Dönhof's position a very difficult one. She seems to have made more vigorous efforts against them, but was even less successful. She was not, like Julie, a favourite with the royal family and the Court generally, but appears to have had a hot temper. While the attachment between her and Frederick-William lasted they were not able to live happily either together or apart.

Countess von Voss noted the progress of the affair in her Diary.

"6 Feb. [1791].—The old Queen cannot bring herself to acquiesce in this new passion of the King's; she invited him for to-morrow, but not the Dönhof."

"9 Feb.—The Queen Dowager has given way; she invited the Dönhof and then went to bed and said she was ill, so as not to appear at her own entertainment."

"14 Feb.—To-day it was actually done. The

[1] Ranke: *Die deutschen Mächte und der Fürstenbund*, I, 287.

old Queen invited her with the King and really saw her. She played lotto with the company, but did not stay to supper."

"16 Feb.—Supper at the old Queen's. The King and the reigning Queen were there, but not the fair one, who is at odds with the King again, for they are always quarrelling."

"19 Feb.—They say all is at an end between the King and the Countess; she will not go with him to Potsdam, but will go away. She reproaches the King that he is still under the influence of the Rietz."

"24 Feb.—The King has reconciled himself with his Countess again. I saw her to-day; she is shockingly altered, as white as a corpse, but she goes on Sunday to Potsdam."

"27 Feb.—The Dönhof came to-day to pay her respects to the old Queen. She looked wretched and I felt sorry for her. She cannot make headway against the Rietz or against Bischoffswerder. It is true that she goes to Potsdam to-morrow, but I do not think that she will long keep her sway over the King. She is not wanting in sense, but she is capricious, and the King is already cooling towards her."

A son of hers, born in January 1792, was given the title of Count of Brandenburg and the name of Frederick-William.

"The King was very good and tender with her," writes Countess Voss, "and gave her fine pearls."

On the 20th of June in the same year is the following entry—

A MYSTIC ON THE PRUSSIAN THRONE

"The Dönhof has suddenly gone away—they say it is for good."

This further matrimonial venture of Frederick-William's gave great occasion to his enemies, both at home and abroad, to scoff at a King who combined so much piety with his amatory tendencies. Catherine wrote in a letter to Grimm: "That lout of a William has just married a third wife; the fellow cannot have enough legal wives. *Pour être un gaillard consciencieux, c'en est un !*" A current epigram stated pithily that while Frederick without wives, or gods, or counsellors was sufficient unto himself, his heir could never have enough of wives, gods and counsellors to satisfy him.

But far more harmful to the State than his matrimonial eccentricities was the increasing power over the King gained by the clique who played on his pious susceptibilities. Wöllner's influence had led him to estrange his people by the narrow illiberality of the religious and press-censorship edicts. Bischoffswerder's advice in foreign affairs was now to set him on to a line of policy not in accordance with Prussia's true interests.

The number of Rosicrucians and mystics who gathered about the King ever increased. The three brothers von Beyer, Hermes, Oswald, Haugwitz and von Arnim were among those of the elect who came into prominence.

A good many of the German Princes were affected by the prevailing tendency to mysticism and the love of the occult, notably Duke Frederick of Brunswick and Prince Eugene of Würtemberg, of whom

Mirabeau declared that with his haggard eyes and wild eloquence he looked like a pythoness.

Goethe was brought into contact with many of these mystics, and he mentions the regret with which he saw men of excellent character imposed upon through their imaginative temperaments by the deceptions of spurious or self-deceived enthusiasts. He introduced such subjects as the Secret Orders and crystal-gazing into some of the pieces he brought out at the Weimar theatre, but found that a disparaging treatment of these themes caused much offence. He could not but be secretly amused, he writes, when the very people whom he had seen egregiously taken in, assured him that such deception was impossible !

There was small prospect of advancement in Berlin for those who did not belong to this set, or were not in favour with its leaders. Bischoffs-werder, moreover, brought into the royal service many of his Saxon compatriots, which naturally aroused much Prussian indignation.

One of these was Count von Brühl, who had long been one of the leaders of the " Strict Observance," and was appointed tutor to the Crown Prince. The appointment was much censured, not only because he was a foreigner and owed his post to his connec-tion with the mystics, but because he was the son of the notorious Saxon minister who had encouraged Augustus III in his extremes of folly and extrava-gance and who had always been the bitterest enemy of Prussia and of the great Frederick.

He was, however, a very different man from his

father—a man of culture, fine character and great talents as well as of charming manners, who won the esteem of even his opponents, so that in the pamphlets which abused the Government for appointing him, his own personality was always respected.

Though Frederick-William's personal popularity among his own people had greatly waned, Prussia actually stood now at the highest point it had ever attained. The easy conquest in Holland had inspired other nations with an idea of the invincibility of the Prussian troops. Count de Ségur described Frederick-William's position now as feared by France, humoured by Spain, exalted by England, regarded by German Princes as the protector of German liberty; Turkey implored his help, Poland his support, Sweden followed his counsels, Denmark gave way before his threats.

And Austria—the hereditary foe and rival, with whom a struggle for supremacy some day was considered inevitable—Austria was in sore straits.

Entangled by his treaty with Catherine in the Turkish war that had turned out a much more difficult matter than he expected, Joseph had his hands more than full with disturbances in his own dominions. Belgium was in open revolt, Hungary so discontented that a deputation of nobles actually asked Frederick-William to suggest a King for them, if they threw off the Austrian yoke.

He suggested Karl August of Saxe Weimer, Goethe's friend, but that Prince was prudent enough to refuse the prospect of such doubtful advancement. Austria was not dead yet, he wrote, and he had no desire to be a second "Winter-king."

The revolution in France was disastrous to Austria's interests, not only by depriving her of her traditional ally, but by spreading the infection of revolt among several of the nations under her sway.

One of the places where disturbances occurred was the Bishopric of Liége, where the original cause of dispute was the trivial matter of the licensing of a gambling-house in Spa. By a sudden and blood-less revolution the people regained many of their lost privileges, and they induced the Bishop to sign a confirmation of the new settlement. Having done so under what they considered peaceful persuasion, but he characterised as compulsion, he fled to Trèves and appealed to the Imperial tribunal, which issued a degree against the rebellious Liégeois and called upon the Westphalian circle to carry it into execution.

Prussia, by right of her possession of Cleves, belonged to this circle, and sent accordingly a contingent of troops. Before this Dohm had been sent from Cleves to inquire into the matter, and he made no concealment of his sympathy with the outbreak.

No opposition was made to the advancement of the imperial contingent, and they took possession of the citadel of Liége in November 1789. But the success of the Belgians in their attempt to throw off the Austrian yoke encouraged the Liégeois to be firm in their demand for a reform of their constitution.

A letter in Frederick-William's own hand urged

on the Bishop the advisability of paying some regard to the desires of his subjects, lest worse might ensue. But this potentate refusing to surrender any of his prerogatives and insisting on the unconditional carrying out of the imperial judgment, Frederick-William in the following year withdrew the Prussian soldiers; the rebellious citizens were able to rout the other imperial troops and they set up a regent in place of the Bishop. But later on, when Joseph's successors had put an end to many of his difficulties by the Convention of Reichenbach, he sent his forces to bring Liége to submission, in contradiction of that very Convention. In spite of Prussian protests the old order of things was restored and the rebellion rigorously put down. Prussian *prestige* suffered severely in the conclusion of this affair.

But before that Convention of Reichenbach there had been a time when war between Prussia and Austria seemed imminent and unavoidable. It was certain that Turkey could not hold out much longer against the two allied Empires, and it was impossible for the other European powers to see with equanimity her provinces divided between her conquerors. The "balance of power" was the fetich of those days, and here the balance of power ran every risk of being upset.

Prussia, moreover, had more urgent cause for anxiety, since it was highly probable that Joseph would seek, with Russia's aid, to get his "indemnification" for the campaign in the West instead of the East.

Therefore the Prussian policy (and the English)

was to uphold Turkey, and a treaty with the Porte was set on foot and at last carried out, being much hindered by the Turkish envoys' interminable delays.

The Austrians had the same difficulty in getting any decisive result in their negotiations about the peace, that was getting more and more to be the object of Joseph's desire in the multiplicity of his other troubles. The Austrian representative declared that though always assuring him of his desire for peace, when it came to discussing the conditions, the Grand Vizier would begin to tell anecdotes or to discuss ancient Rome or modern France.

Hertzberg now believed he saw his way at last to the fulfilment of the scheme on which he had long set his heart. He had worked out an elaborate plan for an exchange of territories in Eastern Europe, which was to achieve the impossible by satisfying everybody. In exchange for what it gained from Turkey, Austria was to restore the Galician provinces to Poland, while Prussia, as the reward of its services in mediating, was to acquire from Poland the long-desired Dantzig and Thorn.

He urged Frederick-William to mobilise his army on the Silesian frontier, thinking it would be a powerful aid to the involved diplomatic intrigues by which he hoped to gain great profit for his country without any of the risks of war.

Hertzberg was too much enamoured of his scheme to realise all its difficulties. It had no chance of success. Turkey was not willing to part with any of its provinces, nor was Poland ready to yield

Dantzig and Thorn, even if there had been a certainty of receiving an equivalent in Gallicia. And England, though in alliance with Frederick-William, would have been far from pleased with the Prussian acquisition of this seaport, which she had contrived to prevent at the time of the First Partition.

Frederick-William was full of confidence in his army, and was not at all unwilling to try conclusions with the hereditary enemy. And it was undoubtedly a favourable moment for settling the long duel for supremacy with Austria.

A great change, however, in the situation was brought about by the death of Joseph II on the 20th of February 1790. His brother Leopold succeeded to his dominion at a moment when the outlook was of the blackest.

Joseph's long illness had been troubled by a constant succession of bad tidings. One after another all his plans had come to grief.

Interesting as a personality, and in many of his ideas far in advance of his times, as a reforming ruler Joseph was a decided failure, and he was conscious of it. " I should like to have written over my tomb," he said : "' Here lies a Prince whose intentions were pure, but who had the misfortune to see all his plans fail.' "

In Mirabeau's phrase, he " did good badly." Too hasty, arbitrary and impatient in his methods, the ideas he failed to carry out were yet living ideas that afterwards came to fruition. " From the torch of his genius," wrote George Förster, the republican, "a spark fell in Austria which will never be extinguished."

Leopold was as different from his brother in character as he was unlike in person. He possessed a Macchiavellian tact and subtlety, was prudent and cautious, and knew how to submit gracefully when submission was profitable. He saw the immediate necessity of soothing his rebellious subjects, of making peace with Turkey and above all of avoiding a war with Prussia at such a highly unfavourable moment.

Overriding the advice of Kaunitz, who thought a threatening attitude the most likely to succeed with Prussia, he wrote a personal letter to Frederick-William of a most conciliatory character.

Frederick-William had himself joined the head-quarters of the army in Silesia. With him now was Lucchesini, the clever Italian, who had been one of Frederick's favourite companions, in whose diplomatic abilities Frederick-William had great confidence. Lucchesini was all for war, and encouraged the King's impatience of the long and intricate negotiations by which Hertzberg hoped to gain a diplomatic victory and to avoid a war which he held to be undesirable, having very little confidence in the assistance of England or any other of Prussia's allies.

Frederick-William's answer to Leopold was to the effect that it was against Prussia's interests to permit of the partition of Turkey's European territory between the two Imperial Courts; that the refusal of Prussia's mediation had necessitated war-like preparations, still he was ready to hold out the hand of friendship, but it must be with the assurance that the balance of power in North and East would be maintained.

Anxious as he was for peace, Leopold would have nothing to say to Hertzberg's plan. The surrender of the larger half of Galicia was too large a price to pay for the small amount of territory that Turkey was to relinquish. And why—as he said to the English ambassador—why should Prussia, who had taken no part in the war, be the gainer by the acquisition of Dantzig and Thorn?

In another letter to Frederick-William (17th June 1790) Leopold declared that he had gone as far in his desire for peace as honour permitted, and offered to send Prince Reuss and Spielmann to Silesia to negotiate.

The little town of Reichenbach was chosen for the meeting, on the 26th of June, of the representatives of Austria, Prussia, England and Holland; and while the discussions were going on, three Prussian armies, one under Frederick-William and the Duke of Brunswick, the others under Möllendorf and Frederick of Brunswick, and two Austrian armies under Loudon and Hohenlohe, were waiting on the frontier.

As the negotiations spun themselves out, Frederick-William wearied of the delay. He feared, too, that the favourable time for a campaign would be lost and winter would come on before the diplomatic wrangles were concluded, and that Austria was playing with him, with this very object in view.

He ordered Hertzberg to insist on the return to the *status quo*, a demand that, since it prevented all accession of territory, Austria had hitherto explicitly refused, and in spite of Hertzberg's arguments and reclamations, reiterated his commands, urging that no more time should be wasted in discussions but that a speedy answer from Austria should be demanded.

"As it is not improbable," Frederick-William wrote on July 20th, "that the Vienna Court will again give only a procrastinating answer, I desire you to set to work without delay upon a war manifesto, so that it may be ready if these people try to befool me again. All my measures are taken; nothing ought to, and nothing shall, stop them but the absolute acceptance of the *status quo*."

Very unwillingly Hertzberg gave up his favourite and long-cherished scheme, and only on the King's direct and reiterated command. All was arranged for the forward march of the troops on the 25th of July, when the unexpected happened, Leopold gave way and declared himself willing to make peace on the basis of the *status quo*. Austria was to take no further part in Russia's war with Turkey; Belgium was to return to its allegiance, but was to have a constitution under the guarantee of England, Prussia and Holland.

Frederick-William in this matter of the treaty was firm and decided; and Hertzberg, to his disgust, instead of taking the lead was compelled to be, as he expressed it, "only a mouthpiece." When the King congratulated him on the conclusion of the

negotiations, the offended minister coldly replied:
"It should be my part to congratulate your Majesty
on the occasion of this treaty, for it is solely and
entirely your work."

At the moment this Reichenbach Convention was
considered a triumph for Prussia and a defeat for
Austria. Kaunitz only signed it, as Hertzberg had
done, on the express command of his sovereign.
Not till later on was it discovered that, as utilised by
Leopold, it was just the reverse.

Great rejoicings prevailed in Silesia at the peaceful termination of the threatening condition of
affairs, and both Frederick-William and the unwilling Hertzberg received ovations. A demonstration of loyal devotion broke out on one occasion
when Frederick-William, impelled by that enthusiasm for nature and country life which was then
the vogue, climbed to the top of a hay-rick; and to
commemorate the occasion the grateful people
erected a monument to him on the Silesian frontier,
with the words: "Den Frieden wahrt sein sichrer
Schild" (His trusty shield is the safeguard of
peace).

Leopold was well aware that he had come out of
the matter better than he could have expected. "It
is the least unfavourable peace we could have
concluded," he wrote to his sister.

The Prussian triumph was short-lived, the victory
hollow and futile. Turkey was the real gainer by
the Reichenbach Convention that freed it from the
grasp of a foe; and England benefited by Turkey's
deliverance. It did not even divide the two imperial

Courts, for Leopold convinced Catherine that he had only bowed to necessity; that he was gaining time to get his finances and his army in order and to quiet his rebellious provinces, when he would be all the better able to stand by her.

His prudent concessions soon brought peace in Hungary; Sweden made peace with Russia; Poland and Belgium considered themselves deserted by Prussia and became bitterly hostile.

Twenty million thalers had been spent on the mobilisation and the preparations for war, and nothing had been really gained.

And yet recent historians, such as Max Duncker and Paul Bailleu, give it as their opinion that the King, in overriding the counsel of Hertzberg in this instance was in the right. While doing every justice to Hertzberg's patriotic zeal and long and faithful service, they consider that he had an overweening confidence in his own skill in diplomacy, and believed that his arguments must infallibly convince his opponents, against their interests. His own scheme of exchange—if it could have been brought about in the face of the opposition of all the parties concerned—would have had even more harmful results. In this matter, according to Duncker, the King showed himself much superior to his minister.[1] Where Hertzberg failed was in neither so sharpening the demands that Austria would refuse them, nor binding it firmly to its contract if it consented. All the stipulations of the Reichenbach Convention

---

[1] *Historische Zeitschrift*, Vol. VII: "Friedrich-Wilhelm and Hertzberg."

that were disagreeable to Austria were afterwards evaded by Leopold.

Meanwhile the Holy Roman Empire was still without its ruler, and at one time there had seemed no certainty that Leopold would be his brother's successor on the imperial throne. Had the League of Princes continued strong and active, it might well have been possible now to separate the imperial crown from the house of Habsburg, or at any rate to impose conditions. But the League was lifeless, and Leopold's election was unopposed. There was no other candidate who had a chance of success.

"I, for my part, believe," wrote Hertzberg to the King, "that you cannot well refuse your vote to the King of Hungary."

Leopold himself declared that he received the imperial crown as a magnanimous present from the King of Prussia.

But his gratitude evaporated in words. Within a short time after the Convention the situation had altered everywhere in Austria's favour, and in spite of all guarantees the revolting Belgians and Liégeois were put down with a strong hand and punished with severity.

In these treaty negotiations it became evident that Hertzberg had lost that influence with the King which he had hitherto maintained. His colleague Finckenstein was enfeebled by age, and Bischoffswerder, without occupying the position of foreign minister, gradually began to play a leading part in the foreign policy of Frederick-William.

THE REICHENBACH CONVENTION

And the policy he pursued was the unfortunate one of friendship with Austria; a friendship that could scarcely be genuine, not only because of conflicting interests, but because each party mistrusted and was jealous of the other. As a Rosicrucian, the reactionary tendency of Austria made it sympathetic to Bischoffswerder. He saw in it a bulwark of monarchical and ecclesiastical authority against the approaching tide of liberalism in religion and politics.

Friendship with Austria, moreover, usually proved more disastrous to Prussia than open enmity, for except during Frederick's time Berlin was no match for Vienna in diplomacy.

At the time of his crowning as Emperor in Frankfort Leopold wrote a most grateful and friendly letter to Frederick-William, thanking him for his support. Though he answered the letter in the same cordial tone, Frederick-William remarked to his ministers: " I only wish this Prince would act as he writes."

Count Goertz, who was present at the election as the representative of Brandenburg, declared that Leopold's chief ministers, Kaunitz, Cobenzel and Colloredo rivalled one another in their hatred of Prussia.

Still the monarch himself was profuse in professions of friendship, and with the prospect before him of coming into possession of Ansbach and Bayreuth it was of importance to Frederick-William to gain Austria's peaceful acceptance of this increase of his territory, which she could not possibly view with pleasure, since it gave Prussia a foothold in South Germany.

The Margrave Alexander of Ansbach-Bayreuth (son of Frederick's favourite sister Wilhelmina) was the last of his line, and with its extinction the Hohenzollern reigning family came into possession through a family compact of ancient date. Prince Henry had once wished to rule over the little principality, but Frederick would not for a moment consider the idea.

In 1789 the Margrave came to Berlin with his "unofficial partner," Lady Craven, to ask secretly for Prussian help in regulating the hopelessly involved finances and the disordered condition of public affairs, for in Ansbach, it was said, "every one ruled except the Margrave."

Hardenberg was the Prussian official sent there in response to this request, and here he had an opportunity of displaying his talent for organisation. The Margrave, who hated the trouble necessary to establishing order, wanted to resign his territory in return for an annuity. There was long hesitation about arranging this, as opposition was feared from Austria or the other German states; and very quietly and unostentatiously it came under Prussian control, while the Margrave still retained the nominal sovereignty. In the summer of 1791 he and Lady Craven departed from the country, leaving the control in Hardenberg's hands, but not till January of the following year was its cession to Prussia publicly announced.

Alexander and "die Lady," as she was called in

Germany, proceeded first to England, but were not very favourably received at the English Court.

Lady Craven was a Berkeley by birth and had made an unhappy marriage. She seems, however, to have put up with her lot for a long time, for she was the mother of seven children before she left her unfaithful husband and travelled abroad. At one time she was friendly with Marie Antoinette; then we hear of her as travelling in Turkey, Greece and Russia before she found her way to this little principality.

The Margrave was at that time in subjection to the charms of the famous French actress, Clairon; but the Englishwoman, who seems to have retained her youthful charm and her liveliness of temperament, completely routed her rival.

On leaving England the pair went to Lisbon, where after a time they were at last able to marry, death having relieved them of their respective legal partners.

The Margrave's subjects, though somewhat surprised at the suddenness of the change, submitted without any difficulty to becoming Prussian, since Frederick-William had the reputation of a benevolent King and Hardenberg that of a good minister.

CHAPTER XIII

SISTOVA AND PILLNITZ

THE year 1790 very nearly saw before its close a general European war. The storm-clouds had gathered very thickly, and the outbreak appeared almost unavoidable. It was the opposition of the British nation to the war policy of the Government that decided the question in favour of peace.

The Emperor Leopold's actions after the Convention of Reichenbach, and his delay in carrying through the promised peace with Turkey caused great anxiety to the Triple Alliance. And as Catherine was still bent on the enlargement of her territory at Turkey's expense, and still looked confidently to Austria for assistance, it seemed likely that the allied Powers would be compelled to take up arms against the two Empires.

So menacing was the outlook that every preparation was made. England was to send a fleet into the North Sea, and Frederick-William was in readiness to make the attack by land. But after a stormy debate in the House of Commons, in which the eloquence of both Pitt and Burke proved unavailing, the motion was negatived; and as without England's help success could not be looked for, the whole plan was abandoned.

It was a time of uncertainty and unrest everywhere. Poland was pre-eminently one of the storm-centres, its internal discords placing it always at the mercy of its enemies.

Lucchesini, the Italian who had so long been one of Frederick's favourite companions, was Prussian ambassador in Warsaw, where he did his utmost to strengthen the party that inclined towards Prussia. Most of the various factions that raged furiously together in that distracted country realised to some extent that one cause of its decay was the weakness of the central power, and had some hopes of the efficacy of a regular royal succession. The Prussian party wanted to offer the crown to Frederick-William's nephew, Prince Louis Ferdinand; others, who favoured Frederick Augustus, the Saxon candidate, were for the marriage of his daughter and heiress with a Prussian prince who should succeed him.

Hertzberg, however, who did not forget how Lucchesini had crossed his plans in the Reichenbach affair, was now very strong against his suggestion of such a union between the two countries. Finckenstein shared his views, and between them they persuaded Frederick-William against his nephew's candidature, in spite of the fact that a great mistrust of Hertzberg's schemes had gradually grown in the King's mind.

Lucchesini then suggested that the question of the Polish succession should be discussed in the Congress that was to take place for the settlement of peace with Turkey. To this Frederick-William agreed, and Lucchesini himself was entrusted with the representation of Prussian interests in the meeting at Sistova.

Russia had refused to send any representative, Catherine, with her usual haughtiness, repudiating the idea of the intervention of any foreign power in her peace negotiations. But the accredited representatives of Austria, Turkey and the three allied powers met in December 1790 in the little town on the Danube, which afforded very poor accommodation for such a gathering.

Sir Robert Murray Keith, the English delegate, described the rooms allotted to them as little larger than pigeon-holes. The Turkish plenipotentiaries, he wrote home, were like oysters. That they *did* move was a fact, but it was very difficult to perceive it. One of them displayed his intimate knowledge of European affairs by inquiring whether Spain were not in Africa.

Not only the deliberate dealings of the Turks made the Congress drag on so slowly, but also the endless differences between the Austrian and Prussian delegates. It was not till August of the following year that their labours were concluded; and even then it was the rapid march of events in France, after the attempted flight of Louis XVI and his Queen and their capture at Varennes, that brought peace to the east of Europe and drew together for a time the two rival powers of Germany.

Before this much had happened in Poland to accentuate the differences between them. Kaunitz, always an opponent of Poland, described to the

Prussian ambassador as a "revolution" the events that occurred there on the 3rd of May 1791.

In the hopes of putting a limit to the foreign intervention in Polish affairs and of strengthening the country to resist further partition, King Stani·slaus suddenly announced in the Diet that the question of a reformed Constitution must be then and there decided. In spite of strong opposition a resolution was passed, embodying among other reforms a hereditary succession to the throne, the abolition of the *liberum veto* and measures of emancipation for the unprivileged classes.

The news of this Polish *coup d'état*, directed mainly as it was against Russian influences, was greeted at first with approval in most of the European capitals. Frederick-William expressed through his ambassador his approbation of the measure, which seemed at first sight to give promise of a better future for the unfortunate land. Hertzberg, however, considered it as a blow to Prussian interests that the succession should be assured to the royal Saxon house, and the Ministerium declared in a report to the King that only the restoration of the freedom of election to the throne (in other words, of the Polish anarchy) could preserve Prussia from exposure to great dangers. Still, as all fear of war with Russia was not over and English assistance could no longer be reckoned upon, it was thought inadvisable to make an enemy of Poland, and the Polish ambassador in Berlin was assured of Prussia's satisfaction with the procedings.

Kaunitz even suspected Prussian intrigue behind

the Polish reforms, and urged upon his master a closer union with Russia; but Leopold, whatever were his real views—and historians differ greatly as to the part Austria played in this matter—expressed a warm sympathy with the "regeneration" of Poland.

But this glimmer of hope for the revival of a national life in Poland soon faded away. The majority of the nobility—the only party with any political power—were against it; and there were too many powerful interests involved in the continuance of the anarchy. Catherine in particular was determined to permit no strengthening of the country whose internal divisions left it at her mercy. Russian promises, Russian threats and Russian gold had brought it about that there was a powerful Russian faction in Poland; and Catherine saw with satisfaction the possibility that a united intervention in French affairs might occupy the attention of Austria, and Prussia leave her—as she expressed it in council—"room to move her elbows freely."

The beginnings of the French Revolution had been watched with far from unsympathetic interest by many in Prussia; the ambassador Goltz was openly in friendship with the leaders of the party. But there, as in other countries, it was little foreseen how great the overthrow would be. Even a keen-sighted diplomatist like Lord Malmesbury declared at late as 1775 that the French monarchy was settled on a foundation beyond the reach of the follies of the Court to shake. With the attack on the excessive privileges of the nobles and clergy most thoughtful men sympathised.

And the first swarm of *émigrés* that descended upon Germany had, by their arrogance and folly, given no favourable impression of their cause. They claimed assistance as a right, and in the expectation of a speedy return to their former power they annoyed and repelled even those who helped them. The weakest States that were nearest to the French frontier suffered the most severely under this infliction. In Trèves the Elector was powerless against their encroachments; they even set up courts of justice.

Freytag relates a characteristic incident that occurred on a Rhine boat. One of the passengers—it was Weber, the author of *Sagen der Weisheit*—was overheard to hum a French song that had the refrain of *Vive la liberté*. Some *émigrés* who were on board attacked him and his unarmed companion, bound them and took them to Coblenz, where, robbed and wounded, they remained in captivity until the advent of the Prussians brought them release.

Later on, when the excesses of the Revolution drove ever increasing swarms of refugees out of their distracted land and plunged them into the depths of adversity, a very different spirit prevailed among them. The best side of the French character came into play; and the cheerfulness, good humour and courage with which they bore their misfortunes and made a jest of their privations were such as no other nation would have displayed.

A MYSTIC ON THE PRUSSIAN THRONE

The French Princes travelled from one European Court to another preaching a crusade against the revolutionaries as the foes of all order, and infinitely increasing the difficulties of the royal pair on the throne, as well as in their eagerness totally misrepresenting the facts. Count Artois declared that "all good Frenchmen were sighing for foreign help," and they even averred that the army would go over to the side of the invaders.

But though they received hospitality and sympathy everywhere — Frederick-William especially giving them liberal help in money—they could not for a long time succeed in obtaining intervention in the royal cause.

From Leopold, as the brother of the suffering Queen, they had naturally expected much, but Leopold was always cautious and slow to move. He avoided any intercourse with them, and the only scheme that appealed to him was that of a Congress of European nations that should preach moderation to the Paris revolutionaries with only a hint of armaments in the background.

There was already a *casus belli*, had he wished for one, for the Empire had suffered aggression at the hands of the French through the deprivation, by a decree of August 1789, of the long-established privileges enjoyed by imperial prelates and landowners who had possessions in Alsace and Lorraine. In the negotiations over this matter Leopold acted with great moderation, that almost bordered on pusillanimity.

Legally the rights of the Empire were affected,

but practically no fair-minded person could really grudge the unfortunate peasants, who had had to pay taxes to the French crown as well as render service to their feudal lords, their liberation from the latter duty; and Prussia certainly was not likely to interfere in order to restore abuses that had already been abolished in her own lands.

But when, after the capture of the royal family at Varennes, the news of their virtual imprisonment and the humiliations to which they had been subjected spread abroad, sympathy for their troubles and apprehension as to their possible fate made Frederick-William all anxiety to take up arms in their behalf.

Long before this there had been discussions between Austrian and Prussian politicians as to the possible necessity of an intervention. Bischoffs-werder was strongly in favour of an active policy, and is said to have been much influenced thereto by Count Rolle, one of the *émigrés*. He and Prince Reuss, the Austrian ambassador, had discussed the matter secretly, and in February Frederick-William sent him to Vienna, where he made a favourable impression upon Leopold, though his free, outspoken manner of carrying out his commission ("comical honesty," they called it) puzzled the crafty Viennese diplomatists and made them think there must be something hidden behind it.

Hertzberg was still nominally foreign minister, but these negotiations were carried out without his knowledge. When Cobenzel asked the amateur diplomatist how the friendly assurances he brought were to be reconciled with the stiff position maintained by the Prussian representative at the Sistova Congress still going on, Bischoffswerder replied that the latter was Hertzberg's policy, which was no longer that of his royal master!

Two new ministers were added to the Cabinet, nominally on account of Finckenstein's age and Hertzberg's weak health. These were Schulenburg-Kehnert and Alvensleben. Schulenburg-Kehnert had gained the favour of Frederick the Great by his management of the commissariat in the " Potato War," and had soon after Frederick-William's accession been obliged to retire, since he absolutely refused to carry out the new fiscal measures which Werder sought to introduce on the abolishment of the Régie.

He was again admitted into the service of the State in 1790, taking the place in the General Directory left vacant by the suicide of his namesake, Schulenburg-Blumberg. The latter minister had superintended the mobilisation of the army in 1789 when war with Austria and Russia had seemed most imminent, but Wöllner had put difficulties in his way and thrown suspicion on his dealings, so that in a moment of despair the unhappy man took his own life. Frederick-William, whose favour this minister had lost solely through Wöllner's intrigues, sent to his widow assurances of his sympathy for her loss and of his recognition of the zealous and faithful services her husband had rendered.

Schulenburg-Kehnert took over also the charge of the mobilisation and the commissariat, and he soon rose so high in the King's estimation that not even Wöllner's jealousy could displace him. He was a bitter opponent of France, while Alvensleben, the other new minister, was more of the Hertzberg school, and advised against joining Austria in a war unless some indemnification for Prussia were definitely promised.

Hertzberg was bitterly affronted by the nomination of these two additional members of the Cabinet, though the King tried to soothe him with the assurance that it was done to relieve him of the too heavy load of work, and further declared that "he would never listen to whispers intended to throw suspicion on a minister whose character and love of his country were so well known to him as Hertzberg's."

Schulenburg and Bischoffswerder and the policy they represented gained more and more ascendancy in the King's councils, and in May (1791) Bischoffswerder was again sent to confer with Leopold, who was then in Italy.

In the Sistova Congress matters were not progressing, Austria and Prussia each laying the blame for the long delay upon the other. The Austrian and Hungarian delegates were on the point of breaking up the Congress, and it seemed as if after all war would be unavoidable, when news came from Bischoffswerder in Milan that Leopold had received him cordially, had ordered a speedy settlement in Sistova, and had agreed to a meeting with Frederick-William at Pillnitz in order to settle the details of a treaty.

A MYSTIC ON THE PRUSSIAN THRONE

It was not, as was first supposed, the news of the intercepted flight of Louis XVI that first induced Leopold to take up a more friendly attitude to Prussia, for this news did not reach him till later. The decision of the English Parliament against interference had reacted disastrously on Austrian interests, since it relieved Russia from the fear of a war with the Triple Alliance. Catherine had no longer need of Austrian assistance, and the cautious and suspicious Leopold thought he read signs of malicious intentions in the St. Petersburg policy. Hence he was glad to accept the hand held out by Prussia.

The bad news from France naturally increased his desire for this alliance. He heard first that the flight was successful, and wrote the heartiest and warmest letters of congratulation to his sister on her escape. Now when the news of their capture reached him, the question whether an effort was to be made to save the French King and the French monarchy became acute.

The idea of actual invasion was not even then openly mooted either by the unfortunate royal pair or by Leopold; it was still through a congress of European affairs that they hoped to find salvation.

Leopold sent out from Padua, on the 6th of July, 1791, an appeal for joint action in support of the French monarchy to the Kings of England, Prussia, Spain, Sicily and Sardinia, and also to the Elector of Mainz as head of the Electoral College.

No one lent so ready an ear to this appeal as Frederick-William, and in spite of the distrust of

Austria that prevailed in the Prussian Cabinet, a provisional treaty was arranged between Kaunitz and Bischoffswerder of a defensive character. It was more advantageous to Austria than to Prussia, since mutual aid was promised in case of internal disturbances, much more likely to occur in the former than in the latter country; and since both agreed to make no separate treaty with another power, which precluded an alliance between Prussia and Russia while it did not compel Austria to give up its old treaty. As to Poland, it was agreed that the Saxon Princess likely to inherit its throne was not to marry a prince of either royal house. The guarantee of the integrity, which Bischoffswerder had at first proposed, was dropped.

It was small wonder that Bischoffswerder was a *persona grata* at the Austrian Court, and that Leopold should specially ask for his appointment to the mission there.

A few weeks before the signing of this treaty came Hertzberg's resignation of the position he had held so long. No only had he been out of favour with the King for some time, but they had actually been working for opposite ends. While Bischoffswerder, in the King's name, was treating with Austria, Hertzberg hoped, by an agreement with Russia, to save at least some part of his great scheme and gain a portion of Polish territory.

On his complaint that some important dispatches were kept back from him, he was told that by the King's wish he was not informed of them. He then asked for permission to retire, which was granted.

A MYSTIC ON THE PRUSSIAN THRONE

His disappearance from the political arena was seen with great disfavour in Berlin, especially by the followers of the Frederician policy and the Rationalist movement. Taken in conjunction with the Austrian Treaty, it was feared that it meant further reaction against the *Aufklärung*, and war, not only against the Jacobins in France, but against all ideas of freedom and progress. Many, and among them Hertzberg himself, believed that Leopold had insisted on his dismissal.

He retired to his country seat near Berlin, but he did not for a long time give up all hopes of regaining the King's favour and the power that he had wielded for so long. He overwhelmed Frederick-William with memorials, warning him against the errors of his present course, but spoiled all prospects of a reconciliation by delivering at the Academy, of which he was Curator, a lecture in praise of that French Revolution against which the King was just about to take up arms.

In the Prussian Cabinet the treaty with Austria met with much unfavourable criticism. Schulenburg had warned Bischoffswerder previously against the craft and subtlety which were concealed, he declared, under the winning manners of the Emperor Leopold. The Cabinet found that Bischoffswerder had exceeded his instructions, and they sought to introduce some modifications and alterations.

The hopes of a European concert, to which Leopold's faith was pinned, showed no signs of fulfilment. England had declined interference, and "without England," wrote Mercy to Marie

Antoinette, "nothing really efficacious can be done." There seemed now, moreover, some hope of a peaceful settlement in France, a possibility of the King's accepting the Constitution and of the re-establishment of order.

The sudden appearance of the Comte d'Artois at Vienna caused some consternation and set rumours afloat, but in reality his visit was most unwelcome to Leopold, who had always kept the *émigrés* at a distance. His appeals and offers were refused, and the only satisfaction he obtained from his visit was a grudging permission to be present at the coming meeting of the two sovereigns at Pillnitz.

On the 25th of August, 1791, Leopold, with the Archduke Francis and General Lacy, arrived at Pillnitz, followed soon after by Frederick-William and the Crown Prince, attended by Prince Hohenlohe, General Manstein and Bischoffswerder. The Comte d'Artois and other French nobles arrived the next day.

A very unflattering description was sent by Spielmann, the Austrian Referendary, to Kaunitz of the "actors on the Pillnitz stage," as he termed them. Of Frederick-William he wrote: "The King is an enormous mass of flesh. He speaks very badly, always disconnectedly, in short broken sentences. He shows very plainly an utter lack of knowledge of affairs. I do not believe I am mistaken at all in thinking that he never was and never will be a man to act from his own determination. It is easily to be seen that all depends upon the impulse he has received from this or that adviser." The

Crown Prince, he declared, looked like a sergeant, and he repeated a report of his character, supposed to have emanated from his tutor, that gave him all the bad qualities of the late King without the least trace of any of the better ones!

The impassioned appeals of the French nobles made some impression upon Frederick-William, but the counsels of the more cool and cautious Leopold prevailed. The final discussions were carried on between Calonne, Spielmann and Bischoffswerder, and the declaration that was issued (Aug. 27th) had in it, as Leopold wrote to Kaunitz, "nothing binding." The two kings stated that they looked on the cause of Louis XVI as a matter affecting all sovereigns; intervention in French internal affairs was only to come about in the event of all the European powers being agreed; and as it was fairly certain that England would not agree, the whole statement had little meaning.

A very different version of the decision was sent to France by the Comte d'Artois, wherein it was declared that the Powers were determined on the work of rescue, and that the Emperor and the King of Prussia had bound themselves to carry it out. This letter, like most of the actions of the *émigrés*, did the utmost harm to the cause of the unfortunate King and Queen, and greatly strengthened the hands of the National Assembly.

For a time, however, after the agreement of Louis to the Constitution, there was a pause in the progress of the Revolution. Leopold on the 12th of November again addressed the Powers whom he had before tried to persuade to a Congress; this time it was to assure them that the danger to the life and honour of the French King was removed, and that there was no longer need for joint action.

Frederick-William was still quite ready to enter the lists in defence of his brother sovereign, but of the sincerity of Austria's intentions there was much doubt in Berlin. At an interview a French envoy had with Frederick-William, the King assured him, with his hand on his sword, that he would gladly hurry to the help of the French King with 50,000 men if the Emperor would only put the same number into the field, but that from that quarter there was nothing to be hoped.

In Paris the desire for war grew stronger, and the tone taken in the dealings with the Emperor more threatening, and at the same time at attempt was made to detach Prussia from the Austrian alliance. General Biron thought it might be possible by arguments or bribery to win over Bischoffswerder and Wöllner, Countess Dönhoff and the Rietz couple, and with their help to bring about a treaty between France and Prussia. He suggested the plan to Talleyrand, who thought well of it and even had some idea of going himself. The choice they finally made of an envoy was not a happy one.

In December the Count de Ségur arrived in Berlin with credentials from King Louis, but at the same time Schulenburg received information respecting him that threw doubt on his loyalty to the monarchical cause. Frederick-William at first declined to receive him; later on he gave him an audience, but only to assure him of the warm interest he took in the fate of the royal family.

Ségur tried to impress upon him how useful a friendship with France might be should Prussia ever find herself unfavourably situated, but he received no encouragement. Frederick-William lost no time in telling the Austrian ambassador of Ségur's visit.

The mission was a failure, and Ségur is said to have been so much annoyed that in the presence of the Prussian ministers he threw his hat on the ground and swore vehemently.

It is perhaps, therefore, not very surprising to find that in his book on Frederick-William II the picture he draws of that king is far from a flattering one.

CHAPTER XIV

THE FIRST FRENCH CAMPAIGN

WHILE Prussian and Austrian statesmen were engaged, like the men in the fable, in disputing over the bear's skin while that animal was very much alive, Berlin was startled by the quite unexpected news of the death of the Emperor Leopold.

Bischoffswerder had again been sent to Vienna, this time at the Emperor's own request, and had scarcely arrived, not even having had an audience, when after a very short illness Leopold expired (March 1st, 1792).

So sudden was the death that rumours of poison were abroad, and both the Jacobins and the *émigrés* fell under suspicion. Frederick-William was inclined to believe in the poison theory, till Bischoffswerder assured him that the death was due to natural causes.

The Archduke Francis, who succeeded his father, was only twenty-four years old. It was doubtful at first how far he would follow Leopold's policy as regarded Prussia and France.

Frederick-William wrote to Bischoffswerder telling him to endeavour to get a clear and decided answer to the question as to war or peace. If Francis showed a disinclination to intervene in French affairs, Prussia must also abandon the design; but if he was ready to proceed, they must at once show that they were in earnest. "Every hesitation," he wrote, "every delay seems to me to be dangerous, dangerous at any rate for the King and Queen of France."

In France itself the war party was rapidly gaining ground. Dumouriez and the Gironde were coming to the front, and Dumouriez was firmly convinced that in the difficult situation of the moment the easiest way out was war.

Whether the two allied powers would have started the hostilities it is difficult to say. The matter was decided by the French declaring war against the Empire on April 20th (1792); the unfortunate King Louis being obliged to appear in the National Assembly and give his assent.

Prussia's recent treaty with Austria would have bound it to take part, even if Frederick-William had not been, as he was, all eagerness for the fray, impelled both by his sympathy for the sufferings of the royal family and his fear of the spread of the revolutionary principles. Doubtless also the hope of military glory had some weight in the scale.

In the army the outbreak of the war was welcomed with delight and little doubt of the result was entertained. With the renowned Duke of Brunswick at the head of the united Prussian and Austrian armies on the one side and the "Paris lawyers" on the other, what but a speedy victory could be expected?

Only a few voices were heard in protest against the war. The King's sister Wilhelmina strongly advised him, in an interview that took place between the two in May, against letting himself be made the cat's-paw of Austria.

And there was a party against it in the Court itself, led by a former tutor of the Crown Prince, Franz Leuchsenring, who belonged to the order of the Illuminati and was a strong opponent of the Rosicrucians. He sympathised warmly with the leaders of the Revolution, and was the centre of the Liberal movement in Berlin, in opposition to the reactionary Bischoffsweder.

Prince Henry was, of course, against the war, but he lived a retired life at Reinsberg and had no influence at all over public affairs.

In May 1792 Leuchsenring was suddenly arrested, and on examination of his papers it was discovered that he was in correspondence with several members of the Jacobin Club. At the same time a Fräulein von Bielefeld, governess to the Princess Augusta, was also arrested.

Rumours soon spread abroad that connected many members of the highest circles, and especially several ladies, with these intrigues. At first it was thought that a revolution in Berlin had been planned, but further examination showed that not against the person of the ruler but only against the clique of his advisers was the attack intended.

It was this affair that brought about the rupture between the King and Countess Dönhoff, whereof mention has already been made.

All that Countess Voss has to say about it is—

"20 June [1792].—The Dönhof has suddenly gone away. They say it is for good."

And on June 24th : " I hear that the poor Dönhoff was mixed up in the unfortunate Bielefeld intrigue, and now I understand that she will not come back. The King went off to the army to-day. Every one wept, and his leave-taking was very touching. In spite of his great faults he is much loved. God grant he may return ! "

There had been a lively scene at Potsdam before Countess Dönhoff took her departure for Switzerland. She had pleaded on Leuchsenring's behalf that he had done no more than try to "imbue the King with sounder principles in policy as well as in morals."

The following extract is from a warning letter of hers to the King about this time—

" I give you up if you engage so light-heartedly in this important and difficult expedition. . . . You will be beaten and driven back from the frontier. Your chivalrous temperament makes you like Don Quixote who ran up hill and down dale to redress wrongs, who attacked everything he met on the way, and fought without calculating either the number or the quality or the strength of his enemies." [1]

Frederick-William evidently resented her interference in political matters, and considered the secret dealings with Paris dangerous.

---

[1] " Je vous abandonne si vous vous engagez avec autant de légèreté dans cette importante et difficile expédition. . . . Vous serez battu et repoussé des frontières. Votre humeur chevaleresque vous fait ressembler à Don Quichotte qui courait par monts et par vaux pour redresser les torts, qui attaquait tout ce qu'il rencontrait sur son chemin, et combattait sans calculer, ni le nombre, ni l'espèce, ni la force de ses adversaires."

THE FIRST FRENCH CAMPAIGN

There is a story told by Paulig of a dramatic attempt at a reconciliation on her part, when she suddenly appeared at Court with her two children and flung herself on her knees before the King, but it was unsuccessful. She afterwards lived at Angemünde, and in the next reign was allowed to return to Berlin to see her children, who were brought up under the care of Hofmarschall von Massow. She lived till 1834.

She was right in thinking that the difficulties of the campaign were very much underrated. Bischoffswerder is said to have cautioned Colonel Massenbach against buying too many horses. "The comedy will not last long; by the autumn we shall be home again." That in a short time the allies would be dictating terms of peace in Paris was very generally believed.

The *émigrés* were answerable for a good deal of the misconception, declaring, as they did, that the nation and even the army itself were ready to rise against the mob that had temporarily got the upper hand. Dampmartin relates that at a council where Frederick-William was present with his ministers, an officer of the Duke of Orléans exclaimed : "Sire, I guarantee your Majesty that in coming away from Alsace I brought the keys of all the fortresses in my pocket"; and that when the Spanish envoy remarked : "I am much afraid, General, that the French may have changed the locks on their gates," the assembly smiled at the idea as at a jest, and never thought of taking it seriously.[1]

[1] Dampmartin, 90.

A MYSTIC ON THE PRUSSIAN THRONE

Two very important factors militated against the success of this campaign. The allies were far from being united in their aims and were full of mistrust of one another; and the Commander-in-chief of the allied forces was not in sympathy with the cause for which he fought.

Disputes had long been going on as to where and how indemnification for each party was to be obtained, whether France or Poland was to suffer amputation, and Haugwitz and Lucchesini on the Prussian, Cobenzel and Spielmann on the Austrian side, made continual suggestions and counter-suggestions. The long opposed plan of Austria gaining Bavaria in exchange for the Austrian Netherlands cropped up again, and might have won the consent of the Prussian Government, had not the Austrians also wanted to add to it Prussia's newly acquired provinces of Ansbach and Bayreuth, a suggestion that deeply incensed Frederick-William and his ministers.

These matters and the Polish question were still unsettled when the war began. There were also great differences of opinion as to the part the French Princes and the other *émigrés* were allowed to take in the campaign, Frederick-William being much more leniently disposed towards them than his allies.

The Duke of Brunswick had a great reputation in France and had actually, not very long before this, been approached with the suggestion that he should undertake the complete reorganisation of the French army. Rarely, if ever, has the instance been

CHARLES WILLIAM FERDINAND, DUKE OF BRUNSWICK.

paralleled that the same general has been offered the command of two opposing sides. He thought it his duty to refuse it, as he also thought it his duty to take up arms for the defence of his over-lord the Emperor, and for Prussia in whose service he had been so long, and was actually still employed. But he sympathised to a great extent with the ideas of the Revolution, was a great lover of France and did not in his heart approve of the war.

His extreme caution and his habit of long hesitation before coming to a decision had grown upon him; he was also possessed of a great dread of losing his reputation, which made him over anxious to avoid risks. The tactics of Frederick the Great in the latter part of the Seven Years' War, when the number and the strength of his foes made it impossible for him to make those swift attacks he loved and restricted him to a cautious manœuvring, were still held up as a model for imitation. There were also too many old generals in the Prussian army, whom the kind-hearted monarch would not compel to retire.

The other States of the Empire showed little zeal in obeying the imperial call to arms. Hesse-Cassel was a praiseworthy exception in that it sent a useful contingent of troops that had seen service in America. Some of those ecclesiastical Electors who had been loudest in crying out against France were the least ready to protect themselves; one circle even brought a complaint in the Reichstag against the passing through of the Prussian troops.

Though the war-cloud had been hanging overhead

for so long, no preparations for defence had been made. The States nearest to France were just those least capable of self-defence, such as the domains of the Imperial Knights and Princes of the Church, like the Bishop of Hildesheim, whose soldiers wore caps inscribed with the motto in Latin : " Give peace in our time, O Lord !" Their forces were troops *pour rire*. In Mainz an army of 2,370 men was commanded by a field-marshal and twelve generals, and apparently needed a president and six councillors to administer its affairs. And at the beginning of the war an order made it permissible—without infraction of their honour—for all officers to refrain from going into action if their domestic affairs did not permit of it !

A Prussian manifesto, issued on the 23rd of June, gave a very reasonable explanation of the grounds on which aid was to be given to Austria in the war that France had declared.

But a very different manifesto was issued on the 25th of July in the name of the Duke of Brunswick as leader of the united armies and addressed to the French nation.

Anything better calculated to destroy all chance of safety for the royal captives and to arouse in French breasts an outburst of national feeling that should unite them against the foreign invader, it is difficult to conceive.

It declared that the object of the allied powers was the re-establishment of the legitimate throne and the authority of the law, and called upon all well-meaning citizens to join the liberators. Those who refused to aid in restoring order were to be treated as rebels. The members of the National Assembly, the Municipality and the National Guard were to answer with their lives for the safety of the royal family. Paris was to submit without delay to the King, who was at once to be set at liberty, and vengeance and destruction were threatened to the city if further injuries were inflicted on the royal family.

It has been the cause for much wonder how the Duke of Brunswick, with his known French sympathies and his habitual caution, could have signed so violent and arrogant a declaration.

That Frederick-William should have approved of it is less astonishing, for he shared with many of his contemporaries the quite mistaken view that the Revolution was the work, not of the French nation, but of the Paris mob alone.

"All the world," wrote Laukhard, the author of *Briefe eines preussischen Augenzeugen*, who served as a private in this campaign, "expected that this manifesto would relieve the allied armies of the necessity of entering France at all."

It is said that the Duke of Brunswick afterwards declared he would have given his life to undo the issuing of that manifesto.

The original idea of a manifesto that was to intimidate the revolutionaries came from the French royal couple themselves, but the outlines that Marie Antoinette sent to Mercy contained no threats. The actual document was worked out by a Herr von Limon and handed by him to the imperial minister

in Frankfort. Schulenburg made some slight alterations, and it was then printed.

Its effect was, as Michelet described it, like that
of a spark in a powder-flask. It was of little use
for King Louis to declare his readiness to defend
his country and the national independence against
the invaders, when his opponents could point to this
manifesto as revealing the real intentions of the
royalists and their friends.

In spite of the excesses of the revolutionary party
and the sporadic outbursts of mob law, the bulk of
the French nation had gained so much relief by the
throwing off of the old feudal burdens that a return
to the former bondage was not to be thought of,
and the idea of this being forced upon them by
foreign invaders aroused that most powerful of all
factors in defence of a country, a national spirit.

The French army was known to be in a deplorable
condition. Lafayette wrote in May that he could
not understand how the Government could declare
war when they were not in the least prepared for it.
Between troops of the line and volunteers they
indeed numbered 300,000, but they were miserably
equipped. Many were armed only with pikes, and
of the guns that were distributed only one in ten was
capable of being fired.

Only in one direction were they superior to the
allies—their artillery. Frederick the Great had
never paid this arm its due. It was despised in his
day and thought beneath the attention of the
noble class to which almost exclusively the officers
belonged.

THE FIRST FRENCH CAMPAIGN

Frederick-William was all anxiety for a speedy forward movement; and it is quite probable that boldness, even rashness might in this instance have been the most successful course, for the deliberate manner in which the Duke of Brunswick and Hohenlohe, the Austrian General, proceeded gave the French time to form a more effective army of defence.

One most unfortunate trait in the Duke of Brunswick's character came frequently into prominence in the course of this war. He did not insist upon his own scheme when the King held a different opinion, but neither did he give it up. He usually appeared to yield, and afterwards tried in a roundabout way to return to his original plan. Either one course or the other might have succeeded; this mixture of the two was hopeless.

The Prussian army was too much encumbered with baggage to make rapidity of movement possible, and yet, owing to bad management, it lacked the things most essential to its well-being. When the troops were before Valmy their bakery was at Verdun and their flour magazine at Trier. The departments did not work together. The master-mind of a Frederick was lacking to oversee and superintend the whole.

The weather throughout this campaign was quite phenomenal. From the day the Prussian army crossed the French frontier it rained almost incessantly, and often in perfect torrents, which greatly aggravated the difficulties of the march and the sufferings of the army.

A MYSTIC ON THE PRUSSIAN THRONE

"Jupiter," wrote Goethe, "is openly branded as a Jacobin—even a *sans-culotte*."

The best description we have of this campaign is from the pen of the poet, who followed his Duke of Weimar to the field and shared in the sufferings of the troops.

The Duke of Brunswick, who had formerly not been friendly to Goethe, remarked to him one day towards the close of the campaign : "I am sorry to see you so uncomfortably situated, yet in one respect it is a satisfaction to me to know of another intelligent and trustworthy man, who can bear witness that it is not the enemy but the elements who have conquered us."

With his keen insight Goethe read the signs of the times in two instances that showed something of the spirit working in the French nation even in the early days of the invaders' success. When Verdun capitulated after a short bombardment, its Commandant, Beaurepaire, drew out a pistol and shot himself in the presence of the civic authorities who had insisted on giving up the place.

And when the allied forces entered the city, a shot fell among their ranks, but without doing any injury.[1] The young French grenadier who had fired it scorned to deny the fact. Goethe saw him—"a fine, well-built young man with a firm glance and a calm demeanour." While his fate was under discussion he was kept, under not very strict surveillance, at the guard-house, close to a bridge over an arm of the Maas. After sitting for some time on

[1] Other accounts say that a colonel was killed.

the parapet, he quietly dropped backwards into the river and was taken out dead.

These were as yet isolated instances. There were many loyalists in Verdun, and when Frederick-William entered the city fourteen young and beautiful girls greeted him with speeches of welcome and brought him offerings of flowers and fruit. Cautious advisers suggested the possibility of poison and warned him against tasting the fruit, but the gallant monarch declined to harbour any such suspicion; he received the fair devotees graciously and ate of their offerings. Three of these—sisters of the name of Watrin—afterwards suffered on the guillotine in Paris for the deeds of that day.

The assertions of the *émigrés* that the French soldiers would flock to join the invaders were utterly falsified by the event.

At first they were unable to stand against the disciplined forces of the Prussians when brought actually face to face. After the capture of Longwy and Verdun it seemed that the way to Paris was open, and in Berlin it was even hoped that the King might be back in time to attend a new opera that was to celebrate the Queen's birthday in October.

But Dumouriez was now with the French troops; an untried general, but one who learned the art of war as he went on. Acting in quite a contrary manner to the cautious orders he had received from Paris, he was at one time in a perfect trap near Grandpré, in which his forces might have been annihilated by a rapid Prussian attack; but the opportunity was lost, and he escaped from the difficulty and was able to bring his scattered detachments together and take up a strong post.

The extraordinary fiasco of Valmy—when after long marching the Prussians at last came up with the foe, and an artillery duel lasting till both sides had fired away all their ammunition was followed up by no attack—has been ascribed to treachery on the part of the Duke of Brunswick or to a secret change in the Prussian policy. It seems really to have been due to a failure in design, to want of concentration. Brunswick hoped by skilful manœuvring to force Dumouriez to vacate his position instead of risking an attack.

There was one critical moment when the explosion of two powder-magazines almost caused a panic in the French army. Frederick-William wanted to seize the favourable opportunity. It is said he rode through the ranks urging a forward charge, calling to the soldiers : " Look at me, which of you offers so large a target for a bullet? "

But the authority is Dampmartin, and Dampmartin is wont to put into the mouths of his personages speeches that bear a strong air of being manufactured afterwards to suit the occasion.

Moreover, it was not the troops that showed any reluctance to attack, but the Commander-in-chief who protested against "such a foolhardy undertaking."

The result of Valmy was a complete change in the feelings of both armies. "We lost more than a battle," wrote General Massenbach, "our *prestige* was gone." And this though the result of the day was utterly inconclusive.

There was deep depression in the German camp. The enemy was on the height before them, just as they had been yesterday; ten thousand cannon-balls had been fired off, otherwise the situation was the same. The French were jubilant. They had stood up against the redoubtable Prussian army and were still unconquered.

Goethe describes the cheerless situation in the German camp; the despondency and amazement, added to by physical discomfort, for the down-streaming rain did not even permit of the lighting of watch-fires. He was called upon for his opinion, as he had often cheered up his companions with an apt saying. This time he had a word of prophetic inspiration. "Here and to-day," he said, "begins a new epoch in the world's history, and you can say that you were present." He realised that Prussia, standing for the old order, was showing its powerlessness against the influx of the new.

The Duke of Brunswick was more than ever convinced of the hopelessness of the undertaking and overwhelmed with a sense of the responsibility that lay upon him.

The army was in a sad plight, in danger of being surrounded, in want of food and clothing, with dysentery and other sickness abounding among them.

It is believed that the seeds of the fatal malady that afterwards carried off Frederick-William, who was of extraordinarily strong physical development, were sown in this campaign.

That he did not spare himself is shown by an anecdote related by Goethe. He found once in his quarters, he writes, an unknown *émigré* of aristocratic appearance, who seemed to be labouring under some great excitement. The poet received him with hospitality, and when his sympathy had awakened some confidence in his visitor, the latter's grievance broke forth, and he complained bitterly of the King of Prussia's cruelty towards the French Princes.

Goethe was amazed, for Frederick-William had always erred on the side of excessive generosity towards these errant royalties. Presently the explanation came out; on leaving Glorieux in the usual deluge of rain the King had put on no overcoat and carried no cloak; the unfortunate French Princes had felt compelled also to renounce such luxuries, and the *émigré* had seen these spoiled darlings, these hopes of the loyalist party, wet through and through, with the rain pouring off their garments!

CHAPTER XV

THE King of Prussia's secretary, Lombard, had
been taken prisoner some time before, and, having
been exchanged during a temporary truce, he brought
back with him propositions from Dumouriez,
together with a present of provisions for Frederick-
William.

Dumouriez hoped—and the idea was long
cherished by the authorities in France—to separate
Prussia, whose King, he declared, was loved and
honoured in France, from the real enemy of both—
Austria.

On the Prussian side there was some hope that
Dumouriez, who was credited with an inclination to
uphold the King and the Constitution, might even
be induced to join the allies. For the dethronement
and imprisonment of Louis XVI in August and
the massacres of September might well have
produced a revulsion of feeling in the French
general.

Colonel Manstein was sent from the Prussian side
to confer with Dumouriez, by whom he was most
cordially received. Manstein, a great favourite with
Frederick-William, had always been opposed to
Bischoffswerder and the Austrian alliance.

But when he urged on Dumouriez to put a stop

265

to the Revolution and to restore the King, he was
shown the decree of the Convent that proclaimed a
republic. This materially altered the case, Dumouriez declared, and he could only promise to do all
he could for the safety of the King's person.

Prisoners were interchanged, and in the ranks as
well as by the commander every effort was made to
show by friendliness to the Prussian army that they
looked on them as brothers; that it was only in the
Austrians they saw foes.

Meanwhile Lucchesini had replaced Schulenburg
at headquarters, and he represented to Frederick-
William that Dumouriez had no authority to treat
for the French nation; that he was probably only
gaining time for reinforcements to come up, or
trying to embroil Prussia with Austria.

A council of war was held, and very few agreed
with Frederick-William's proposal to give battle.
Indeed, sickness had made such terrible ravages
among the troops that the number capable of fighting was seriously reduced. What with this sickness,
the scarcity of food, the severity of the weather and
the badness of the roads, a retreat would have been
advisable, even had not the alarming news come that
Custine was making a dash into German territory
and threatening Frankfort.

During the retreat the negotiations were continued, though on the Prussian side it was less with
a view to their leading to anything definite than with
the hope of facilitating the return through the gorges
and over the passes of the Argonne. Two envoys
from the Convent were so well received in Prussian

headquarters that the mistrust of the Austrians was aroused.

As Dumouriez had now turned his attention to the Belgian Netherlands, where he hoped to be joined by all the disaffected Austrian subjects, and part of the Austrian army was detached to defend Lille and Luxemburg, the Duke of Brunswick resolved to give up the campaign for that year.

The sufferings endured in this retreat of the invading Prussian army can be well conceived from Goethe's narrative. " In these six weeks," he wrote, "we have suffered more fatigue, want, anxiety, misery and danger than in our whole lives."

Longwy and Verdun had to be abandoned. The invincible Prussian army, instead of marching to Paris and being welcomed there as liberators of the country, had found a nation united against them, and were forced to retreat in this miserable plight.

And in still more startling contradiction to the expectations that had been aroused was the next news that came. Only a few battalions of Austrian troops had been left to guard the Palatinate with the aid of a few regiments belonging to the Elector of Mainz, and Custine, who was in command of the Rhine army, saw his chance. He marched thither with 1,800 men, compelled after a short fight the Mainz troops to surrender, and took Spires, with its important magazine, and Worms. Instead of the allies dictating terms in Paris, here was the French army on German ground taking one fortress after another.

The consternation in the neighbouring German

States was great, and the unsound condition of the Empire was clearly manifested in the way they met the common danger. While the rulers displayed their cowardice in promptly taking to flight, the learned classes were themselves mostly imbued with the revolutionary spirit and prepared to welcome the French, and the masses were simply indifferent.

In Mainz itself the fortress had been neglected, and it was not till after the capture of the Elector's troops that hasty preparations were made for its defence. The Elector fled to Würzburg, followed by the nobles and *émigrés*, and on the first demand for surrender the all-important fortress was actually given up.

There were many in Mainz who had welcomed the Revolution; clubs had been formed of "Friends of Freedom and Equality." The French leaders' dreams seemed to have a prospect of realisation that France's example of liberty should gradually spread over and republicanise the rest of Europe.

The warmth of welcome given to the invaders was, however, somewhat dashed when the French leader exacted enormous war contributions.

Frankfort, the imperial free city that had so lately seen the crowning of the last of the Emperors, was not so ready to don the cap of liberty and wear the tricolour; but the town was insufficiently fortified for resistance, and the French entered it in October.

Meanwhile Dumouriez with the Belgian division of the army had gained a victory over the Austrians at Jemappes, taken possession of Mons, and almost cleared the Austrian Netherlands of the imperial troops.

The one cheering episode in this campaign was due to Frederick-William's insistence upon an attack on Frankfort, and was carried out against the wishes of the Duke of Brunswick. The Prussians, with troops from Hesse-Cassel and Darmstadt, appeared before Frankfort at the end of November, and the city was retaken, the French being driven back upon Mainz.

On the King's entrance into the city he was enthusiastically welcomed by the citizens. People pressed to touch his cloak, and the honour of holding his stirrup was fought for. In his speech he particularly praised the dauntlessness of the Hessian contingent, whose coolness made him think he was assisting at a Potsdam manœuvre instead of a bloody siege.

The rescue of Mainz had to be postponed till the spring.

At the very time that French generals were treating with Prussia about the safeguarding of the royal family, events in Paris were marching fast towards the culminating deed of the King's execution.

The mockery of a trial began on the 11th of December, and on the 21st of January the long-drawn-out sufferings of the unhappy Louis XVI, borne with such patience and fortitude, came to an end. "He was probably," wrote Sybel, "the only man in Paris who had peace in his mind that day."

On Frederick-William the news of the execution made a very painful impression. For several days he took little or no food, and was in a state of deep depression.

In Vienna execrations of the bloody deed found vent, but angry words were not followed up by actions.

And in the Prussian ministry attention had for some time past been a good deal diverted from France and directed to Poland.

Even while the allied armies were preparing for their invasion of France, the question that was occupying most keenly political and diplomatic circles in Europe was not France, but Poland. And this was due to Catherine. She had long had her eyes on the country, and the only question for her was: Could she seize it all while her neighbours were otherwise engaged, or would she be compelled to offer a sop to Prussia and Austria to content them while she swallowed the rest?

She had at one time promised to send 18,000 men to help the allies against France; but no one put much faith in the promise, the general opinion being that the troops might get as far as Poland, but no farther.

She had refused to recognise the Polish *coup d'état* of May 1791, and as there was always a faction in Poland working in the Russian interest, it was not long before an appeal was made to her from inside that disunited country, from nobles who were unwilling to lose their *liberum veto* and their right to elect a King.

She was, of course, ready to respond to their appeal for help—if, indeed, she had not suggested it—and as soon as the Peace of Jassy (January 9, 1792) had put an end to the war with Turkey she began the work of "restoring order" in Poland.

To Prussia suggestions were made by Count Ostermann, her vice-chancellor, for common action against Poland. Russia, he declared, would never permit the growth of a Power of the first rank on her western frontier.

Frederick-William had at the time expressed his complete sympathy with the constitutional movement in Poland. The Polish Cabinet, however, had always looked on it disapprovingly, and Count Goltz had made it clear to the Polish King that in giving up the old order of things the agreement with Prussia was virtually abandoned.

Frederick-William, in discussing the matter with his ministers, expressed his own opinion in these words—

"Russia is not far from the idea of a new partition of Poland; that would certainly be the most effectual way of limiting the power of a Polish King, be he hereditary or elective. Yet I doubt if a suitable compensation for Austria can be found by this means, and also whether the Elector of Saxony would accept the crown after so much of the power of Poland had been shorn away. Still, if we could succeed in indemnifying Austria, the Russian scheme would be the most favourable for Prussia, it being understood, however, that we get the whole of the left bank of the Vistula and are thus enabled to round off that wide frontier, now so difficult to protect.   That is my judgment of the Polish matter." [1]

Of the morality, or otherwise, of the action there seems to have been no question in the mind of Frederick-William, any more than there was in that of Frederick the Great at the time of the First Partition.   And we have not advanced very far in international morality since that day.   Nations still grab what they can, and it is only those who get no share of the spoil who recognise the sin and the injustice.

Accordingly a general agreement with Catherine's plans was expressed to the Russian ambassador in Berlin, and the co-operation of Vienna was also sought.   Leopold, it was believed, would not have consented, but after his death Catherine succeeded in overcoming the influences in Vienna that were hostile to her plans.

On the 14th of May an assembly of nobles at Targowitch issued a protest against the new Constitution, which was followed up by a declaration from Catherine that she looked upon it as an affront, seeing that she had guaranteed the former one.   She further declared that as the friends of Russia had suffered oppression, she found herself compelled to send troops into Poland.

The Polish constitutional party called on Prussia for assistance, but Lucchesini declared that Prussia had had no share in the innovations, and did not feel called upon to take up arms in defence of the new Constitution.   Count Potocki hurried to Berlin

[1] For German text *see* Appendix I.

to appeal personally to Frederick-William, but to no avail.

Though the first action was fairly claimed as a victory by the Poles, they had to give way before a further Russian reinforcement. King Stanislaus offered to resign his crown, but this was not what Russia desired at that moment. It was intimated that his joining the Targowitch Confederation was preferable, and this he did in spite of his former declaration that he would give his life for the maintenance of the Constitution declared on the 3rd of May.

Thus died the last flicker of hope for Polish liberty. The Russian party in Poland was now supreme. Poniatowsky, Kosciusko and other patriotic officers either resigned their posts or left the country. It lay at the mercy of its greedy neighbours.

In the fear lest Catherine might sieze the whole of Poland, Prussian troops were sent to the eastern frontier while the negotiations were going on between Goltz and Ostermann; and in December the Prussian ministers were able gleefully to inform Lucchesini that the Czarina had given her consent to "a stroke of business that ensures us a brilliant indemnity, which we should never have obtained if the decision had been left to our trusty ally, Austria." [1]

In this Second Partition of Poland, which was between Russia and Prussia only, the latter not only regained the districts that had once been wrested

[1] *See* Appendix II.

from Germany, including the long-coveted towns of Dantzig and Thorn, but also acquired a portion of purely Polish territory.

The reason given in the "Declaration of H.M. the King of Prussia concerning the march of the Prussian troops into Poland" of the 6th of January, 1793, was a feeble attempt to put a gloss of respectability upon an unscrupulous action. It spoke of the adherents of the new Constitution—which Frederick-William had at the time received with approbation—as proselytes of the Jacobins, and justified the investment of the country by Prussian troops as a measure necessary to hold the revolutionary party in check and to maintain order.

At a confederation at Grodno in May the members were compelled by Russian threats or induced by Russian bribes to agree to the new arrangement.

Austria professed—especially in England—much indignation at this new partition, in which it had no share; but at the same time the instructions to Cobenzel in St. Petersburg were that he was in the first place to try to bring about the Bavarian exchange, and, failing that, he must endeavour to obtain for Austria a portion of Poland equal in size to that which Prussia had acquired.

Austrian influence was far less powerful now at the Berlin Court than in the previous year. The failure of the first campaign had greatly increased the animosity between the two countries. The Austrians attributed the lack of success to the Duke of Brunswick's hesitancy; the Prussians suspected their allies of keeping back their troops with a view to a stroke for Bavaria.

Moreover, Bischoffswerder, the chief promoter of the Austrian alliance, was temporarily out of favour. The King, a great admirer of the virtue he found it so difficult to practise, had always looked up to Bischoffswerder as a pattern of morality, almost above earthly weaknesses.

Now, by a malicious stroke of fate, it happened that a mass of correspondence which had been captured by French outposts was rescued. Among this was found and brought to the King's notice a series of tender epistles from Bischoffswerder to Mme. Pinto, one of two fascinating sisters, the other being the wife of Lucchesini.

It was a blow to Frederick-William's faith in his mentor, and one that he did not get over for a long time. Indeed, the power of the Secret Orders over him was thereafter considerably lessened.

Bischoffswerder did not deny the letters, but declared that his passion was a serious one, and his one desire was to marry Mme. Pinto, to which—as Hennet de Gontel gaily remarks—there was but one slight impediment, to wit, Mme. Bischoffswerder. A divorce removed her, and Bischoffswerder married his fair correspondent.

Another minister who fell into disfavour about this time was Schulenburg. The failure of this French campaign brought about a complete change in his opinions, converting him to the views of his colleagues Finckenstein and Alvensleben. Not being able to persuade the King to a similar conversion, he retired early in 1793 from the ministry.

His successor was Count Haugwitz, who was destined to have a powerful, and in many respects a disastrous, influence on Prussian politics. He belonged to the Rosicrucian Order, and first attracted Frederick-William's notice by his writings. Of suave and attractive manners, with a face that was supposed to bear a resemblance to the usual conception of Christ, with a show of enthusiastic piety combined with the broad-mindedness of a man of the world, he won his way rapidly into the King's favour. He did not disdain to pay court to Mme. Rietz, and his aristocratic appearance lent a grace to her gatherings. Owing to Finckenstein's age and Alvensleben's weak health he soon gained a leading place in the ministry and the chief control over foreign affairs.

In February a council was held at Frankfort, and the plan for the next campaign was arranged between the Duke of Brunswick and the Austrian General Wartensleben. It was recognised that the enemy had been underrated, and that the attack must be made this time with increased forces and better preparation.

The successes of the previous year had aroused an extraordinary spirit of martial ardour in France, and the Convent was able to send vast numbers into the field. Though for lack of military knowledge and organisation they were rarely able to stand against the disciplined Prussian troops when it came to an actual engagement, yet the subjugation of

these untried troops, inflamed as they were by a
national spirit and the love of liberty, was impossible to the smaller, well-schooled army that still
relied on the Frederician traditions.

Von Cölln found in the French successes a proof
that the day of standing armies was over, that a
nation in arms was what the times demanded.

The disfavour with which the Emperor Francis
had seen the partition of Poland had caused
Cobenzel and Spielmann to lose ground in his
favour, and the man who came to the front now in
Viennese politics was that bitter enemy of Prussia,
Thugut.

This minister's real name was Tunicotti; the wits
of Vienna had dubbed him "Thunichtgut" (Do-
no-good), for which Maria-Theresa's amiability had
substituted Thugut. In spite of his low birth, his
great talents and skill in intrigue had raised him to
a position of immense influence in the aristocratic
Austrian Court. He was unscrupulously bent on
the aggrandisement of Austria, and the Prussian
Cabinet recognised that under his leading the policy
of Austria would be more than ever inimical.

After the taking of Frankfort Frederick-William
spent some months in that city, where his Court was
the meeting-place of German and French princes
and nobles and foreigners of distinction.

It was the final flicker of eighteenth-century
brilliance before it faded out and gave way to the
new order of things.

Amid the strife of politicians and the preparations for a second campaign there came here at

Frankfort a refreshing interlude, where the King watched with interested and sympathetic eyes the playing out of a youthful love-idyll.

From his own words in a letter written on the 22nd of March we see the impression made upon him by the young Princess who was afterwards to be the good genius of his successor and the ideal of womanhood to the Prussian nation—

"Since my last letter I have had no time for writing; we have lived in continual festivities, which are due principally to the presence of strangers of rank, especially Princess George of Darmstadt and her two lovely grandchildren, the daughters of Prince Charles of Mecklenburg.

"When I saw the two angels for the first time—it was at the entrance to the theatre—I was so struck by their beauty that I was quite overcome when the grandmother presented them to me. I very much wished my sons might see them and fall in love with them. The next day they (the sons) were introduced to them at a ball, and were quite enchanted with them. I did my best that they should see them often and learn to know them well.

"The two angels are, as far as I can see, as good as they are beautiful. Now love was there, and it was very soon decided to marry them. They have agreed, and the betrothal will soon take place, probably in Mannheim. The elder will marry the elder and the younger the younger."[1]

According to Dampmartin Princess Louise was so fond of her younger sister that she declared it

[1] For original text *see* Appendix III.

CROWN PRINCESS LOUISE AND HER SISTER.

would be impossible for them to part, and therefore the Crown Prince urged his brother Louis to marry the younger sister.

Goethe shared Frederick-William's enthusiasm for the charming pair when he saw them a few months later on the occasion of their paying a visit to the King's camp at Bodenheim. Coming as they did in the midst of the turmoil of war, they might well be taken for celestial appearances, he declared, and added that the impression they made upon him would never be effaced.

It was indeed a good fortune that gave the Crown Prince a wife who had the intelligence to recognise the sterling goodness underlying his stiff manners and awkward shyness.

The Duke of York was in Frankfort at the time. He was nominally in command of the Hanoverian troops, Field-marshal von Freytag being associated with him. This Prince, the second son of George III, was described by Mirabeau as a mighty hunter, a mighty drinker, an indefatigable laugher, but without grace, presence or politeness. He had married in 1791 Frederika, the daughter of Frederick-William by his first marriage. Lord Malmesbury wrote of her at the time: "She is far from handsome, but lively, sensible and very tractable, and if only a tenth part of the attachment they now show for each other remains, it will be very sufficient to make an excellent *ménage*."

He relates elsewhere that the young couple were so eager for matrimony that they would not wait till the day fixed by Frederick-William, and the ceremony took place before the news arrived that the Great Seal had been put to the King of England's permission.

The Duke of York had suggested an English alliance for the Crown Prince, but against this Frederick-William had an objection. " The King," Lucchesini wrote to the Berlin Cabinet, "is determined never to consent to such a marriage, since it is a known fact that English Princesses without exception sacrifice every other consideration to the interest of their house and their mother-country, and let themselves be led by the representative of England. His Majesty remarked : ' Either the husband of an English Princess is a man of firm character, then there is no end to the intrigue of the English ambassador; or he is weak and easily led, in which case the English Cabinet deal with him as they will.' " [1]

Having succeeded in providing his son with the bride he so much desired for him, Frederick-William in arranging her household was anxious that his old and valued friend the Countess von Voss should take the place of Mistress of the Robes.

The Countess was still in mourning for her husband and busy in settling the affairs of her estate, and she was at first somewhat unwilling, but with the most flattering pertinacity the King argued away her grounds of dissent and finally persuaded her to take the office. The extreme youth of the Princess made it desirable that she should have a lady of

[1] Heigel, II, 97.

the Countess's experience and known faithfulness about her.

The following letter was addressed to the Countess by the King when the matter was settled, and is dated from his headquarters at Türckheim on the 6th of August, 1793—

"MADAME,

"I have received with your letter of 27th of July the jewels of the Order of the Red Eagle with which I had decorated your deceased husband. I regret sincerely that he could not longer wear this mark of my esteem, and my feelings in regard to him are too well known by you for you to doubt as to the share I take in your sorrow.

"As regards the rest, you would do very wisely to write, as you suggest, to the Princess Royal, to inform her yourself of my choice of you to fill the position of Mistress of the Robes. Such an attention is sure to please her, and will prepare her in advance for the friendship I feel sure she will soon have for you."

He closed the letter with the usual beautiful little formula, which even the free-thinking Frederick employed in his familiar correspondence: "*Je prie Dieu qu'il vous ait dans sa sainte et digne garde.*"

CHAPTER XVI

FRENCH AND POLISH CAMPAIGNS

AFTER the Princesses had left Frankfort, Frederick-William's attention was again turned to the war. Already the Duke of Coburg, strengthened by Prussian and Hanoverian troops, had cleared the Maas district of French and raised the seige of Maastricht, but had not followed up the victory. Dumouriez was ordered to give up his attack on Holland and come to the rescue.

Dumouriez was anxious to gain a battle in order that, crowned with victory, he might make the step he contemplated, that of joining the allied forces, putting a stop to the Reign of Terror in Paris, and establishing a constitutional monarchy. But his defeat at Neerwinden by the imperial troops on the 18th of March shattered these hopes; it was not as a conqueror at the head of an army, but as a defeated general followed by only a handful of soldiers that he went over to the enemy.

Frederick-William was anxious that Prussia should also have its share in the glory of overthrowing the republican armies. A decisive victory, he wrote to the Emperor, would be doubly important now, "for it is not, as in ordinary war, only a partial and transitory interest that is at stake, but the welfare of all nations, all thrones, of humanity itself."

FRENCH AND POLISH CAMPAIGNS

And so he went forth again as the champion of
the old order, unaware that it was a hopeless contest, since the fiat had gone out that it was to yield
its place to the new.

To re-conquer Mainz was the first aim of the
Prussians. The French party in this city had gained
the upper hand, and a Rheno-Germanic republic
was formed as an offshoot of the great Mother-
republic. Three deputies went from the city to
Paris; among them George Förster, one of the most
ardent adherents of the revolution in Germany, who
was bitterly disappointed with a nearer view of the
apostles. of liberty and brotherhood. He died,
almost broken-hearted, in the next year. Another
was Adam Lux, whose courageous effort to save
Charlotte Corday brought him to the guillotine.

Mainz had been strongly fortified during the
winter, and the garrison was commanded by General
Doyré with Kléber under him. Merlin de Thion-
ville was also there as one of the commissioners from
the Convent—"the revolution incarnate," as he
was nicknamed. He had paid great attention to
the fortifying of the city, and during the siege was
to be seen daily on the ramparts, even personally
pointing the cannon, whereby among the Prussians
he earned the title of the "Fire-devil."

General von Kalckreuth was in command of the
allied armies. A sortie on the night of the 30th of
May nearly had serious consequences for the Prussians, whose camp at Marienborn was attacked; only
the discipline of the troops enabled them to rally
from the confusion into which they were thrown.

283

A MYSTIC ON THE PRUSSIAN THRONE

Those same *émigrés* who had flattered Frederick-William with the title of Agamemnon when they were urging him to undertake the war, were ready now, because the city did not fall with the first attack, with the prophecy that it would be a siege as long as that of Troy.

Not until heavier guns were brought from Holland was much damage done, but these soon wrought havoc and destruction in the place.

Goethe was here also, and he risked his life again and again to watch, with a fascinated horror, first the flight of the shell, and then the outbreak of flame that showed it had done its deadly work.

But though churches and public buildings were destroyed and suburbs brought to ruin, no outposts had fallen into the besiegers' hands, no breach had been made, and there was no lack of provisions when the city capitulated. The conditions obtained were very favourable, the beseiged being allowed to withdraw with all the honours of war in return for a promise not to take up arms against the allies for a year.

With Mainz recovered and the French troops driven back across the frontier, with the army of Belgium beaten at Farmars and Valenciennes, the outlook for the French Republic was threatening indeed. The country itself was in the throes of confusion; a firm stand was at last beginning to be made against the terrorists, the planners of massacres and *noyades*. A vigorous prosecution of the war on the part of the allies stood a better chance of success now than ever before.

FRENCH AND POLISH CAMPAIGNS

But Prussia seemed content to rest upon its laurels; the Emperor Francis was more anxious about incorporating Valenciennes into his possessions than about the further carrying on of the war, while the English under the Duke of York separated themselves from their allies to besiege Dunkirk.

And the set-back proved only momentary. Carnot, who had now control over the French armies, sent Houchard to save Flanders, and after a hotly contested fight at Hondschoote the siege of Dunkirk had to be abandoned.

The Convent had its own methods of ensuring zeal and efficiency among those in command of its forces. Because Houchard did not make the most of his victory he was recalled and guillotined. A French general of those days fought with the alternative before him of victory or the scaffold.

Houchard was replaced by Jourdain, who engaged with the Austrians for two days at Mattignies, and though the issue was doubtful, the final result was the Duke of Coburg's retreat.

That the Prussians did not now press forward was mainly due to want of funds. The Duke of Brunswick, with recollections of the last campaign in his mind, would undertake nothing without the amplest preparations and precautions.

"I do not understand the Duke," Frederick-William is reported to have said; "he is always in want of 500 men. If I give him 200,000, he will ask me for a second army in order to be in a condition to act with the first."

And the Prussian treasury was exhausted by the previous year's campaign, by the fitting out of this one and the siege of Mainz. In the Prussian Cabinet the opinion was rapidly gaining ground that the country had already done more than as a member of the Empire it was bound to do. Why—as the Prussian envoy at the Diet of Regensburg inquired —why should it strain its exhausted resources to fight France and conquer Alsace for Austria, while that country was intriguing with Russia against Prussian interests in Poland?

Thus, to the wonder and relief of the French, the Duke of Brunswick contented himself with parrying their attacks. When, however, they were emboldened to surprise and attack him at Pirmasens, in the moment of alarm and danger he forgot his punctilious prudence and became once more the resolute leader, driving back the French in spite of a desperate resistance.

But instead of taking advantage of the victory, the old methods of excessive precaution were taken up again. General Valentini complained in his memoirs that "the natural, practical views of the King were thwarted at every turn."

Soon after this victory at Pirmasens Frederick-William left the seat of war in the west to go where he was induced to believe his presence was more imperatively necessary—the newly acquired province of South Prussia.

There had been no opposition offered to the entry of either Russia or Prussia into their new possessions. Catherine's threat that a refusal would be

looked on as a declaration of war had been efficacious in inducing the Diet at Grodno to agree to
Russia's "indemnification." But to Prussia they
were less subservient, and there was a strong suspicion in Berlin that Austria was encouraging the
Polish discontent.

Therefore the King was strongly advised to let
the Duke of Brunswick continue the campaign, and
transfer his personal attention to Polish affairs.
Lucchesini had great trouble in inducing him to
take this step; after gaining his consent he had
scarcely left the King when he was called back.
He had thought better of it, said Frederick-William
in some excitement; he would rather remain. To
leave the army on the eve, possibly, of a decisive
engagement would injure his reputation. After
long discussion Lucchesini again persuaded him;
and to prevent any possibility of retraction he wrote
that same day to the Czarina announcing the King's
intention.

Frederick-William arrived in his new dominions
in October. The cession of territory had been per-
force consented to in the Diet, but in gloomy silence.
Von Hoym, the Silesian minister, declared that it
was only the nobles who protested, that citizens and
peasants welcomed the change as a deliverance from
slavery and oppression. Certainly speeches of welcome and offerings of flowers from young girls
awaited the King in the cities he visited, but the
chief impression he received from his visit was that
a great part of the new possession was practically
a desert, and that the feeling of the people was such

that it would take a long time to reconcile them to becoming a portion of the Prussian kingdom.

In the early part of this year there had been a faint echo in Silesia of that revolt of the populace which had uprooted the dynasty in France. It is a matter for wonder that the call to throw off the bondage of the Middle Ages did not meet with a stronger response in the German states.

The origin of the trouble was the dismissal of a Hungarian tailor, whose cause the journeymen workers took up so hotly that they destroyed the house of Werner, the president of the Council.

Hoym was the Silesian minister, occupying a post that was independent of all control save that of the sovereign. He was a man who had done much for the country and the people under Frederick-William, especially in the direction of road-making and in measures for dealing with fire and for the care of the sick.

At the beginning of the riot the authorities were slack, then, taking alarm, they called in the troops to assist. Hoym was horrified when he learned that thirty-seven had been killed and more wounded. He stopped the tumult by gentler measures, reinstating the man who had been dismissed, sending deputies about the country to soothe the people, giving pensions to the relatives of the men who had been killed, and even refraining from punishing the rioters.

It was on Frederick-William's return to Berlin in this year that the Brandenburg Gate, which had been begun in 1789, was opened for the first time. In building this, Langhaus had taken the Propylæa of the Acropolis as a model, so that it is less heavy and sepulchral than most of the Berlin architecture of Frederick-William's period with its semicircular windows and gates that look like grave-portals.

On this return of the King, though not an occasion for much triumph, there was also for the first time heard the strains of the song "Heil dir in Siegerkranz," the words for which were composed by a Dr. Schuhmacher in Lübeck.

In the French campaign, after Frederick-William had left the army, there was little done. It was now the Austrians under the impetuous Wurmser who were for pressing forward, and the Prussians under the cautious Duke of Brunswick who held back. It was not only his own hesitancy that restrained him now; the Prussian ministry were, almost to a man, against the zealous prosecution of the war. The idea of restoring the French monarchy was realised to be hopeless. It was no faction they were fighting against, but the French nation—a nation intoxicated with enthusiasm for liberty, a nation to whom political freedom was the religion for which they were ready to fight to the death.

The war had become a defensive war in protection of those States of the Empire that were exposed to the attack of their fiery neighbour as well as to the contagion of its example.

For the impetuous young French Republic was full of a proselytising zeal, and its emissaries saw a hopeful soil for the germination of the new seed in the decaying German Empire. It is not to be wondered at that the upholders of the old order saw French intrigue in everything; that the "contumacy" of the Poles, for instance, was attributed by Lucchesini to Jacobin influence.

It is not to be wondered at, either, that a reactionary tendency was noticeable in the policy of all the German rulers, and that stronger measures were taken against the spread of revolutionary principles.

Two young French generals won their way to the front in this year's campaign, who compensated for their want of experience by their zeal, resolution and daring, and made out of the undisciplined masses a powerful weapon for attack.

Hoche, who had command of the Moselle army, was only twenty-five and of plebeian birth, but a born leader of men. To Pichegru, who had more military training, was given the beaten and disorganised Rhine army, but the difficulty of his task did not discourage him, and the vigorous conduct of the war testified to the skill of these two leaders. The three days' fight at Kaiserslautern ended indeed with a French retreat, but as usual the victory was not followed up or utilised.

But when Hoche and Pichegru united their forces they soon succeeded in driving Wurmser out of his entrenchments to Weissenberg, and finally over the Rhine.

Success was with them also in the north, where the Duke of York was obliged to give up the siege of Dunkirk, and in the south, where Toulon was captured, and the name of a young Corsican officer came first to the ears of a world that was soon to be filled with the sound of it.

FRENCH AND POLISH CAMPAIGNS

This second campaign ended everywhere with the retreat of the allies, and in December the Duke of Brunswick laid down the command. He was "morally sick," he told Lord Malmesbury, of the continual interference of the King's military advisers; his relations with Frederick-William had never been cordial, and the result of the two campaigns was not likely to make them more so. He was succeeded in the command by General Möllendorf.

The Prussian distaste for the war had not unnaturally been increased by the dubious issue of this second campaign, and that any preparations were made for continuing it in the following year was due to Frederick-William's personal initiative.

The want of means was the greatest and most pressing difficulty. The States of the Empire were willing enough that Prussia should defend them at its own expense, but that was no longer possible. The suggestion that the Prussian army should, since it was acting as an imperial army, be supported as such, was objected to by Austria, as raising Prussia to a position of too great importance. The Austrian counter-proposal was that each State should act in its own defence, but much time would be required to raise forces in any way adequate to the task.

The Prussian kings had always believed in the necessity of a war-chest filled with actual specie for the prosecution of a campaign, and the possibility had not dawned upon them of leaving the payment of war expenses as a debt to a future generation.

A MYSTIC ON THE PRUSSIAN THRONE

It was then that recourse was had to English gold. On January 1st, 1794, Frederick-William took Lord Malmesbury aside, and after assuring him of his hatred of the French principles and his readiness to combat them, told him also of the impossibility of his doing so without subsidies.

Malmesbury had been sent to Berlin for the purpose of inducing the King of Prussia to continue the war with France. There was an inclination in England to believe that the alleged want of funds was only a diplomatic manœuvre, an excuse for not continuing the war. George III, in an interview before Lord Malmesbury left for Berlin, said to him: "I believe that the King of Prussia is an honest man, though a weak one. You must first represent to him, that if he allows his moral character the same latitude in his explanation of the force of treaties as he has allowed it in still more sacred ties [referring to his marriage], all good faith is at an end, and no engagement can be binding."[1]

Malmesbury's Diary at this period makes frequent mention of the Bethmann story. At Frankfort earlier in this year Frederick-William had again fallen a victim to the attractions of a young lady, and, had she been willing, it is probable another left-handed marriage would have taken place, for Frederick-William had learned to look upon polygamy as a natural royal prerogative.

Mlle. Sophie Bethmann (or Bettmann—the name is variously spelt) was the daughter of a rich banker

[1] *Malmesbury Diary*, III, 7.

at Frankfort, and is described as intellectual, well educated and well-formed.

Malmesbury writes of her as "very artful and ambitious. Had made the King of Prussia believe she really loved him for *his* sake, and that no other woman ever had; this had disposed him to go all lengths—even that of left-handed marriage."

He describes her as "well-made, but not handsome." Elsewhere he writes: "Mlle. Bethmann professes to love the King, but that her principles prevent her giving way to it; she is all sentiment and passion. The King of Prussia inclines to believe all she says, and calls her 'une fille bonne et précise.'"

She showed herself, Philippson says, grateful, devoted and full of affection for the King, but she refused the offer he made of this doubtful kind of alliance.

Malmesbury believed that Lucchesini worked against the connection, having learned from a description of her character, given by her cousin, that she was not likely to be tractable, *i. e.* to be of use to him in swaying the King. But Malmesbury was very suspicious of the wily Italian just then, declaring that by his intrigues he had removed from the King's confidence every one whose influence was favourable to England and Austria, and he was in a frame of mind to see Lucchesini's hand in everything.

On the other hand, he at this time put faith in Haugwitz, the man who has been called the evil genius of Prussia, and who certainly acted in a double-faced manner in the matter of the English treaty, committing his master to language he had never intended.

Malmesbury had written home to his Government that without the Prussian troops there could be no hopes of a favourable issue; and England offered to provide two-fifths of the twenty-two million thalers required to put an army of 100,000 men into the field, if Austria, Holland and Prussia would between them do the rest, Prussia to be afterwards indemnified by conquests from France.

This also Austria refused. An imperial decree was issued on the 20th of January, ordering the arming of all the States on the frontier, and many of the governments made an effort to rouse their people to arms. But the French made light of this decree, knowing that in many cases the only rising that was likely to take place would be one against their own rulers.

An army led by Frederick-William himself would, Heigel believes, have given a very different turn to the whole matter; but while endless negotiations were going on, the favourable moment for an attack passed; and since all assistance to the maintenance of his troops was refused by the States of the Empire, Frederick-William in March ordered their retirement to Westphalia, leaving only the contingent of 40,000 men he was bound by treaty to supply for the defence of the Empire.

This caused an outcry in Vienna, where the Archduke Charles and the Prince of Coburg were anxious to keep up the Prussian alliance, as offering the only chance of success in the struggle against the Revolution.

And England was very unwilling to see Prussia leave the field. Malmesbury was a bitter opponent of revolutionary France, and he did his utmost, even going beyond his instructions, to bring about a workable agreement.

Haugwitz met the representatives of England and Holland at the Hague in April (1794), and concluded that treaty that was afterwards the cause of so much friction. The two parties saw the matter from diametrically opposite points of view, and the equivocal language of the treaty was differently understood by each.

The English were accustomed to buying German soldiers to fight their battles for them. Many of the rulers of the small States gained the means for their ridiculous pomp and extravagance by this shameful traffic in the lives of their subjects. Therefore when the English Government, in conjunction with Holland, agreed to pay £50,000 a month till the end of the year, £300,000 to put the army in motion, and £100,000 on their return, they considered that they were buying the services of the Prussian troops and that he who "paid the piper had a right to call the tune."

The Prussian Government saw the matter otherwise. If it was to the interest of the Maritime Powers that the war against France should be continued, and the Prussian army was the only one in a position to carry it on by land, it was only fair that they should provide the money for its con·

tinuance. Frederick the Great had received subsidies from England during the Seven Years' War, but he did not for a moment consider that he forfeited thereby the right to conduct the campaign as he thought best.

The actual wording of the treaty rather favours the English view, since the 62,400 men were to be placed, "after a military agreement between England, Prussia and the States-General, where the Maritime Powers considered most suitable for their interests (nach einem militärischen Einverständniss zwischen England, Preussen und den Generalstaaten wo die Seemächte ihren Interessen am angemessensten erachten)."

While the English Government considered the last part of this sentence the most important, the Prussians laid the stress on the " military agreement," and thought that while Möllendorf needed the troops to defend the Rhine districts, they should not be drawn off to protect Belgium and the coast of the North Sea.

What with this fundamental difference of opinion and the English dilatoriness in sending the subsidies —in spite of Lord Malmesbury's pleading for a prompt delivery it was not till July that the first instalment was received—the treaty brought satisfaction to neither party, and each looked on the other as having failed to carry it out.

And now when at last matters appeared to look favourable for a vigorous joint attack on France, Poland again distracted the attention of Frederick-William and the Prussian ministry.

FRENCH AND POLISH CAMPAIGNS

This year (1794) saw a 'desperate attempt to regain their freedom on the part of a handful of true Polish patriots, who, if they arose too late to save their country, yet made its downfall sublime by their heroism.

Amid a generation of self-interested schemers and crafty politicians, Kosciusko gives us the spectacle of a man with a pure and single-hearted devotion to the cause of his country.

The outbreak began with General Madalinski's refusal to obey the Russian order for the disbanding of his troops. The revolt spread; Kosciusko took the command of the insurgents and won a victory over the Russians, compelling them to leave Warsaw.

It was characteristic of Lucchesini that he considered this rising "a most advantageous event for the interests of the Prussian monarchy," since its repression would give the opportunity for further conquests of territory.

He persuaded Frederick-William, not without a great deal of difficulty, again to set out for Poland, hoping that his presence would put a stop to the wrangling between the Russian and Prussian commanders.

Frederick-William reached Wola on the 3rd of June, and on the 6th repelled a Polish attack at Rawka, where his nephew, Prince Louis Ferdinand, particularly distinguished himself.

A few days later the Prussians took Cracow, and then followed up Kosciusko towards Warsaw, whither he had withdrawn after his retreat.

A MYSTIC ON THE PRUSSIAN THRONE

The town was ill prepared for a siege, its inhabitants were divided into factions, and it would probably have yielded under a resolute attack. Frederick-William was all for storming Praga and then entering Warsaw in triumph as his ancestor, the Great Elector, had done. But the over-cautious hesitancy, that was the bane of the Prussian military policy at this period, found its advocate this time in Bischoffswerder, and the King was persuaded to abandon this idea for the slower process of a siege. Even this was given up a short time afterwards, owing to news of risings in the newly acquired districts of South Prussia behind them, owing also to lack of munition and to illness among the troops.

Von Boyen, in his description of this campaign, attributes this somewhat inexplicable retreat to Russian counsel influenced by jealousy. He writes that a resolute attack would have finished the campaign, that Frederick-William inclined to it, and had actually set the army in motion, when the Russian general, Prince von Nassau, asked for an interview with the King and rode apart with him, after which the march was countermanded. It was a change most disastrous to Prussia's glory.

Probably the King's state of health had also something to do with the lame issue of this campaign. Symptoms had begun to appear of that painful dropsical malady which was to prove fatal a few years later. The seeds had been sown during the fatigues and discomfort of the retreat from Champagne; the bad water in Poland aggravated the malady.

FRENCH AND POLISH CAMPAIGNS

In personal bravery Frederick-William was not lacking; the Hohenzollerns were ever soldiers born. On one occasion in this Polish war his intrepidity led him to expose himself imprudently; he was surrounded by the enemy, and would have been taken prisoner had not his second son, Louis, while the agitated generals were hesitating as to what was to be done, hastily assembled some squadrons and dispersed the enemy.

Frederick-William came back to Potsdam in September, glad to be out of Poland and longing to lead his troops in the Rhine country into action. But those who saw him doubted whether this would ever be possible again. Haugwitz, when he waited on him in the Marble Palace, was shocked at the alteration in his appearance. He could scarcely believe, he declared, that it was the same man.

The Prussian troops in Poland, left under the command of Schwerin, did nothing beyond controlling the unrest in South Prussia and defending their own position. Indeed, at one time the Poles, after taking Bromberg, even threatened Thorn and Dantzig, and some of the Berlin garrison had to be sent off to defend Prussian territory.

It was not till Suwarroff, with the main Russian army, appeared on the scene that the Polish rising was put down and that Praga was taken after a desperate battle. Kosciusko was made prisoner at the battle of Matschiewics by General Fersen who treated the wounded hero with much consideration, till he received orders to send him prisoner to Russia.

CHAPTER XVII

THE PEACE OF BASLE

DURING all this year a regular conspiracy had been going on among Frederick-William's ministers and advisers to induce him to put a stop to the French war.

It had been from the beginning the most unpopular war that Prussia had ever waged. The spirit of the nation was Prussian, not imperial, and this was a war that did not actually concern Prussia itself, but had really devolved into a struggle between France and Austria for the possession of Belgium.

Almost the only man in the country who still had the cause at heart was Frederick-William himself. The idea of being the champion of the Empire and the upholder of law and order (which to him meant monarchical authority) against the forces of the Revolution was too dear to him to be abandoned without a struggle.

In the army there was much less resentment against the foe they were nominally fighting than against their Austrian allies, which accounted a good deal for the lukewarmness with which operations were conducted. Only a few fiery spirits like Blücher and Prince Louis Ferdinand showed any zeal for combat.

THE PEACE OF BASLE

And one of the foremost strivers for peace was the Commander-in-Chief, General Möllendorf.

He had won a victory over the French at Kaiserslautern in May, but since he and his allies could never work in unison it remained fruitless. The Maritime Powers were anxious to have the troops in the Netherlands, but Möllendorf refused to leave the Rhine country, where he remained on the defensive. He was well aware that a decided forward policy would not be to the taste of the Ministry in Berlin.

Thus the French, after being largely reinforced, were again able to take the offensive, and they succeeded after a desperate struggle in driving the Prussians from the so-called Schanzli—the strong positions that were the key to the whole cordon of the allies from Spires to Trèves—and obliging them to fall back on Donnersberg.

In Belgium the French were everywhere victorious, and some historians have maintained that Austria intended to abandon it, that the Duke of York was purposely betrayed at Tourcoing, and that they were ready to make peace with France at any price. The truth, however, appears to be that it was due to over-anxiety and bad management on the part of the Duke of Coburg, whose health had given way. Nor was his successor Clerfait the resolute leader that the emergency demanded. Old, feeble, irresolute and without sufficient troops to cope with the inspirited and enthusiastic foe, he was driven further and further back till the left bank of the Rhine was in French hands.

A MYSTIC ON THE PRUSSIAN THRONE

England and Prussia were both equally dissatisfied with the result of the treaty of April.
Malmesbury had an unenviable position between
the two, at one moment writing urgent appeals to
his Government to send the promised subsidies, and
at another trying to induce the Prussian leader to
take his troops to the Netherlands. Haugwitz helped
to confuse the issues, for while his words to Malmesbury were to the effect: "Only send the promised
subsidies and you shall dispose of our army as
you will," to Möllendorf he declared that the
higher political interests of the State made any
such co-operation inadmissible. His complaint to
Malmesbury about Frederick-William's inclination
towards peace, due to the Jacobin proclivities of the
mystics in whose toils he lay, was a deliberate dis-
tortion of the facts for diplomatic purposes. The
delay of the English in sending the money, and the
uncertainty as to its continuance, were useful arguments to the ministers when they urged the King
to make peace.

Since General Möllendorf was not allowed by
the Berlin Cabinet to carry on the war in a whole-
hearted manner, had he wished it, his anxiety for
peace is not surprising; but that he should be one
of the first to enter into secret negotiations with the
enemy is rather remarkable for a Commander-in-
Chief.

He consulted Lucchesini on the matter, who
declared that the King would never consent to treat
with the regicides. He himself had no such objection, and he pointed out that Mazarin had negotiated

with Cromwell, but he knew how strongly Frederick-William felt on the subject. This difficulty was removed on the 18th Thermidor by the fall of Robespierre; and the coming into power of a more moderate faction raised the hopes of the peace party.

Möllendorf was one of the most urgent advocates of peace. He complained of the French that they did not scruple to attack him on three, four, or even five consecutive days! He complained of the English that they wanted to control his operations, of the Austrians that they made outrageous demands upon him and blamed him for their own mishaps, of his officers for their want of resolution—being himself of all the most irresolute.

His first negotiations with the enemy were kept secret from the King.

The French were well informed of all movements in Prussian political circles, and as they had long hoped to find in their neighbour an ally instead of an enemy, they were ready to meet half-way any advances in the direction of peace. They had an excellent diplomatist in their Swiss ambassador in Baden (Aargau). Barthélemy was a zealous servant of the Republic, though no Jacobin. He and his colleague Bacher in Basle kept a close watch on Prussian affairs and sent frequent information to Paris.

To these two came an emissary from Möllendorf, ostensibly to arrange about exchanges of prisoners, but really to open negotiations.

It rather upset Möllendorf's plans that at this

moment Prince Hohenlohe, who knew nothing of these dealings, should gain (on Sept. 20, 1794) the most brilliant victory of the whole campaign at Kaiserslautern, the third battle that occurred at that place. The Prussian cavalry especially distinguished itself by deeds that recalled the glories of the Seven Years' War. The Commander-in-Chief received the victor with a very notable lack of enthusiasm, and almost apologised for the victory to the Swiss go-between.

Frederick-William was bombarded on all sides with enteaties to give up the war, and he must have had much more resolution than he is usually credited with, or he could not have held out so long.

The Jewish banker Ephraim wrote him a remarkable memorandum, urging peace on the strange grounds that the French were irresistible, being intoxicated with liberty as the Turkish soldiers were —by common report—with opium before a battle. The King thought he traced the hand of Hertzberg in this appeal. Hertzberg had written again and again, pleading for the termination of the war, and at last received a rebuff of a sharpness quite unusual with the good-natured monarch.

Wöllner was now among those who clamoured for peace, but he had lost ground considerably in the King's favour, and his letter pleading for it in his usual high-flown and bombastic phrases remained unanswered. Bischoffswerder, on the other hand, had regained much of his former influence, and he who had done so much to bring on the war was now equally anxious to bring it to an end.

THE PEACE OF BASLE

Lucchesini was sent to Vienna in September with the object of inducing the Emperor to defend Maastricht and also to send 20,000 men to Poland in accordance with the treaty. He not only brought back the news that the Emperor declared his inability to furnish the contingent, but also the conviction that a secret understanding existed between the Russian and Austrian Courts—a suspicion that later events verified.

Then in October came the news that the English refused any further payment of the subsidies, on the ground that the stipulations of the Hague Treaty had not been carried out.

About the same time Struensee gave a deplorable report as to the state of the finances, and a committee was appointed to consider how means for another campaign could be obtained. Struensee and Alvensleben made counter-proposals, both of which fell through, and the result of the consultation of Prussia's most experienced officials was a report of nineteen pages that only suggested an internal loan and a slightly increased coinage of kreuzers and groschen. At the same time the Committee expressed in all loyal submission its desire for peace, assuring the King that it was the wish of the whole nation, and that the French war was so unpopular that the burden of taxation would be much more willingly borne if people knew that it was only for the purpose of putting down the disturbances in Poland.

Very reluctantly did the King take the first step in withdrawing 20,000 men under Hohenlohe and ordering Möllendorf to hold the remainder in readiness to retreat into Westphalia and Ansbach. " God knows how I feel this retreat," he wrote to a confidant, "and how it goes against the grain with me ! "

But still he had no idea of concluding a separate peace, and any turn of events that seemed to offer a possibility of finding means to continue the war, or at least of making such preparations for it as would enable him to conclude a satisfactory peace, was welcomed by him hopefully.

Möllendorf, anxious for peace as he was, was yet unwilling to leave the Rhine strongholds until an armistice had been obtained. He sent Meyerinck to Potsdam, where in an audience with Frederick-William he told him of the secret negotiations that had been going on. He also told him—and this was what had most effect on the King—that the States of the Empire were hoping to obtain peace through him, and that the Elector of Mainz would make the proposition with all the due formalities. Indeed, Möllendorf had already induced the Elector to address a petition to the King, as head of the League of Princes, that he would "procure peace for the Empire, for which all Germany would be grateful to him."

Frederick-William agreed that the troops might remain by the Rhine; only Hohenlohe with his 20,000 was to march off at once. He also sent Meyerinck back to Basle, to find out with certainty if the French were as willing to make peace as he affirmed.

In his efforts to work on the King Struensee had

looked everywhere for assistance, and at last had recourse to Prince Henry. Since the beginning of his nephew's reign, when his hopes of ruling through him failed, Prince Henry had lived in retirement at Rheinsberg. A reconciliation was now brought about; they had an interview in Sans Souci on the 25th of October, and a few days later Prince Henry sent him a memorandum with his views explained in full, to which the author himself and at the time many others attributed the conversion of the King to the policy of peace.

The Imperial Diet at Regensburg was wavering very much at this time on the question of peace. On the 13th of October the war party had the upper hand, and it was resolved to get together a quintupled contingent to carry on the war. But on the 24th their desire for peace was so manifest that the Austrian envoy wrote home very bitterly about it. All the deputies except the Austrian and Hanoverian approved of the proposal of the Elector of Mainz, and though the Emperor wrote strongly against it and urged the collection of more troops, a resolution was sent him in December, begging him to conclude a peace in conjunction with his ally, the Prussian King.

The news of Kosciusko's defeat in October seemed to promise an end to the Polish war, and when the Maritime Powers again approached Frederick-William, he showed an inclination to listen to them that greatly alarmed his ministers, and "it needed all their ingenuity to make him at least hold fast to the demand that before any further dealings England should pay the overdue subsidies." [1]

In November came the news that the ruthless Suwarroff had stormed Praga and forced Warsaw to surrender. Frederick-William was so roused by it that without consulting any of his ministers he hurriedly dispatched an envoy to stop the movement of Hohenlohe's troops; for it was the impossibility of keeping up a war on both eastern and western frontiers that was the strongest argument for peace.

The idea of going himself to the Rhine sprang up anew in him. He told Bischoffswerder that things were going to improve in that quarter, and that while he spoke he felt a strange spiritual uplifting, which seemed to him a supernatural confirmation of his words.

His ministers were very much alarmed at this independent action on his part, and as Hardenberg's efforts to obtain contributions from Hesse-Cassel, Darmstadt, Trèves and Zweibrücken were at last successful and might render possible a continuance of the war, they sent him a memorandum, begging that a diplomatist should be sent to Basle to carry on negotiations with the French. They assured him that Holland and Austria had already begun treating secretly with France and that Prussia ought not to be the last.

This might not have moved him if it had not been for the letter from Haugwitz accompanying it. With a clever understanding of the King's temperament and opinions, he used the arguments most

[1] Bailleu: *Hist. Zeitschrift,* LXXV.

likely to tell. The German Princes, he declared, looked to Frederick-William for the protection which the Emperor, who subordinated the German to the English interests, denied them. He begged him not to leave any longer in uncertainty the friends who laid their fate in his hands, but to send at once a diplomatist to Basle, and Goltz was the man suggested.

Thus it was not with the idea of deserting the Empire, but rather as leading it in the way of peace as Prussia had led it to war, that Frederick-William took the decisive step. On the 1st of September he informed his Cabinet and Prince Henry, through letters in his own hand, that he was sending Goltz to Basle.

The great difficulty in the way of a settlement was the question of Mainz and the left bank of the Rhine, already in French hands; and while the negotiations were going on, the possibility was not forgotten that another campaign might be unavoidable.

General Massenbach had been summoned to Berlin to draw up a plan of operations. He has left it on record that the King's advisers were trying to persuade him to make peace at any price, Bischoffs-werder among the foremost. Massenbach relates that in a conversation with Prince Henry he recalled the occasion when the young King Louis XIV hesitated about conferring with Cromwell under the conventional title of " Brother," and Mazarin's reply to his scruple was : " Well, then, call him Father ! " " You are the man for me," cried Prince Henry in delight; "you have grasped my views entirely."

Of his audience at Potsdam he relates that he only saw Frederick-William's eyes light up once, and that was when he spoke of the gallant deeds of Blücher at Kaiserslautern.

The news of the negotiations, of course, soon leaked out, and great indignation was displayed by Prussia's allies. Lord Malmesbury was in Brunswick at the time, arranging for the unfortunate marriage between the Prince of Wales and the Duke's daughter Caroline, and he expressed his opinion in no measured terms.

The peace preliminaries were interrupted by the somewhat sudden death of Goltz. Hardenberg, who was sent to replace him, did not belong to the "peace at any price" party; he was at first mistrusted by the French as being a Hanoverian, and consequently "half English."

Though the Republic was in a very insecure position, between the deposed Terrorists on the one hand and the reactionaries on the other, and though its difficulties were increased by the prevailing famine, the Committee knew that Prussia had gone too far now for retreat, and Barthélemy's instructions were to be firm and unyielding.

As Hardenberg also took a firm stand, the discussions might have been indefinitely protracted, had not a new tumult in Paris alarmed the Committee into consenting to suggestions that they had before imperatively refused, on condition that the peace should be concluded immediately.

Hardenberg believed that he had won a diplomatic victory, for he wrote to the King that the peace was advantageous, secure and honourable (vortheilhaft, sicher und ehrenvoll). The Berlin Cabinet was delighted, and Frederick-William trusted that he had found the "golden mean"; that the nation's desire for peace was gratified without Prussia's entering into that alliance with France of which its enemies suspected it.

A political blunder the treaty may have been, but to see in it an act of treachery on the King's part is to do him great injustice.

Roughly summarised, the treaty stipulated that the French troops were to retire from Prussian territory on the right bank of the Rhine; the question of the left bank was to be left in abeyance until the Empire made peace with France. Meanwhile the peace was to be extended to all those imperial states which should within three months join the Prussian system. A line of demarcation was to be drawn through Münster and Cleves to Limburg, beyond which neutrality was to be maintained; and to all the northern States that would retire with Prussia from the war, peace and security of transit were to be assured. In a secret article Prussia promised not to interfere in favour of the Orange dynasty in Holland, and agreed in the event of a final peace giving France the left Rhine bank, to surrender her possessions there in return for compensation in some other quarter.

On the 7th of May the treaty was officially announced in the Diet. Some of the States had already decided to throw in their lot with Prussia; others, like Baden, were only prevented from doing so by the proximity of the Austrian troops. In the Diet no open opposition was made to the treaty, except by Austria and Cologne. It was not till afterwards, when the Austrian victories under Arch-duke Charles enabled the Empire to hold up its head again and relieved it momentarily from the dread of France, that the States turned against Prussia and saw in Austria their protector.

In Northern Germany the treaty met with approval. The philosopher Kant, now an old man, was inspired by it to dream and write of a state of society in which war should be no more. The satisfaction of all those around him reconciled Frederick-William to the measure he had so long resisted.

Austria's indignation at this treaty was not likely to make her more complaisant in the matter of the partition of Poland. Indeed, if the Emperor had had his way, Prussia would have been altogether excluded this time. Catherine was not disposed to go quite so far; but the hope of getting Cracow and Sandomir had to be abandoned, and Prussia's share of the spoil in the treaty between the three Powers signed at St. Petersburg on October 24th, 1795, was comparatively a small one.

This was the third and final partition, after which Stanislaus laid down the crown and Poland, as a separate nation, ceased to exist.

The new acquisition brought at first no relief but rather an increase to the financial burdens of the State, for with it Prussia took over the Polish debt to Holland.

THE PEACE OF BASLE

It was in the matter of these Polish domains that came, after these partitions, into the possession of the crown, that Frederick-William was so shamefully deceived by his officials. He was induced to permit their sale at ridiculously low prices, in the belief that improved methods of agriculture were to be introduced and the prosperity of the country greatly increased.

Count Hoym himself took the lead in these iniquitous transactions; Rietz, Bischoffswerder and Triebenfeld were among those who profited by them. Chancellor Goldbeck got wind of what was going on and at first remonstrated, but was afterwards persuaded to silence by a share of the spoils. Zerboni, a South Prussian official who threatened to disclose what he had learned about some of these deals, suffered a severe imprisonment through the machinations of Hoym, who completely deceived his royal master.

When the increasing illness of the King made them fear the possibility of his successor's discovery of their malpractices, the lands were hastily sold to other owners.

In these last few years of Frederick-William's life, with ever increasing illness and suffering, he spent most of his time in the Marble Palace at Potsdam. Much as he loved on special occasions a display of pomp and magnificence, he kept up here no royal state, but lived in a simple way such as would befit any rich commoner. There was not even a military guard at the palace. He had bought the barren island called the Pfaueninsel, where he had a little residence built in the form of a ruined fortress, which now became a favourite place of retirement.

Of the way he spent his time we are told that five hours daily were devoted to work, two hours to music and the rest to reading, mostly in French, and to walks in the garden. His tall figure was a familiar sight in the New Garden, where, simply dressed and wearing no orders, but with a stout stick in his hand, he would walk, followed by the two big dogs, for whom he had as great an affection as Frederick for his little Italian greyhounds. Winter and Carnival time brought rather more social activity.

One of his favourite companions in these last years was St. Paterne, a French writer who had been his correspondent before his accession. Other *émigrés* with whom he frequently associated were de Boufflers, the Baron des Escars, the Abbé de Balinière and Mesdames de Sabran and Radaillac.

The mystics had fallen somewhat out of favour. The policy they had induced him to follow had not been a success. And he found that all his officials were against the persecuting policy of Wöllner and Hermes. The King's own standpoint in this controversy between orthodoxy and free-thinking, which was the primary cause of his unpopularity in the latter part of his reign, is best explained by a letter in his own hand, addressed to a respected theologian who belonged to neither extreme.

" I considered it my duty to make regulations and take measures for the upholding and the recognition (Erkenntnis) of the teaching of Christ. If all had

PORTRAIT GROUP OF FREDERICK-WILLIAM II AND FAMILY.

gone according to my will and wish, much more would have been done. Still the evil has been partly checked. But it had unfortunately gone very far, and the fear of man rules in the heart of many of those who ought to fight against the evil. Others again want to rush in with fire and sword. Both often place good at a disadvantage with regard to evil."

The "rushing in with fire and sword" is believed to refer to Hermes, whose zeal was intemperate. That clause in the Religious Edict which spoke of tolerance and the putting of constraint on no man's conscience as long as he kept his opinions to himself and avoided "trying to convince others or to lead them astray or to make them waver in their faith," was the foundation whereon an inquisitorial commission was built up, which examined into the teaching at colleges and schools, and the doctrines preached in sermons, and instituted tests for the appointment of ministers.

The movement known as the "Aufklärung" had had its day; it was giving way now before the light that was spreading over Germany from the little Duchy of Saxe-Weimar. Goethe and Schiller in their *Xenien* poured the vial of their ridicule upon the school that had found its chief exponent in Nicolai; and the reign of dry utilitarianism was over.

Berlin began to increase greatly in population soon after the peace of Basle. Foreigners weary of war flocked there where peace was for a time assured. The most intellectual coterie there at this time was that of the Jews, who had a little world of their own; which, owing mainly to the brilliant social qualities of two women, Rahel Levin and Henrietta Herz, attracted members of other worlds, being infinitely more interesting than the military and aristocratic circles.

One of the most important events in this reign concerning Prussia's domestic policy must find a brief mention here. The merit of introducing a new code of laws belongs, however, not to Frederick-William but to his uncle. As early as 1746 Frederick had charged the Chancellor Cocceji to work out a unified code for the whole nation, to replace the former involved system that varied in each district. In 1751 the matter was dropped and not taken up again till 1780, when the task of preparing it was given to Carmer.

On Frederick-William's accession he approved of the scheme, and in 1788 he gave Carmer the Order of the Black Eagle. By his desire it was published, that the opinion of deputies from the different districts might be obtained, and it was ordered that it should come into force in June 1792.

It met, however, with passionate opposition in certain localities, especially from what came afterwards to be known as the Junker party, who objected strongly to the innovation of marriages between the nobility and those who did not belong to that privileged class being made legal.

Carmer was a man of liberal views, and the code as he designed it was much in advance of his times, at any rate for Prussia. Provincial justices appealed against its introduction as dangerous to monarchical principles. Wöllner meddled in it, and of course smelt out some free-thinking principles. It was suspended for a time, and then the King asked the opinion of Goldbeck, the Silesian minister of justice, and wanted him and Carmer to work together at its completion. Carmer held out for his own views, but the effect of the French Revolution was to arouse a dread of any measures that gave power and independence to a bureaucracy, and when it finally came into force, it was shorn of much of its constitutional character.

Still, such as it was, it constituted an immense advance on the statutes that had preceded it.

CHAPTER XVIII

THE LAST YEARS

THE Crown Princess had more than justified the good opinion Frederick-William had formed of her from the first. On her entry into the city in the end of 1793 Louise had taken captive the heart of the Berlin populace by a warm-hearted, spontaneous act that delighted the crowd who came out to greet her.

Among the many ceremonies arranged in her honour was her welcome at the Potsdam Gate under a triumphal arch by eighty small children dressed in white and holding garlands. When one of the smallest ones recited a verse in her honour, the Princess was so moved that she caught up the little reciter in her arms and kissed her, an act that had not been arranged for in the programme and that scandalised Mme. Voss.

The Countess was, indeed, often shocked by the young couple, who were happy in each other's society, very simple in their tastes, and without much regard for that rigid etiquette on which the worthy Countess set such store.

But she thoroughly appreciated the goodness of Louise, though she found her reserved at first, and did not for some time make her way into her confidence.

318

THE LAST YEARS

"The Princess is really worthy of worship," she wrote on December 31, 1793, "so good, and at the same time so charming, and the Prince is such an honest, excellent man that one does not grudge him the rare happiness of such a marriage, the possession of such an angel."

On the occasion of her first birthday in her new home Frederick-William presented her with the summer residence of Oranienburg, which he had had newly decorated for her. The ladies and gentlemen of the Court were attired as peasants and came to welcome her, offering her the key of the Palace with appropriate verses.

At the end of a long and happy day the King asked her if she still had a wish ungratified. The only thing left for her to wish for, said Louise, was a handful of gold to give to the poor. "How big?" asked the King. "As large as the heart of my generous papa," was her answer, and she had no reason to be dissatisfied with the result.

The two young couples—for the wedding of her younger sister with Prince Louis had taken place two days after her own—lived very closely united. The serpent in this paradise appears to have been Prince Louis Ferdinand. This Prince, who had distinguished himself by bravery in the field and was considered by some as the most gifted of the Hohenzollerns, was a cause of great anxiety to Countess Voss, at first by paying too much attention to the Crown Princess, and when she made it impossible for him to approach her, by transferring his attention to her sister. Princess Louis was only fifteen, was less guarded than her elder sister and more susceptible to flattery, and her husband was not such a stay to her as was the Crown Prince to Louise.

The Countess writes with relief on April 15th, 1795 : "All went to Potsdam for some months, and the influence of bad men came to an end."

In October 1795 a young Prince was born, the future Frederick-William IV; the Countess writes of happy and peaceful times, of summer and winter spent in Berlin, spring and autumn in Potsdam.

At the end of the year 1795 Mme. Rietz took it into her head to travel. Up to this time she had made a comparatively moderate use of her influence with the King and her powerful position in a society that was quite ready to cringe to a royal favourite.

But this journey seems to have had a deleterious effect upon her character. She went first to Vienna, but the haughty Austrian aristocracy had no welcome for her. In Naples she made the acquaintance of Lady Hamilton and of that eccentric nobleman the Earl of Bristol, Bishop of Derry.

This most unclerical divine was the son of that Lord Hervey satirised by Pope. He had made himself popular in Ireland by identifying himself with the Nationalist cause, and took a prominent part in the formation of the Volunteer Convention. He assumed an almost royal state in Dublin, driving in a coach drawn by six horses and attended by a bodyguard of light dragoons. He generally dressed in purple, with diamond knee- and shoe-buckles, and wore white gloves from which hung gold fringe and tassels.

He afterwards retired to Italy, where, in spite of advancing years, he led a merry life, his social talents making him a popular member of a cosmopolitan society. He was credited with being a lover of Lady Hamilton's until Mme. Rietz came upon the scene, when he soon joined the circle of admirers that vivacious lady gathered round her.

She had never been a beauty, but she still retained her fine neck and figure, and she was a brilliant conversationalist, having an original mind and the gift of expressing herself in choice language, possessing, moreover, that magnetic power which makes its owner always a social centre.

Lord Bristol openly acknowledged himself her slave; he wore her portrait set in brilliants upon his breast, and when she returned to Berlin he followed in her train.

Her new friends in Italy persuaded Mme. Rietz that she had been too modest, and that as the favourite of a King she was entitled to have social rank and landed property. At her entreaty Frederick-William gave her the title of Countess Lichtenau.

The news of his increasing illness brought her back to Berlin; and Lord Bristol induced the King to give her the estates of Lichtenau and Breitenwerder, as well as presenting her with the houses in Berlin and Charlottenburg which she occupied, a dowry for her daughter and a large sum of money for herself.

From this time, too, she forced herself into prominence, and the King was weak enough to yield to her desire to be acknowledged as a sort of left-handed partner, to be introduced at Court, and even to be invited to festivals among the royal family. This naturally gave great offence to the exclusive Berlin aristocracy, and the hatred the Countess Lichtenau earned by her arrogant assumption of her new privileges was not even satisfied by her subsequent disgrace.

Countess Voss makes occasional mention in her diary of the regret with which she, the faithful and devoted friend of the royal family, saw the momentary triumph of the adventuress.

In the summer of 1796 the King made a stay at Pyrmont, in the hope that the use of the waters might check the progress of his disease. The improvement, however, was only temporary.

The winter saw him back in Potsdam, and this winter was an eventful one in the royal family.

On the 19th of December Countess Voss writes : "there was a play acted at the Lichtenau's; she had sent tickets for us all. Our ladies and cavaliers went, but not I. She gave herself great airs at this festival, so people told me afterwards. The King was also there. God knows how all this troubles and worries me on his account."

"Dec. 21.—We and all the Court dined with the King. Princess Louis left early. She was anxious because the Prince had fever."

"Dec. 23.—Prince Louis is seriously ill. He has

a great deal of pain, and they fear a kind of bilious fever."

"Dec. 24.—Prince Louis is so seriously ill that all are anxious about him, and this was a painful damper on all the Christmas joy."

"Dec. 25.—Prince Louis is rather quieter. . . . There was a Court at the reigning Queen's, where the King, too, appeared for a moment."

"Dec. 26.—Ah! there is no hope for our poor Prince Louis. We went across very early to the Prince's, then Selle was sent for, but he said the same thing!"

"Dec. 28.—A heavy, unlucky day! Poor Prince Louis died this evening at a quarter to eleven. . . . The King and Queen were both with him a long time, and the parting scene at his death-bed was heart-breaking. . . . The Crown Prince and the other brothers and sisters wept aloud."

"Jan. 1, 1797.—There was a family dinner, but quite among ourselves, for the Crown Prince is unwell and has a very bad sore throat."

"Jan. 2.—Our anxiety about our Prince is indescribable."

"Jan. 3.—The Crown Prince is very bad and in great danger—cannot breathe, cannot speak or swallow. The doctor calls it an inflammatory quinsy. . . . Towards evening he had a little relief. The King came late and stayed two hours by his bedside, then came the Queen too."

"Jan. 5.—The King comes every evening, goes into the sick-room to the Crown Prince, who is rather better. He is always specially gracious to

me. The old Queen (Elizabeth-Christine, wife of
Frederick the Great) is very ill, and I am alarmed
about her."

"Jan. 7.—The King comes every evening. The
old Queen dreadfully ill. I go twice a day to see
her."

"Jan. 9.—The Prince is much better to-day, but
must not leave his room. God has heard our prayer
and given him back to us."

On the 13th of January the old Queen died. She
left most of her property to Frederick-William, for
whom she seems always to have had an affection.

At Prince Louis's funeral, the Countess tells us,
the Court was in mourning for the Queen-Dowager
also, and consequently the ladies had to wear two
long black veils, one of which hung down in front,
so that they could scarcely recognise one another.

In February Frederick-William's third daughter,
Augusta, was married to the Electoral Prince of
Hesse-Cassel. The eldest daughter (by the first
wife) was now settled in England; the next,
Wilhelmina, had married Prince William, after-
wards King of the Netherlands.

On the 14th of March the Countess writes—

"We dined with the King, and the Landgrave of
Cassel was also there. Then we went to the Princess of Orange, and in the evening there was an
opera at the Lichtenau's, at which the whole Court
was present. The performance was very fine, but
when one thinks what that woman is and how objec-
tionable the connection, it is dreadful to be obliged
to see her. Last of all there was a family supper

at the Queen's, where we did nothing but weep, because poor Princess Augusta of Cassel is going away to-morrow."

"March 15.—The Prince of Cassel and his wife really left to-day. The King was very much moved, and the Crown Prince and his brother accompanied them as far as Magdeburg. The King came at seven in the evening and stayed two hours with us. Himmel played the piano. The King was very sad."

On the 22nd of March the Crown Princess gave birth to a son, "a splendid boy." The King had already gone to Potsdam, writes the Countess, but Köckritz drove there at once to announce it, and came back very pleased, rewarded with presents. This was the child destined to be the first Prussian ruler in whom was vested the headship of the German nation.

On the 3rd of April the Countess writes of his baptism—

"I carried the royal child and brought him to the King. The names were Friedrich Wilhelm Ludwig, but he will be called Wilhelm. After the ceremony the King gave the little Prince back to me, and was very gracious to me."

"April 9th.—The King is unwell. The Lichtenau came to see me and talked to me a great deal about him. This person says more than she can prove (als sie wahr machen kann). She is dreadful!"

"April 10.—At one o'clock came the Chamberlain with a kind little letter from the King and a crystal medallion set with large diamonds which he sent me as a present. I was overjoyed at so much kindness on his part, and went to the Princess and to all in the Palace to show the medallion."

The King's letter was as follows—

"I know, Madame, that your attachment is sufficient to keep ever present in your memory the moment when at the baptism you presented to me the youngest of my grandsons. I flatter myself, however, that you will remember it all the better by my proving that I do not forget it either, and I beg you to accept in memory of this day the slight token of esteem with which this letter is accompanied, being, Madame, your very affectionate

"FREDERICK-WILLIAM.

"*Potsdam*, April 9th, 1797."

In her diary she writes on May 7th: "We had dinner with the King in his garden. Ah! he has fallen away very much. I am in despair at seeing him, how rapidly he changes."

"May 14.—This afternoon we went with all the company to the King in his new garden. He is better. We had a great collation there. The Queen was there also, and the Lichtenau and all the King's children."

"May 16.—The Princes dined in Sans Souci and found the King rather better, but he did not come to table. Yet he had been on horseback to watch the review."

"June 4.—First Whitsun holiday. All went to church. Prince Henry came to dinner; at four o'clock we went to the operetta that the King gave; all the Court was also there, and the Lichtenau and

a number of people. The King is worse again; they say he must go to Pyrmont. God grant that he may return! He was very lively in spite of his pain, talked to me a great deal and stayed at supper till eleven o'clock."

"June 6.—. . . In the evening we went to the King's in Charlottenburg, who showed us his new rooms. There was a concert and then supper. The King was very gentle and friendly, spoke and laughed a good deal. God preserve him to us!"

"June 16.—This evening there was a little concert at the King's, and I found him much better than yesterday, in very good temper and very much occupied about his journey."

The visit to Pyrmont in the previous year having afforded him some slight relief, the King had determined to try it again. His physicians had ordered complete rest, but being pretty well assured that he was past their help, Frederick-William sought rather to forget his pains in such relaxations as were still open to him. He often had long spells of fainting and suffered from difficulty in breathing, but is said to have been, in spite of his sufferings, always gentle, kindly and courteous.

"Princess Louis is to travel with him" (the Countess added), "and I wish we were also going, so that he should not be so much alone with the Lichtenau."

She had her wish later, for on the 18th of July she writes—

"Thank God! good news of the King! He would much like my master and mistress to come

to Pyrmont, and me with them—that delights me
greatly. . . ."

"July 23.—Reached Pyrmont and dined with the
King, whom I found, I am sorry to say, much worse
than I expected. French play after ball, and supper
with the King, where there was nobody but my
party, Countess Lichtenau and myself."

At Pyrmont there was a brilliant circle gathered
round the dying King, not only members of his own
family and of other German royal houses, but many
distinguished foreigners, among them the Crown
Prince of Denmark and two of the English Princes.

On his return to Potsdam his weakness increased.
Once he was sufficiently well to be able to ride, and
made his appearance at parade, as the Countess
chronicled with delight.

On the 25th of September she wrote : " The birthday of our beloved King. God restore him to
health ! . . . In the evening a ball in Monbijou,
where the Queen has had a very pretty winter garden
made. The King appeared and talked to the
Spanish ambassador, and then a long time to me.
He told me about his portrait that he wanted to give
to the Crown Princess, and he sent it to me directly
after dinner. I admired a little porcelain snuff-box
that he now carries with him, and he made me accept
it. He was wonderfully kind and friendly to me.
Unfortunately he did not stay to supper, but supped
at home with the Countess, which is much more
restful for him."

Seeing that the end could not be far off, the
Lichtenau's friends were urgent with her that she

should make sure of her possessions and go away while there was yet time. But she refused to leave the man to whom she had made herself necessary, and she hoped that her assiduity in nursing him and consoling his sufferings would soften the hearts of his family and lead them to forgive her.

Bischoffswerder and Haugwitz were with him daily for the hours of work; his French friends helped to cheer his evenings. Haugwitz relates how the dying man in these last days talked with him about the events of his reign, and did not conceal from himself the faults he had made. "The war with France," he said, "should never have been undertaken. If you had only been with me then! Luckily we came out of it with nothing worse than a black eye." [1]

He spoke with satisfaction of the system of neutrality, which must be maintained, he said. "Do not forsake my son; give me your hand upon it." He raised his swollen hand, which had lain stretched out upon the table.

That visit to Berlin to attend the fête the Queen gave for his birthday was his last. Soon music and conversation were too much for him, but he liked being read to aloud. The device was now employed of bringing oxygen into the room by means of air-balloons, in order to obviate the difficulty of breathing.

On the 7th of October he was induced to pass a highly necessary edict shortening the time of mourning, especially in the case of royalty. For the rules

[1] Bailleu : *Hohenzollern Jahrbuch*, 1897.

were so rigidly fixed in those days that fines of from five to fifty thalers were exacted for non-compliance.

"I am in deadly anxiety," writes the Countess on October 15th, "about our poor dear King, who, they say, is unconscious and must be dreadfully ill."

"Oct. 13.—We dined alone at home, although the Queen had invited us there, but in the evening we had to go to her on account of this Princess of Baden. It was a big supper, and a lot of people were there. I think it is too bad (zu stark) at this dreadful moment!"

Countess Voss evidently had no great liking for the Queen. A few days later she writes: "We had to go again to Monbijou—to be bored!" It is not the only hint she gives of her society being somewhat wearisome.

"Oct. 15.—The Queen was with him in Potsdam and saw him. He lies on a *chaise longue*, speaks very indistinctly, but was pleased to see her. The children drove there too."

The diary mentions the Countess of Lichtenau preventing the King from seeing his family, but this has been proved to be an error on the writer's part. Having given such very unflattering portraits of the King from the pens of Frenchmen, it is a change to be able to quote the following passage, written by the French ambassador in Berlin a little later—

"The harmony among the Princes of the Prussian royal house is exemplary. The King loves his children above the ordinary, and they on their part are boundlessly devoted to their father. History will pronounce its verdict upon Frederick-William as King; as man there can be but one opinion among those closely connected with him as to his honesty, his goodness and his domestic virtues." [1]

Moreover, the diary itself contradicts the notion, for it mentions that the Queen, his children and the Crown Princess visited him frequently.

The Queen even thanked the Lichtenau for her care of the suffering man. But the Lichtenau saw, it is stated, a look in the eyes of the Crown Prince that made her feel it would have been wiser to have taken her friends' advice and retired to England. By that time it was already too late; there were guards around the Palace to prevent any one leaving it.

On the 15th of November, the last day of Frederick-William's life, the Countess Voss writes—

"The Queen drove with the Crown Prince to Potsdam; the latter came back very sad. He found the King very ill, and went, to distract his mind, to the theatre, but soon came back and stayed with us alone, much depressed."

The next day the end came, and Frederick-William was released from his long sufferings.

By some manœuvring on the part of those around him the Lichtenau was kept away from him at the last. She was herself ill from over-exertion and want of rest, and being made to believe that he was a little better, she was persuaded to leave him for a few hours in order that she might get some sleep.

Countess Voss relates how the news came to his family—

[1] *Hohenzollern Jahrbuch*, 1897, p. 133.

331

"Nov. 16.—A huntsman came with the news that the King is dying. The Crown Prince wanted to go at once, but then he hesitated and did not go till nearly noon. At one o'clock came the dreadful news that the King had died at nine o'clock. I went up in my powder-mantle just as I was, to inform the present Queen. The Radziwills were with her; we all cried together about him. I was half dead with grief, could not eat, and drove out in the afternoon to Potsdam. There I found the present King, and wished him happiness and blessing. The deceased had already been carried to the Palace by the first battalion."

"Nov. 17.—I have not slept. I went twice to the dear departed to see him. He is very thin, but not altered. . . . We drove back to Berlin and drank tea with the Queen-mother, who is really grieved. My Queen is quite overwhelmed and upset, and the King is too. Both are truly very sad, and the young King, in his noble way of thinking, would gladly have waited longer for the crown, to keep his father with him."

The new King, whose long reign comprised both the fall and the regeneration of Prussia, was a singularly simple-minded, upright and well-meaning man.

Modest and ingenuous, the words with which he greeted his ministers on his first appearance at a council were: "You have lost your best friend; will you take me instead (wollen Sie mich annehmen)?"

In person he was tall and had the blue eyes of the Hohenzollerns, but an awkward constraint of manner and a difficulty in expressing himself gave strangers a less agreeable impression of him than his character deserved. He had also a great difficulty in making up his mind, but nevertheless such a dread of being ruled by others that he distrusted men of strong character, a trait that long prevented him from availing himself of the services of such a man as Stein.

He carefully avoided his father's faults. The royal household offered a picture of quiet family happiness that was something quite new in the reigning houses of Europe. A rigid economy was introduced, to bring the finances into order.

The Countess of Lichtenau had read his glance aright. It is said that when she approached him on the day of his father's death, he said to those around him: "Take that woman away out of my sight." She and Saint-Ygnon, a French *émigré* who had returned with her from Italy, found themselves under arrest, and were kept strongly guarded.

She was charged with the abstraction of valuable State papers. But the Commission before which she was summoned after a long period of imprisonment were unable to convict her of anything criminal, and she was released, though deprived of her houses and estates and reduced to a small pittance. Those who had been readiest to flatter her were the first to desert her in her downfall.

Her after career was not edifying. She married a young musician, who soon deserted her through jealousy; then a Hungarian officer, with whom she had no better fortune. When Napoleon came to

Berlin she was in great poverty, and through his intercession with the King of Prussia she had some of her confiscated property restored. She lived in Berlin till her death at the age of sixty-six. Her daughter, the Countess de la Marck, had an equally chequered career, marrying first a German count, then a Polish nobleman, and finally a French captain.

Wöllner, after the death of his protector, had no scruple in helping his successor to undo the work he had begun, but in spite of his abject submission he was dismissed in March 1798 without the pension for which he pleaded.

Bischoffswerder was also dismissed some months after the new King's accession. He died in 1803, in time to escape the knowledge that for the Prussian collapse under the Napoleonic storm the journalists, looking around for a scapegoat, had laid all the blame on the shoulders of the men who influenced Frederick-William II, and that he especially was to be long the target for every kind of abuse, in which the truth was buried under a mass of exaggeration.

And in this he was like his royal master. Frederick-William was called to a task of quite exceptional difficulty. The system that Frederick had kept going by sheer force of will, by unceasing toil and relentless rigour, was no longer tenable. When the breath left his body the Frederician system was bound to collapse. To reorganise the whole system of government, at a time when the struggle between the old order and the new was actually

beginning, without statesmen accustomed to responsibility by his side, a superman was required. And
more than one Napoleon does not arise in a
generation.

That he failed in the task is indubitable. But the
legends started by Mirabeau and echoed by others
of his doing no work for his people, of his being
sunk in base pleasures, have been disproved now
that the facts are better known.

Germany is a country where above all others the
battles of conflicting opinions are fought out with
bitterness. In the struggle between orthodoxy and
free-thinking all the bigotry was not on the side of
the orthodox. And when Frederick-William made
his futile but well-meant attempt to bring back the
erring into the orthodox fold, he exposed himself
to the bitterest attacks from all the opponents of
religion, among whom were many unscrupulous men,
ready to exaggerate every scandal and spread every
discreditable rumour about him.

In the retrospect of her life the Countess Voss
thus writes of the King, whom she knew better,
perhaps, than did any one else, whose faults she did
not spare, and to whom, with all her reverence for
etiquette, she could speak on occasions pretty
plainly—

"The good, never-to-be-forgotten Prince who
followed him " (*i. e.* Frederick the Great) "seemed
made to make his people happy; a character full of
mildness and warm, heart-felt benevolence; there
was also energy in him, and he would have proved
it well, if mischance had not so willed it that low

and bad influences gathered round him and got possession of him, and he had lost all mastery over his own passions. This was also the cause of his early death; he was taken before his time, and ah! not mourned nearly so long as he had well deserved! And yet he was so kind, so true a friend in need, and, if one may use the simple expression, such a true-hearted, honest man!"

APPENDIX I

"RUSSLAND ist nicht weit vom Gedanken einer neuen Teilung Polens entfernt; das wäre freilich das wirksamste Mittel die Macht eines polnischen Königs zu beschränken, sei er nun erblich oder wählbar. Indes zweifle ich, ob sich dabei eine angemessene Entschädigung für Oesterreich finden liesse und ob nach einer solchen Beschneidung der polnischen Macht der Kurfürst von Sachsen noch die Krone annehmen würde. Immer aber wäre, wenn es gelänge Oesterreich zu entschädigen, der russiche Plan der günstigste für Preussen,—wohl bemerkt, dass Preussen dabei das ganze linke Weichselufer empfinge und diese weite, jetzt schwer zu deckende Grenze sich dann wohl abgerundet fände. Das ist mein Urteil über die polnische Sache."

APPENDIX II

". . . Ein Geschäft, dass eine glänzende Entschädigung sichert, das wir niemals abgeschlossen hätten, wenn die Entscheidung unserem treuen Bundesgenossen Oesterreich überlassen gewesen wäre."

z   337

APPENDIX

APPENDIX III

"Seit meinem letzten Briefe habe gar keine Zeit zum Schreiben gehabt; wir haben in lauter Fêten gelebt, die besonders durch die Anwesenheit hoher Fremden veranlasst wurden, nämlich des Prinzess George von Darmstadt und ihren beider herrlichen Kindeskinder, der Töchter des Prinzen Karl von Mecklenburg.

"Wie ich die beiden Engel zum ersten Mal sah, es war am Eingang der Komödie, so war ich so frappirt von ihrer Schönheit, dass ich ganz ausser mir war, als die Grossmutter sie mir präsentirte. Ich wünschte sehr, dass meine Söhne sie sehen möchten und sich in sie verlieben. Den anderen Tag liessen sie sich auf einem Ball präsentiren und waren ganz von ihnen enchantirt. Ich machte mein möglichstes, dass sie sich öfters sahen und sich kennen lernten.

"Die beiden Engel sind, so viel ich sehen kann, so gut als schön. Nun war die Liebe da, und so wurde kurz und gut resolvirt, sie zu heirathen. Sie gaben sich das Jawort und die Versprechung wird bald vor sich gehen, wahrscheinlich in Mannheim. Der ältere heirathet die älteste und der jüngste die jüngste."

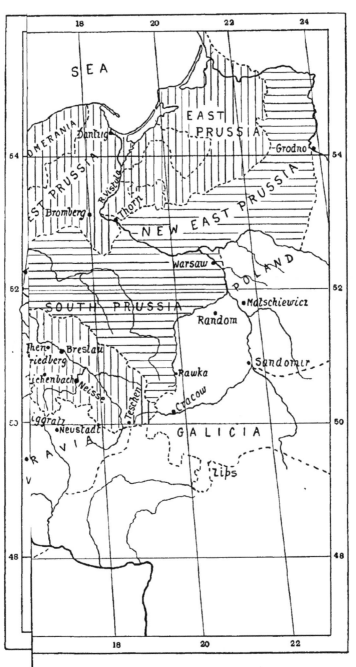

ntal lines the new possessions acquired during his reign.

PRUSSIA (1786-1797)

Perpendicular lines indicate Prussian territory at the accession of Frederick William II,; horizontal lines the new pos

INDEX

INDEX

INDEX

INDEX

LIST OF AUTHORITIES

Allgemeine Deutsche Biographie.
ALLISON : *History of Europe.*
AUSTIN, MRS. : *Germany, 1760-1814.*

BAILLEU : *König Friedrich-Wilhelm II u. der Genesis des Friedens v. Basel.*
BAILLEU : *Vor hundert Jahren.*
BARANIUS, A. W. : *Versuch einer Biographie der Gräfin Lichtenau.*
BERNER : *Geschichte des preuss. Staates.*
Boyen, H. v. (published 1889).

Cambridge Modern History.
CAPEFIGUE : *La Favorite d'un Roi de Prusse.*
CARLYLE, TH. : *Frederick the Great.*
CASSEL, PAUL : *Eine Apologie des Königs Friedrich-Wilhelm II* (1886).
CLAPHAM : *Causes of the War of 1792.*
COELLN, FR. V. : *Vertraute Briefe über die inneren Verhältnisse am preuss. Hofe seit dem Tode Friedrichs II.*
COXE : *History of the House of Austria.*

DAMPMARTIN : *Scènes de la Vie privée de Frédéric-Guillaume II* (1811).
DOHM, C. V. : *Denkwürdigkeiten, 1778-1806.*
DUNCKER, MAX : "Friedrich-Wilhelm II und Hertzberg." *Hist. Zeitsch. VII.*

ENSE, VARNHAGEN V. : *Denkwürdigkeiten.*

FITZMAURICE, LORD EDMUND : *C. W. F., Duke of Brunswick.*
FÖRSTER, J. G. : *Briefwechsel.*
Frédéric, Œuvres de (pub. 1788).
FREYTAG, G. : *Bilder aus deutscher Vergangenheit.*

GOERTZ : *Denkwürdigkeiten.*
GOETHE, J. W. v. : *Aus meinem Leben.*
GOETHE, J. W. v. : *Belagerung von Mainz.*
GONTEL, E. HENNET DE : *Un Roi de Prusse bigame.*

HAHNKE, ELIZABETH CRISTINE.
HARDENBERG : *Denkwürdigkeiten* (ed. by L. Ranke).
HEIGEL, C. T. : *Deutsche Geschichte* (1899).
HERTZBERG, E. F. v. : *Recueil des Deductions,* etc. (1789-92).
HODGETT, BRAILEY : *House of Hohenzollern.*
Hohenzollern Jahrbuch.
HUDSON ; *Life of Louisa.*

LIST OF AUTHORITIES

KOHUT: *Freimaurerei.*
KOSMANN: *Leben u. Thaten Friedrich-Wilhelms II.*
KÖPPEN, F. V.: *Die Hohenzollern.*

LAVISSE ET RAMBAUD: *Histoire Générale.*
LECKY: *Leaders of Public Opinion in Ireland.*
Lichtenau, Confessions of Countess.

MACKINTOSH, SIR JAMES (1848).
MALMESBURY, LORD: *Diaries.*
MALMESBURY, LORD: *Letters from 1745-1820.*
MANSO: *Geschichte, 1763-1815* (1819-20).
MASSENBACH, C. V.: *Memoiren zur Geschichte.*
MAUVILLON: *Ferdinand v. Braunschweig.*
MENZEL, C. A.: *Zwanzig Jahre, 1786-1806.*
MIRABEAU, H. COMTE DE: *L'Histoire Sécrète de la Cour de Prusse.*

NICOLAI, C. F.: *Anekdoten.*

ONCKEN: *Allgem. Geschichte.*
ORANGE, PRINCESS WILHELMINA OF: *Erinnerungen,* ed. S. B. Volz.

PAULIG, F. R.: *Friedrich-Wilhelm II.*
PHILIPPSON, MARTIN: *Geschichte des preuss. Staatswesens vom Tode Fr. d. Gr. bis zu d. Freiheitskriegen.*
PHILIPPSON, MARTIN: "Friedrich der Grosse" (in *Der Neue Plutarch*).
PREUSS, J.: *Friedrich der Grosse.*

RANKE, LEOPOLD V.: *Die deutschen Mächte u. d. Fürstenbund.*
RANKE, LEOPOLD V.: *Hardenberg.*
RIOUST, M. N.: *Joseph II par lui-même.*

SCHMETTAU, C. V.: *Mémoires Raisonnées.*
SCHON: *Beiträge.*
SCHUBART: *Vaterlands Chronik, 1791.*
SCHWEBEL, O.: *Gesch. der Stadt Berlin.*
SEELEY: *Life and Times of Stein.*
SÉGUR, L. P. DE: *Histoire du Règne de Frédéric-Guillaume II.*
SOREL: *L'Europe et la Révolution française.*
SOREL: *La Decadence de la Prusse après Frédéric II.*
STADELMANN: *Preussens Könige in ihrer Tätigkeit für die Landeskultur.*
SYBEL: *Oesterreich u. Preussen.*
SYBEL: *La Révolution française.*

THIÉBAULT, D.: *Mes Souvenirs de vingt ans de séjour à Berlin.*
TREITSCHKE, H. V.: *Deutsche Geschichte im neunzehnten Jahrhundert.*

Universal Magazine, 1764.

VOSS GRÄFIN, S. V.: *Neun u. sechzig Jahre am preuss. Hofe.*

WAITE, A. E.: *Real History of the Rosicrucians.*
WILLERT, P. E.: *Mirabeau.*
WOLF, A.: *Oesterreich u. Preussen.*

Richard Clay & Sons, Limited, London and Bungay

Lightning Source UK Ltd.
Milton Keynes UK
UKHW022021020621
384830UK00002B/166

9 781010 338376